OECD's Multilateral Agreement on Investment

OECD's Multilateral Agreement on Investment

A Chinese Perspective

Chen Huiping

Xiamen University Law School
Fujian, China

KLUWER LAW INTERNATIONAL
THE HAGUE / LONDON / NEW YORK

Published by:
Kluwer Law International
P.O. Box 85889, 2508 CN The Hague, The Netherlands
sales@kli.wkap.nl
http://www.kluwerlaw.com

Sold and Distributed in North, Central and South America by:
Kluwer Law International
101 Philip Drive, Norwell, MA 02061, USA
kluwerlaw@wkap.com

Sold and Distributed in all other countries by:
Kluwer Law International
Distribution Centre, P.O. Box 322, 3300 AH Dordrecht, The Netherlands

A C.I.P. Catalogue record for this book is available from the Library of Congress

Printed on acid-free paper

ISBN 90-411-8893-2
© 2002 Kluwer Law International

Kluwer Law International incorporates the imprint of Martinus Nijhoff Publishers

I want to thank Professor An Chen, my former Ph.D. director, for his valuable input on this book and for his preface. Gratitude should be given to Dr. Marcel Brus, my supervisor at Leiden University, for his encouragement to write and his suggestions for revision of the book. I also want to thank Ms. Yu Zhanmin and Mr. Tian Xiuwen for their kind helping in typing part of the book.

Preface

OECD's Multilateral Agreement on Investment (MAI) was intended to be an international investment code and represented the new trends of multilateral investment legal frameworks. Being scholars of international economic law, Chen Huiping, my colleague and former Ph.D. student, and I, began to follow the MAI negotiations ever since 1997 when they were made public. In view of the significance of the MAI for the development of international investment law, it is important and urgent to study the MAI from Chinese and developing countries' perspective.

In 1999, Ms. Chen wrote her Ph.D. dissertation of which the MAI was the main subject. Her dissertation won high appraisal and evaluation from Chinese scholars. In 2000, she had a good chance to do further research on the MAI in Leiden University, the Netherlands. The abundant resources, her hard work, her deep insight and her good command of English enable her to do detailed study on the MAI from Chinese perspective and write this book in English.

The MAI does not belong merely to the developed countries, it also has impacts on the developing countries, so it is necessary for developing countries to have a say in such an international instrument. Ms. Chen is one of a few scholars from developing countries who make detailed analyses and comments on the MAI. Therefore, I believe this book is of high value and I am glad to accept her invitation to write the preface for her book.

An Chen
Chairman of Chinese Society of International Economic Law
Professor of Law, Xiamen University, Law School, China

Contents

OECD's Multilateral Agreement on Investment

1. Introduction

The Organization of Economic Cooperation and Development (OECD) is the "Rich Man's Club" of the developed countries in the world. The inward and outward investments in these developed countries account for at least two-thirds of foreign direct investment (FDI) in the world. Therefore, a comprehensive and effective multilateral framework for investment is of necessity and urgency for these countries. In 1995, OECD member states launched negotiations among them to create a Multilateral Agreement on Investment (MAI).[1] The intended MAI would be negotiated and adopted inside the OECD and then open for accession by any other states, the developing countries in particular. After almost three-year negotiations, an MAI Negotiating Text was made public in April 1998. The Text was the main result of the work of expert groups and the Negotiating Group, but had not yet been adopted by the Negotiating Group. Due to the facts that there existed many disagreements among these developed countries, the developing countries protested the MAI texts for procedural and substantive reasons, and the non-governmental organizations (NGOs) of environment, human rights, labour, etc. opposed the MAI negotiations, the OECD had to declare in December 1998 to stop the negotiations on the MAI.

Although the OECD's intention to create an MAI inside OECD failed, they decided to advocate negotiations on such a multilateral investment agreement in the World Trade Organization (WTO). In the meanwhile, the WTO is ambitious to formulate multilateral rules for foreign investments in the near future. It established a Working Group on the Relationship between Trade and Investment after its first Ministerial Conference in Singapore in late 1996. Its purpose is obvious, that is, they try to find out the relationship between trade and investment and then they have reasonable excuse to negotiate investment rules in WTO—a global trade organization. In WTO's fourth Ministerial Conference in Doha in November 2001, most developed countries tried again to list investment as one of the issues to be negotiated in the new round of negotiations but failed. The Conference decided to revert to this issue two years later. However, the study on the relationship between trade and investment in WTO continues, and there exists such a possibility that some time in the future a formal negotiation on investment rules would be held in WTO.

---

[1] The negotiating text (draft text) of the MAI is available at http://www.oecd.org/daf/investment/fdi/mai/negtext.htm.

On the other hand, the United Nations Conference on Trade and Development (UNCTAD) considered it necessary for the interest of developing countries to study the multilateral investment rules. According to the Midrand Declaration in May 1995, the "Commission on Investment, Technology and Related Financial Issues" was set up in UNCTAD to study the Possible Multilateral Framework on Investment (PMFI) so as to strengthen the understanding of this subject and to build the capacity of developing countries in international investment negotiations. At present, the Commission has convened several conferences on this subject and achieved positive results.

The above facts show that the international society is trying to create a multilateral legal framework for international investment in the past and future years. Therefore, it is sure that the OECD's MAI Negotiating Text will exert substantial impacts on such a framework. But both the MAI negotiations and the MAI Text have serious flaws and defects and are against the interest and standpoints of developing countries. So it is necessary to analyze and comment on the MAI from the developing countries perspective, with the hope that the future investment negotiations wherever they will be held will absorb the participation of developing countries, consider their special interest and reflect their demands and standpoints.

This book consists of nine chapters. Chapter One is an introduction to the book. Chapter Two analyzes the background of the MAI negotiations, briefly reviews the process and results of the negotiations and makes the author's comments on the negotiations. Chapter Three analyzes and evaluates the main features of MAI provisions and the approaches adopted by the MAI. Chapter Four studies the scope of application of the MAI through the analysis of the respective definitions of investor and investment in the MAI, and points out that the purpose of broad definition is to broaden the MAI's scope of application. Chapter Five analyzes and comments on the MAI's general principles of treatment accorded to foreign investors and their investments, and points out that the MAI's provisions in this regard have negative impacts on developing countries. Chapter Six introduces respectively the MAI's specific rules of treatment accorded to foreign investors and their investments in such new areas of international investment as performance requirements, investment incentives, key personnel, privatization, as well as monopoly, state enterprises and concessions. Chapter Seven analyzes and comments on the MAI's treatment provisions on investment protection, i.e., the fair and equitable treatment and full and constant protection and security treatment as the general treatment, and the specific treatment with regard to expropriation and compensation, protection from strife and transfers. Chapter Eight introduces and evaluates the MAI's dispute settlement mechanism: the state-state procedure and the investor-state procedure. Chapter Nine is the conclusion.

2. An Overview of the MAI Negotiations

2.1 INTRODUCTION

The efforts to make a comprehensive and effective legal framework for international investment first originated from the end of the Second World War and continued therefrom. Unfortunately, only agreements on some specific investment sectors such as the Energy Charter Treaty (ECT) and the General Agreement on Trade in Service (GATS), and the agreements on some specific aspects of investment activities such as the Agreement on Trade-related Investment Measures (TRIMs) and the Agreement on Trade-related Aspects of Intellectual Property Rights (TRIPs), were concluded. In 1990's, globalization of economy and liberalization of investment characterized the international economy and therefore an effective comprehensive investment agreement was in urgent need for those capital-export and capital-import countries. As a leading developed country, the United States pursued in the Uruguay Round to sign an enforceable multilateral investment agreement in the newly established WTO. But this suggestion was strongly opposed by developing countries. Then the United States considered that any negotiations on investment agreement in WTO would be refused by developing countries, so it would be better for such an investment agreement to be negotiated in the OECD and the developing countries could join in the agreement later on if they liked.[1] But European countries and Canada regarded WTO as the proper forum for investment negotiations because they wanted a level playing field including developing countries' interests.[2] Finally, the position of the United States was taken by all OECD countries. In September 1995, the OECD launched official negotiations on an international investment code—Multilateral Agreement on Investment (MAI).

The OECD consisted of 24 developed countries in 1994. From 1995, Mexico, Czech, Hungary, Poland, and Korea acceded to the OECD one by one. Now there are 29 member states in the OECD. The OECD members are the most important capital-export and capital-import countries in the world. For example, in 1980's and the early 1990's, the OECD members accounted for 95% of the total exported capital and 75% of the total imported capital in

---

[1] A. Böhmer, "The Struggle for a Multilateral Agreement on Investment—an Assessment of the Negotiation Process in the OECD", 41 *German Yearbook of International Law* (1998), p. 275.
[2] Id.

3

the world.[3] That is why the OECD has always paid much attention to and played a pioneer role in international investment rules. In 1961, the OECD adopted the Code of Liberalization of Capital Movements and the Code of Liberalization of Current Invisible Operations. In 1976, the OECD adopted the Declaration on International Investment and Multilateral Enterprises. The Declaration consists of four parts: OECD Guidelines for Multilateral Enterprises, The National Treatment Instrument, Conflicting Requirements Imposed on Multilateral Enterprises, and International Investment Incentives and Disincentives. Until now, these investment rules are still the main rules regulating the investment among OECD countries. Therefore, it is no surprise that OECD took the lead in commencing the negotiations on the Multilateral Agreement on Investment.

The MAI was intended to be the state-of-the-art agreement to level the playing field, based on the existing OECD investment documents. The MAI was to be concluded among OECD countries and then open to any other countries. R. Ruggeiro, the former Director-general of the WTO, described the MAI as "the constitution for a single global economy".[4]

2.2 BACKGROUND OF THE MAI NEGOTIATIONS

2.2.1 Economic Background

From the end of the Second World War to the end of 1970's, the focus of the developed countries was on their own economic recovery from the War and their economy was in gradual development. Therefore most of their domestic capitals were invested inside the countries. On the other hand, more and more colonial countries gained independence from their metropolitan states. As a result of the cherishing of their economic independence and autonomy, they were more willing to be self-reliant in their economic development. They set up strict rules for the inflow of foreign investment. This accounts for one of the reasons why a global comprehensive investment agreement could not be concluded during that period.

Since 1980's, the economy of developed countries has reached quite an advanced level and the investment between them have been getting more and more active. The national power of developing countries has been consolidated and the development of economy gradually takes the focus position among their national affairs. Therefore, many developing countries including China tried to open their doors to absorb foreign investment so as to meet the capital demand in these countries. More and more foreign investments from developed countries come into developing countries. To sum up, foreign direct investments flowed into both developed countries and developing countries were in a surge in that era. The following table gives

---

[3] OECD, *Towards Multilateral Investment Rules*, 1996, p. 19.
[4] C. Raghavan, "Investment rules not dead, yet", *South – North Development Monitor* (SUNS) (Email edition), Issue 4156, Feb. 20, 1998.

concrete figures as to the FDI inflows to both developed and developing countries.

Foreign Direct Investment Inflows 1985–96, US$ billions

	1985–90	1992	1994	1996
World	141.9	173.8	238.7	349.2
Developed Countries	116.7	119.7	142.4	208.2
Developing Countries	24.7	49.6	90.5	128.7
Least Developed Countries	0.6	1.5	1.0	1.6

Source: UNCTAD (1997) Table B.1.[5]

The above data show that the total amount of FDI in 1996 is more than twice as much as that from 1985 to 1990. The FDI invested in developing countries in 1996 is more than four times as much as that from 1985 to 1996. From 1985 to 1990, the FDI invested in developing countries accounts for less than one fifth of the total FDI in the world. But in 1996, the figure has exceeded one third.[6] FDI in 1990's increased very fast and played a more and more important role in almost every country's economy. International investment and international trade constitute the two important pillars of the world economy.

International investment was also greatly stimulated by the constant and liberal development of world trade. In the traditional trade model, commodities were produced in one country and then transported to another country for sale. In modern trade model, commodities are directly produced, through the establishment of invested enterprises, in those countries with great potential market or with cheap labour and abundant natural resources. As to the trade in service, it is mostly conducted through the "commercial presence" (i.e., solely-owned enterprises, joint ventures or branches) established in different countries. Foreign investment is thus promoted and the pace of development of investment gradually exceeds that of the trade. Foreign investment and international trade are interrelated and build up together new model of world economy.

The multilateralization of investment activities is the characteristic of international investment in modern time. In the past, foreign investment came from one capital-export country to another capital-import country. This kind of investment concerned only two countries and could be well protected by traditional bilateral investment protection treaties. Nowadays, transnational corporations (TNCs) are distributed among many different countries. The great development of communication technology and financial service makes it possible that TNCs formulate their global strategy and accordingly arrange and organize their economic activities in different areas

---

[5] Cited from E. V. K. FitzGerald, R. Cubero-Brealey and A. Lehmann, "The Development Implications of the Multilateral Agreement on Investment: A Report Commissioned by the UK Department for International Development" (21 March 1998), p. 10.
[6] Id., pp. 9–10.

so as maximize their profits. For instance, they may scatter their production process and distribution links in different countries, i.e., establishing a factory in the country with cheap labour, setting up a distribution base in some key areas from where it is easy to enter into other large markets, and establishing after-sale service branches in those areas with more consumers of high-tech products and certain services. Thus, the activities of one TNC may concern many different countries. The bilateral investment treaties can not provide sufficient protection for this kind of foreign investment.

In summary, the dramatic increase of FDI, the new patterns of investment and the multilateralization of investment activities make developed countries realize that it is of urgent need to create an international investment code to fully regulate the FDI. Such an investment code should be able to protect the interests of developed countries and their native investors, and to accelerate the development of investment liberalization.

2.2.2   Legal Background

Since 1980s, there has been great development in domestic laws concerning foreign investment, bilateral investment treaties (BITs), regional investments agreements and multilateral trade-related investment agreements. However, there still exist inherent limitations in the regard of investment protection.

With the further development of their native economy, developed countries gradually loosen their legal control over foreign investment and strengthen the protection of foreign investment. As to developing countries, in their domestic legislation concerning foreign investment, they also relax their restrictions on the admission of foreign investment and the control over them after their admission in order to absorb more foreign investment. For example, in 1996, 98 liberalizing changes were made in the regulatory FDI frameworks of 65 countries (10 developed and 55 developing countries).[7] Moreover, many investment incentives including tax holidays and tax reductions are taken by many developing countries to encourage the inflow of foreign investment. The above facts are regarded by developed countries as an indication of unilateral promotion of investment liberalization by developing countries.[8]

On the other hand, developing countries still reserve their control and restrictions on the screening of foreign investment, performance requirements, percentage of equity, etc. These practices are considered as discriminatory treatment to foreign investors and barriers to market access. Foreign investment is thus made in uncertainty.[9] Moreover, the purpose to attract more foreign investment results in increased competition of more preferential

---

[7]   A. Böhmer, *supra* note 1, p. 272.

[8]   E. V. K. FitzGerald, etc., *supra* note 5, p. 13.

[9]   "Multilateral Agreement on Investment: Report by the Committee on International Investment and Multilateral Enterprises (CIME) / and the Committee on Capital Movements and Invisible Transactions (CMIT)", May 1995 (hereinafter referred to as the "MAI Report (1995)"), available at http://www.oecd.org/daf/cmis/mai/mairap95.htm.

measures among developing countries and thus makes it more costly to absorb foreign investment.[10]

The limitations of the effects of bilateral investment agreements (BITs) with regard to the protection of foreign investment are increasingly obvious. Being an important international regime, BITs always play a key role in the protection of foreign investment. BITs are concluded not only between developed countries and developing countries, but also between developing countries. By the end of 1997, there have been 1513 BITs concluded by 169 countries, three fourths of which were concluded in 1990's.[11] This phenomenon reflects the swift growth of international investment, on one hand, and the increasing attention paid by different countries to the protection of international investment, on the other hand. However, if BITs are used as main means to provide comprehensive protection for FDI, it is necessary to require more than 180 countries in the world to sign BITs one another and the total amount of BITs will reach more than 20,000. It is well known that signing a BIT is a time-consuming and effort-consuming task. The economic costs can be imagined if every country signs a BIT with all other countries in the world. Moreover, the treatment and protection of foreign investment provided by different BITs may be different, and therefore the more BITs there are, the more differences there exist. The inevitable outcome is that the treatment and protection of international investment in the world, even in one same country, is not uniform. As a consequence, the function and effects of BITs will be greatly affected and discounted. In contrast, a multilateral investment agreement can possibly overcome the above shortcomings of BITs.

The number of regional investment agreements is increasing in this period. Examples are: the Unified Agreement of the Investment of Arab Capital in the Arab State (1980), Agreement on Promotion, Protection and Guarantee of Investments among Member States of the Organization of the Islamic Conference (1981), Community Investment Code of the Economic Community of the Great Lakes Countries (CEPGL) (1982), Revised Basic Agreement on ASEAN Industrial Joint Ventures (1987), and APEC Non-Binding Investment Principles (1994).[12] Though the North American Free Trade Agreement (NAFTA) is a trade agreement, its Chapter Eleven is specifically concerning investment. Similarly, the regional investment agreements have their own shortcomings and limitations.

At the multilateral level, there is not a comprehensive investment agreement. But many trade agreements did mention the issue of investment. In the WTO regime, the General Agreement of Trade in Service (GATS), the Agreement on Trade-related Investment Measures (TRIMs), and the Agreement on Trade-related Aspects of Intellectual Property Rights (TRIPs) have relations with international investment. Foreign investment is also a key subject in the Energy Charter Treaty (ECT). There is a demand for multilateral investment agreement.

---

[10] E. V. K. FitzGerald, etc., *supra* note 5, p. 12.
[11] UNCTAD, *World Investment Report 1998*, p. 59 and 117.
[12] As for all the regional investment agreements, see UNCTAD, *International Investment Instruments: A Compendium*, vol. II, Regional Instruments, United Nations, New York and Geneva, 1996.

All the factors in the above economic and legal background constituted the causes of the negotiations of the MAI. The proposed MAI would build on OECD's present regional investment instruments, consolidate the results achieved by other multilateral agreements relevant to investment, and create new disciplines in order to provide a comprehensive framework for international investment.[13]

2.3   A BRIEF INTRODUCTION TO THE PROCESS OF THE MAI NEGOTIATIONS

2.3.1   The First Phase of the Negotiations

In 1991, OECD's Committee on International Investment and Multinational Enterprises (CIME) and the Committee on Capital Movements and Invisible Transactions (CMIT) started to study the issue of multilateral investment. In June 1994, the OECD Ministerial Meeting made a mandate to appoint CIME and CMIT to formally launch to explore the major issues of a multilateral framework on investment. The technical and analytical work was undertaken by five working groups which were composed of independent experts. The five groups dealt respectively with liberalization obligations under existing OECD instruments, liberalization obligations in new areas, investment protection, dispute settlement, and the involvement of non-Members and institutional matters.[14] The two committees presented to the OECD Council Meeting at Ministerial level in May 1995 a report entitled "Multilateral Agreement on Investment".[15]

After reviewing the above report, the OECD Ministers issued a mandate to commence immediately the negotiations in the OECD aimed at reaching a multilateral agreement on investment.[16] The proposed MAI would provide a broad multilateral framework for international investment, set high standards for investment liberalization and investment protection and contain dispute settlement procedures. The MAI would be initially negotiated and reached among the OECD member states. It would be a free-standing international treaty open to all OECD Members and the European Communities, and to accession by non-OECD Member countries.[17] The MAI was intended to be concluded by the time of the Ministerial meeting in 1997.

The MAI negotiations were based on the report presented by CIME and CMIT. It may be said that the analyses work by the two committees on international investment is an important preparatory job in the earlier stage of

---

[13]   R. Geiger, "Towards a Multilateral Agreement on Investment", 31 *Cornell International Law Journal* (1998), no. 3, p. 474.

[14]   Annex to the "MAI Report (1995)", *supra* note 9.

[15]   The "MAI Report (1995)", *supra* note 9.

[16]   "The Original Mandate", available at http://www.oecd.org//daf/investment/fdi/mai/mandate.htm#Mandate.

[17]   "A Multilateral Agreement on Investment: Report by the MAI Negotiating Group", May 1996 (hereinafter referred to as the "MAI Report (1996)"), available at http://www.oecd.org/daf/cmis/mai/mairap96.htm.

the MAI negotiations. In effect, the investment chapter of the NAFTA is the prototype of the above report and its annexes. The report expanded those provisions of the NAFTA to all economic sectors and to all OECD member states.

In September 1995 the Negotiating Group was constituted to commence official MAI negotiations. There were 30 negotiating members including the delegations from 29 member states and the European Commission. The Group was chaired by Mr. Frans Engering (Netherlands); Mr. Alan P. Larson (United States) and Mr. Akitaka Saiki (Japan) were vice-chairmen.[18] The Group gathered in Paris to hold a meeting once every six weeks. Many expert groups were established, such as the Expert Group on Dispute Settlement and Geographical Scope, Expert Group on Intellectual Property Right, and Expert Group on Special Topics. These groups were subordinate to and under the leadership of the Negotiating Group. They worked on some specific technical issues and matters and prepared proposals for the discussion of the Negotiating Group. Those unresolved problems were submitted to the Group for final solution. WTO, IMF and ICSID were invited as observers to participate in the meetings of the expert groups and the Negotiating Group.

In May 1996, a progress report was presented by the MAI Negotiating Group to the OECD Council meeting at Ministerial level.[19] The report declared that the framework for the MAI had been basically fixed and the substantive issues had been examined. It was agreed that a broad definition of investors and investments would be given so that the MAI would provide comprehensive coverage.[20] The ambitious "top down" approach would be adopted in drafting the provisions on national treatment, most-favoured-nation (MFN) treatment and transparency.[21] The dispute settlement mechanism would include both state-state procedure and investor-state procedure.[22] Possible mechanisms for standstill and rollback and for the listing of country specific reservations had been identified.[23]

However, some outstanding issues still remained.[24] There were controversies on the definition of investments and how it would be applied. Other unresolved matters are: how to realize the achievement of a high level of liberalization; how to apply the general principles of treatment to such new areas as investment incentives, performance requirement, privatization, monopolies/state enterprises/concession, etc.;[25] how to apply the commitments under the MAI to all contracting parties at all levels of government; and how to deal with measures taken in the context of regional economic integration organizations (REIO).

---

[18] Id.
[19] Id.
[20] The broad definition of investors and investments will be discussed in detail in Chapter Four of this book.
[21] The "top down" approach will be discussed in Chapter Three of this book. The national treatment, MFN treatment and transparency will be discussed in Chapter Five of this book.
[22] The dispute settlement mechanism will be discussed in Chapter Eight of this book.
[23] Mechanisms for standstill and rollback will be discussed in Chapter Three. The issue of country specific reservations will be discussed in Chapter Five of this book.
[24] "The MAI Report (1996)", *supra* note 17.
[25] The new areas will be discussed in Chapter Six of this book.

In October 1996, the Negotiating Group began to have a discussion on the environment issue, as a result of the worry by international societies about the potential impact of the MAI on national and international environmental regulations.

Until January 1997, the Negotiating Group had come to consensus as to the basic purpose, structure and provisions of the MAI and developed a preliminary draft of the MAI. The negotiations were intended to be completed on 26 May 1997 in the OECD Council meeting at the Ministerial level.[26]

From the first beginning to January 1997, the negotiations were proceeding behind closed doors among the negotiating countries.[27] They focused mainly on the developing of articles and the settlement of disagreements among different negotiating members. Neither the basic stipulations nor the draft of the MAI were made known to the public. As a consequence, not much attention from the press or the public was given to them.

2.3.2   The Second Phase of the Negotiations

In February 1997, the negotiating text of the MAI was made public on the internet by a Non-governmental Organization (NGO).[28] Since the draft MAI was considered as existing serious shortcomings as to the negotiating process and substantive contents, it was protested by many NGOs, civil societies in developed countries as well as developing countries throughout the years of 1997 and 1998.[29] The MAI negotiations came into an uneven phase.

As a result of the international protest of the MAI and the substantial disagreements among OECD countries as to some specific provisions of the MAI, the OECD declared in March 1997—two months before the intended time for the conclusion of the MAI, that they needed more time to discuss and solve these disagreements.[30]

In the OECD Council meeting at Ministerial level in May 1997, the MAI Negotiating Group presented another progress report.[31] The report declared that most elements of the MAI had been drafted but there were still many controversies among the negotiating parties as to the special issues, environment and labor, and the carve-out of tax, RIEO and culture.[32] The admission of investment and the list of country specific reservation were two most

---

[26]   Center for Economic and Policy Research, "The Multilateral Agreement on Investment: Timeline of Negotiations", available at http://www.cepr.net/globalization/MAI/maihist.html.
[27]   TWN/R. Bissio, "NGOs gear up to start anti-MAI campaign", 4091 *SUNS*, Nov. 6, 1997.
[28]   IPS/J. Achieng, "Experts snub OECD's proposed investment pact", 4109 *SUNS*, Dec. 2, 1997.
[29]   TWN/R. Bissio, *supra* note 27; IPS/J. Achieng, *supra* note 28; M. Khor, "NGOs in OECD countries protest MAI", 4155 *SUNS*, Feb. 19, 1998; TWN, "NGOs criticize MAI-type investment approach at UNCTAD", 4230 *SUNS*, June 12, 1998. The substantive contents of the MAI will be further discussed in the following chapters.
[30]   Center for Economic and Policy Research, *supra* note 26.
[31]   "Multilateral Agreement on Investment: Report by the MAI Negotiating Group", May 1997 (hereinafter referred to as the "MAI Report (1997)"), available at http://www.oecd.org/daf/cmis/mai/MAIRAP97.HTM.
[32]   Id.

difficult issues. In view of the above disagreements and the protest from outside the negotiations, the Ministers decided to extend one year to sign the MAI so as to solve the outstanding problems and intensify the dialogue with non-OECD countries.[33] They hoped to conclude the Agreement in time for the 1998 Ministerial Meeting.[34]

In the OECD Council meeting at Ministerial level in April 1998, the chairman of the Negotiating Group presented another report.[35] The focus of the negotiations in the past year was on some political issues, labor and environmental issues, the treatment of intellectual property, exceptions with respect to national security, public order, measures taken in the context of a REIO, culture, subsidies, health, social services, and aboriginal and minority issues. The report stated that it was not possible to conclude the negotiations at this Council meeting as scheduled by last Council meeting at Ministerial level.[36] Taking into account the difficulties confronted by the negotiations and the general concern by international society, Ministers decided to extend a period of time to give assessment on the MAI Text.[37] Moreover, the negotiating parties might have more time to conduct further consultations and dialogues with other social interest parties so as to acquire their support. The next meeting of the Negotiating Group would be held in October 1998.[38]

On October 14, 1998, French Prime Minister L. Jospin announced that France had decided not to participate in the MAI negotiations scheduled for October 20–21, 1998.[39] Six days later, the Negotiating Group gathered in Paris again to continue the MAI negotiations. But because of the withdrawal of France the meetings were switched from intended formal negotiating sessions on the language of the MAI to discussions of how to proceed with the MAI.[40] No result was reached so the Group hoped to meet again by the end of 1998.[41] On October 22, 1998 the OECD Executive Committee in Special Session convened the senior representatives of 29 member states. The MAI was also discussed in this meeting. It was suggested that further consultations with non-members, and societies including business, labor, NGOs, consumers and other organizations be intensified, so as to solve effectively

---

[33] "Ministerial Statement on the Multilateral Agreement on Investment: OECD Council at Ministerial level", 26 May 1997, available at http://www.oced.org//daf/investment/fdi/mai/minstate.htm.
[34] Id.
[35] "Multilateral Agreement on Investment: Report by the Chairman of the Negotiating Group" 28 April 1998 (hereinafter referred to as the "MAI Report (1998)"), available at http://www.oecd.org/daf/cmis/mai/report98.HTM.
[36] Id.
[37] "OECD Ministerial Statement on the Multilateral Agreement on Investment (MAI)", Paris, 27–28 April 1998, available at http://www.oecd.org/news-and-events/release/nw98-50a.htm.
[38] Id.
[39] C. Baumgartner, "The Demise of the Multilateral Agreement on Investment", *Colorado Journal of International Environmental Law & Policy Yearbook* (1998), p. 46; M. Vallianatos, "Update on MAI Negotiations", Oct. 27, 1998, available at http://www.flora.org/flora.mai-not/7582.
[40] M. Vallianatos, *supra* note 39.
[41] "Opening Statement by Mr. Donald J. John, Secretary-General Consultations on the Multilateral Agreement on Investment", Paris, 20 October 1998, available at http://www.oecd.org/news-and-events/release/nw98-100a.htm.

the issues concerned by civil societies.[42] However, as a matter of fact, the French withdrawal left the other negotiators no other options but to stop the negotiations since it was impossible for OECD countries to reach consensus on the intended MAI. Soon after that, other countries such as Britain, Australia, Canada and Germany dropped their efforts on and support of the MAI.[43] The MAI negotiations were in fact blocked completely.

On December 3, 1998, the OECD senior officials responsible for investment policy had an informal meeting in Paris.[44] In view of the disagreements among member states to the MAI Text, and the strong protest in international society, the meeting decided not to continue with the MAI negotiations. But lessons were drawn from the failed MAI negotiations that the formulating of international investment rules in future times needs closer cooperation among governments in a more transparent way, and broad participation by non-members and social circles.[45]

Finally, the MAI negotiations which had lasted more than three years ended without any agreement.

2.3.3   Outside the MAI Negotiations

The intention of the OECD is to negotiate the MAI inside its member states and then make it open to all other countries. So at the beginning of the negotiations, no non-OECD countries were invited to participate in the negotiations, and almost no information about the negotiating text of the MAI was released. The negotiators did not realize the importance of information exchange with non-parties until the negotiating text was made public and received much criticism and opposition.[46] Ever since then, the OECD had organized a series of symposiums and dialogues with non-member countries, NGOs and civil societies. They also admitted those non-OECD countries interested in the MAI to participate in the negotiations as observers. These countries are: Argentina, Brazil, Chile, Hong Kong (China), Slovak Republic, Estonia, Latvia and Lithuania.[47]

The main symposiums and dialogues are: Policy dialogue with Dynamic Non-Member Economics in Wellington (New Zealand), April 1995;[48] Symposium in Brazil with Latin countries in February 1997;[49] Symposium in

---

[42]   "OECD Chairman's Statement under Secretary of State Stuart Eizenstat (USA) Executive Committee in Special Session", Paris, 23 October 1998, available at http://www.oecd.org/news-and-events/release/nw98-101a.htm.
[43]   C. Baumgartner, *supra* note 39, p. 47, and its footnotes of 56 and 57.
[44]   "OECD Informal Consultations on International Investment", 3 December 1998, available at http://www.org/daf/cmis/ii/iindex.htm.
[45]   Id.
[46]   In the MAI Report (1997), it was first addressed that it was necessary to intensify the consultations with non-members, NGOs and civil societies.
[47]   "The MAI Report (1998)", *supra* note 35.
[48]   For details of the dialogue, see OECD, *Towards Multilateral Investment Rules*, 1996, pp. 41–113.
[49]   OECD, *The multilateral Agreement on Investment: State of Play as of February 1997*, OCDE/GD (97)38.

Korea in April 1997, 12 Asian and Middle countries attended;[50] Special Session held in Paris for representatives from non-OECD members on the MAI in September 1997, under the auspice of the OECD;[51] Symposium on the MAI with African countries in Egypt in October 1997;[52] Consultation of OECD Negotiators with NGOs on the MAI.[53]

However, according to the above-mentioned materials, in these symposiums and dialogues, the OECD only introduced to the participants the main contents of the MAI and the progress of the MAI negotiations. There were either no consultations or just one or two briefings/discussions with NGOs.[54] The Chair of the Negotiating Group also admitted that non-OECD member countries *"be kept informed* about the MAI. ... *receive* the latest information about the state of play of the negotiations"(emphasis added).[55] Then the benefits from joining the MAI were advertised to non-members. The alleged benefits included the access to the "Parties Group", the enjoyment of rights, protection, treatment and legal security offered by the MAI, and greater attractiveness for more foreign investment.[56] But whether these benefits are really available and practicable for developing countries is worthy of doubt. In fact, consultation with developing countries and NGOs is only the name, the essence is to peddle the MAI to developing countries.

2.4 REASONS FOR THE FAILURE OF THE MAI NEGOTIATIONS

The OECD occupies a leading position in international direct investment, therefore it is active in taking the initiative to make multilateral rules for investment. The MAI negotiations were the reflection of its ambition. But, the negotiations failed at last.

There are two categories of reasons for this failure. One is that the MAI could not balance the interests, benefits and obligations among developed countries. The other is the protest from developing countries, NGOs and civil societies.

Outwardly, the failure of the negotiations is caused by the disagreements between developed countries, particularly disagreements between the United States and European countries, on such issues as measures taken by

---

[50] OECD, *The multilateral Agreement on Investment: State of Play as in April 1997*, OCDE/GD (97)114.
[51] OECD, *Proceedings of the Special Session on the Multilateral Agreement on Investment Held in Paris on 17 September 1997*, OCDE/GD (97)187.
[52] "Symposium on the MAI", 20 October 1997—Cairo, Egypt, available at http://www.oecd.org/daf/cmis/mai/shelton.htm.
[53] "OECD Negotiators Consult with NGOs on the MAI", available at http://www.oecd.org/news-and-events/release/nw97-91a.htm.
[54] M. Vallianatos, *supra* note 39.
[55] F. Engering, "The Multilateral Investment Agreement", 5 *Transnational Corporations*, no. 3 (December 1996), p. 160.
[56] J. R. Shelton, "Opening Address", *The multilateral Agreement on Investment: State of Play as of February 1997*, p. 6.

REIO, culture, country specific exceptions, dispute settlement mechanism, environment and labor.[57] The essence of these disagreements is that the developed countries could not find a balance on their different interests, benefits and obligations in drafting the MAI. To be further, it is the incisive contradictions among developed countries that are the main obstacles for the negotiations. The following examples will prove this proposition.

During the process of the negotiations, the European Union (EU) countries vigorously advocated the exclusion of the measures taken by the REIO from the MAI. They held that the REIO measures should be an exception to the most-favoured-nation (MFN) treatment of the MAI. The reason is obvious, that is, the EU itself is the largest REIO in the world. The members accord beneficial treatment to each other, but they do not want to share these benefits with those non-members. Non-members represented by the United States and Japan resolutely opposed the proposition of the EU.

Culture industry includes press, newspapers, broadcast, television and films. According to the domestic legislation of France, Italy and Canada, foreign investors are not allowed to set their feet in the culture industry. In the MAI negotiations, these countries insisted on the carving-out of the culture issue. On the contrary, the United States recreation industry, particularly its movie industry such as the Hollywood, is so flourishing that it is ambitious to invest abroad. Therefore, the United States advocated the inclusion of the culture industry in the MAI.

As a result of the above-mentioned "top-down" approach, each contracting party is allowed to give a list of those measures inconsistent of the MAI and the sectors to which the MAI does not apply as the "country specific exceptions". The lists, subject to the agreement of all contracting countries, will come to effect as an annex to the MAI. In the negotiations, the negotiating parties took advantage of this favorable provision to issue several hundred pages of proposed exceptions.[58] The long list of exceptions would not only weaken the effect of the MAI, but also aggregate the difficulties of the negotiations.

In 1998, Canada became one of the countries opposing the adoption of the MAI.[59] The reason was that Canada was sued by three foreign investors in 1997 and 1998 according to the investor-state dispute settlement mechanism of the North American Free Trade Agreement (NAFTA).[60] Since the MAI has a similar investor-state dispute settlement mechanism, the cases arising from

---

[57]   M. Vallianatos, *supra* note 39.
[58]   A. Böhmer, *supra* note 1, p. 286.
[59]   C. Baumgartner, *supra* note 39, p. 45.
[60]   The three cases are: Ethyl Corp. v. Canada, for details, see "Ethyl Corporation vs. Government of Canada: Now Investors Can Use NAFTA to Challenge Environmental Safeguards", available at http://www.citizen.org/pctrade/cases/Ethylbri.htm; S. D. Myers Inc. v. Canada, for details, see "NAFTA Case Shows Risks, Secrecy", available at http://www.canadians.org/release38.html; "Canada Slapped with NAFTA Lawsuit against Another Environmental Law", available at http://www.citizen.org/pctrade/nafta/cases/canada.htm; "US Company Seeks Compensation from Canada under NAFTA", available at http://lawmoney.oyster.co.uk/public/news/hotnews/news9809/news980904.2.html; Sun Belt Water Inc. v. Canada, for details, see "U.S. Lawsuit on Canadian Fresh Water Exports Pours More Cold Water on NAFTA, Says Council of Canadians", available at http://www.canadians.org/release55.html.

the NAFTA made Canada worried that the adoption of the MAI would lead to more cases against Canada.

Another reason for the failure of the negotiations is the protest of developing countries, NGOs and civil societies. They complained that there existed material shortcomings in both the process and the substance of the negotiations.[61] Just as R. Bissio, the Director of the Third World Institute, concluded that the problem was not the MAI *per se*, but the principles and policies behind it, and it was not that the MAI was bad because it was secret, but rather it is secret because it was bad.[62]

As far as the process is concerned, the MAI negotiations were conducted behind closed doors at the first stage. Only the negotiating delegates and the high financial officials of the OECD members were aware of the negotiations and the content of them. Developing countries from Asia, Africa, South America and Central America neither knew about such negotiations nor participated in them. The reason for not inviting non-OECD countries to take part in is, according to the Chair of the Negotiating Group, "...mainly because experience shows that the more countries are involved, the slower the pace of work."[63] To probe to the roots of the matter, this was a strategy of developed countries. They focused only on their own interests and viewpoints. They did not at all want developing countries to be involved in it nor to consider the interests and views of developing countries. This practice which was lack of transparency is easy to disregard the need and target of developing countries. Even one of the OECD official realized with hindsight that "the participating governments made a mistake in negotiating within tightly set deadlines without exposing key concepts of the agreement to public debate at an early stage."[64]

The negotiations of the MAI were not open to developing countries, but the resultant MAI was to be open to developing countries. This is unfair. Moreover, the MAI was to be imposed in a package on some non-OECD countries. For example, in the new negotiations for a renewed Lome Convention between the EC and the ACP countries, the ACP countries were pressured to accept the MAI as part of the new agreement.[65]

As far as the substance is concerned, the negotiating text of the MAI would injure the national sovereignty. France, Germany and some other parties shared the same viewpoints with developing countries that the contents of the MAI would lead to a decline of the national sovereignty with regard to economic matters.[66] The draft MAI did not give full consideration to the labor and environment. This is another reason for NGOs, civil societies and developing countries to protest the MAI. Even France and Canada requested for strict rules in this respect.[67] The draft MAI accorded sufficient rights to foreign investors, but did not set any binding obligations for them. The rights and the obligations of foreign investors are critically uneven and

---

[61] TWN/R. Bissio, *supra* note 27.
[62] TWN, *supra* note 29.
[63] F. Engering, *supra* note 55.
[64] R. Geiger, *supra* note 13.
[65] TWN/R. Bissio, *supra* note 27.
[66] A. Böhmer, *supra* note 1, pp. 273–274.
[67] Id., p. 274.

unbalanced. The MAI was described as "a world constitution for powerful multinational enterprises", "a charter of rights and freedoms for multinational enterprises", or to give company executives a "higher category of citizenship" through the provisions of the MAI.[68] Hereby lists only the main shortcomings of the MAI. More detailed comments on the substance of the MAI will be given in the following chapters.

The Asian Financial Crisis burst out in 1997 had negative impacts on the adoption of the MAI. Developing countries realized that the government should retain the capacity to control the inflow of short-term capitals. The MAI's inclusion of stocks and bonds in the scope of investment and its encouragement of free flow of capitals would interfere with the capital market of developing countries. The Asian Financial Crisis gave warn to developing countries in negotiating an agreement on international investment.

The developing countries' dissatisfaction with the process and substance of the MAI negotiations is in essence the reflection of the contradiction between the developed countries and the developing countries in international investment. This is the first time that the major negotiations by developed countries were frustrated because of the opposition of developing countries.

2.5   CONCLUSION

Although the MAI negotiations by the OECD failed, and although the OECD decided to give up the MAI, we should learn some lessons from the MAI negotiations for future negotiations for investment rules, no matter where they are to be negotiated, in the OECD or in the UNCTAD.[69]

First, in procedure, the negotiations should be performed in a forum where almost every country in the world can equally participate. The negotiations should be in a transparent way. Only when such an investment agreement is negotiated and agreed by every country can it gain respect and receive observation. The negotiations should also pursue the dialogues with NGOs, civil societies and interest groups which should also have a say in such negotiations.

Second, in substance, the articles of the investment rules should take into account both the interest and viewpoints of developed countries and the current situations of developing countries. So the standards should not be too high to be acceptable by both developed and developing countries.

Third, attention should be paid to the concerns of human kinds such as environment and labor in drafting investment rules.

---

[68]   Id.
[69]   After the death of the MAI, EU countries prefer the WTO to be the forum for investment rules, but developing countries prefer to make investment rules in the UNCTAD. See "OECD Ministerial Statement on the MAI", *supra* note 37; IPS/D. D. Sarkar, "MAI principles alive and kicking, analysts say", 4310 *SUNS*, Oct. 27, 1998.

3. General Features of the MAI and the Approaches Adopted by the MAI

3.1 INTRODUCTION

As mentioned in Chapter Two, the negotiating text was built on the existing legal regimes on foreign investment. It not only covers all the issues addressed in those legal regimes but is at the state of the art. On the other hand, the MAI has its own innovations and also deals with some issues uncovered by the existing legal regimes. It can be said that the MAI represents the new trends of multilateral framework for international investment. It has had substantial impacts on recent bilateral investment treaties and regional investment regimes and it is sure to play an important role in any future investment regimes. Therefore, it is valuable and necessary to examine the features of the MAI as a whole and the approaches adopted by the MAI to realize its target.

The original intention, purpose and main theme of the MAI are set forth at the very beginning in its Preamble: "wishing to establish a *broad* multilateral framework for international investment with *high standards* for the liberalization of investment regimes and investment protection and with effective dispute settlement procedures.... To create a free-standing Agreement open to accession by all countries...." (emphasis added).[1] The purpose to create such a high standard agreement is to "enhance international co-operation with respect to investment and the development of world-wide rules on foreign direct investment" and to promote "the efficient utilization of economic resources, the creation of employment opportunities and the improvement of living standards".[2]

The above statement briefly summarizes the features of the MAI which are concretely practised by the MAI's follow-up rules. To be specific, the MAI was intended to be an effective comprehensive world-wide investment code; it is an agreement with broad scope of application; the standards for the treatment and protection of investors and investment are the highest so far; the enforcement mechanism of the MAI is very strong and effective; the governments' obligations and the foreign investors' rights are uneven and unbalanced.

---

[1] See the Preamble of the MAI.
[2] Id.

In order to raise the level of existing liberalization and meet the end of high standards for investment protection, the MAI negotiators adopted some special approaches different from those adopted by other international agreements, such as "country-specific exceptions", "top-down", "standstill" and "rollback". These approaches will be discussed in detail in Section Three of this chapter.

3.2   GENERAL FEATURES OF THE MAI

The MAI is about non-discrimination and liberalization in foreign direct investment. It has the following features.

3.2.1   An Intended Comprehensive Legally Binding World-wide Investment Code

So far, there is not a comprehensive binding agreement dealing specifically with international agreement in the whole world. The trade-related investment agreements in the WTO regime are only the norms dealing with the investment activities relevant to trade. The Energy Charter Treaty (ECT) is an agreement dealing with both trade and investment in the energy sector. The North American Free Trade Agreement (NAFTA) is only a regional agreement dealing with both trade and investment. The MAI negotiators were ambitious to make the MAI a comprehensive binding universal investment code.

The MAI is a comprehensive agreement dealing specially with the complete field of international investment. It covers both substantive norms and procedural norms in foreign direct investment. It was to constitute a special organ "Parties Group" to be responsible for the operation of the agreement. It gives detailed stipulations to the definitions of investors and investments, general standards of treatment and specific disciplines for investors and investments, and the treatment of investment protection. It also provides detailed procedures for the settlement of disputes between different contracting states, and between contracting states and investors. The whole agreement is 145-pages long.

The MAI negotiators planned to make the MAI to be an independent and free-standing, binding and effective investment agreement in the OECD first and then it would be open to accession by other non-OECD countries. The sole purpose is to make it a universally applicable investment code. In contrast, the former OECD investment instruments such as the Codes of Liberalization and the Declaration on International Investment and Multilateral Enterprises are non-binding instruments applicable only among OECD members.

3.2.2   Broad Scope of Application of the Agreement

The scope of application of an investment agreement depends on how broad the agreement defines investors and investments. Normally, the broader the definition is the broader the scope of application will be. The MAI gives broad definition to both investors and investments.

Investors in the MAI include almost all natural persons and economic entities such as company, partnership, branches, etc.[3] In other words, almost every natural person and economic entity can enjoy the treatment and protection offered by the MAI.

Investments in the MAI include not only traditional foreign direct investment but also indirect investment such as shares, stocks, bonds, debentures, etc.[4] Even more, they also include rights connected with investments such as intellectual property rights, concession rights, property rights, etc. On the contrary, most investment agreements including bilateral investment agreements (BITs) only apply to direct investment rather than indirect investment.

The MAI may be applied to all investment activities in both market access phase and operation phase: establishment, acquisition, expansion, operation, management, etc.[5] Most investment agreements only apply to the operation phase rather than the market access phase. The MAI applies to all contracting parties, to all economic sectors, and to all treatment and measures taken by all levels of governments (central, federal, state, provincial and local governments).[6] The treatment and measures cover laws, regulations, and administrative practices.

The purpose of the MAI's broad application is to promote investment protection and investment liberalization.

3.2.3 High Standards for the Treatment and Protection of Foreign Investors and their Investments

The MAI emphasizes not only the investment protection just as most investment agreements do, and the treatment of investors and investments which is not the focus of most investments agreements. Moreover, the standards provided by the MAI for the treatment and protection are the highest, compared with other investment agreements.

As for the standards for the treatment, the MAI provides that each contracting party should accord national treatment and most-favoured-nation (MFN) treatment. The two principles of treatment should be accorded to both foreign investors and investments. They should also apply to the phase of market access and the phase of operation.[7] In addition, the MAI developed new rules of treatment in some new fields not satisfactorily covered by the present OECD instruments, such as performance requirements, investment incentives, privatization and monopoly, etc.[8] The reason for the highest standards is to raise the level of liberalization of investment.

---

[3] As for the definition of investors, see the MAI, Chapter II, Definitions, Art. 1. The definition of investors will be discussed in detail in Chapter Four of this book.
[4] As for the definition of investments, see the MAI, Chapter II, Definitions, Art. 2. The definition of investments will be discussed in detail in Chapter Four of this book.
[5] The MAI, Chapter III, National Treatment and Most Favoured Nation Treatment, paras. 1, 2 and 3.
[6] This will be further analyzed in Chapter Five of this book.
[7] The treatment standards will be discussed in detail in Chapter Five of this book.
[8] The rules of treatment for special issues will be discussed in Chapter Six of this book.

As for the standards for the protection,[9] in addition to the national treatment and MFN treatment, the MAI established a minimum standard for treatment which requires of each contracting party to accord to investments fair and equitable treatment and full and constant protection and security. The treatment may not be less favourable than that required by international law. Moreover, the MAI developed some specific and strict rules for expropriation and compensation, protection from strife, transfers and subrogation. All these may provide sufficient protection for foreign investors and their investments.

3.2.4   Strong and Effective Enforcement Mechanism of the MAI

The present OECD investment instruments are lack of an effective enforcement mechanism. The commitments of members thereunder are urged to be enforced by the peer pressure. The MAI negotiators considered that the whole agreement would be like a paper tiger without strong dispute settlement mechanism.[10] Therefore, they put forth effort to reinforce the enforcement mechanism so as to ensure that each contracting party would undertake its agreement commitments under the Agreement. The dispute settlement mechanism of the MAI covers state-state dispute settlement and investor-state dispute settlement.[11] The means of settlement include negotiations, consultation and international arbitration.

On the other hand, the withdrawal procedure is very strict, or even unreasonable. The contracting parties may not withdraw from the agreement within five years once they accede to the MAI. Even if they withdraw from the agreement, the MAI shall continue to apply for a period of fifteen years.[12] That is to say, if one country accedes to the MAI, it shall undertake the commitments under the MAI for at least twenty years. This kind of withdrawal procedure is quite rare in international agreements. The high cost of withdrawal from the MAI will surely prevent countries from withdrawing.

3.2.5   Uneven and Unbalanced Relations between the Governments' Obligations and the Foreign Investors' Rights

The MAI establishes a series of rights and responsibilities. But the rights granted in the Agreement go only to foreign investors and corporations; while the responsibilities go only to governments.[13] Since foreign investors

---

[9]   The protection standards will be discussed in Chapter Seven of this book.
[10]   F. Engering, "Keynotes Address", *Multilateral Agreement on Investment: State of Play in April 1997*, OCDE/GD (97)114, p. 8.
[11]   For a detailed discussion of the dispute settlement mechanism, see Chapter Eight of this book.
[12]   The MAI, Chapter XII, Withdrawal.
[13]   "Everything you Wanted to Know About the Multilateral Agreement on Investment (MAI)", available at http://www.citizen.org/pctrade/mai/what%20is/maievery.htm; L. Wallach, "Testimony of Lori Wallach", Thursday, March 5, 1998, available at http://www.citizen.org/pctrade/testimony.htm. The commitments of contracting states and the rights of foreign investors will be shown in the following chapters.

are not parties to the MAI, the MAI can not impose any obligation or respon-sibility on them. Therefore, foreign investors do not undertake any binding responsibilities in host country, for instance, the responsibilities to observe laws and regulations of the host country. The rights and obligations of foreign investors are critically unbalanced. That is why the MAI is consid-ered as "A Bill of Rights for International Investors" or "Corporate Bill of Right".[14]

Although the MAI negotiators agreed to annex the OECD Guidelines for Multilateral Enterprises to the MAI,[15] the Guidelines themselves are not legally binding. According to an OECD official, attaching the Guidelines to the MAI will enhance its political appeal, but will not affect the non-binding nature of the instrument.[16] Therefore, the MAI is still lack of binding rules governing the behavior of investors.

3.3   COMMENTS ON THE FEATURES OF THE MAI

The MAI is the first attempt to combine in one multilateral investment agree-ment the disciplines in three key areas of foreign direct investment rule-making: investment protection, investment liberalization and dispute settlement.[17] The whole MAI is compared to a large and strong building.[18] The broad definition of investor and investment is the wide foundation of the building. The heavy obligations of contracting parties in investment pro-tection and liberalization are the walls of the building. The dispute settle-ment system is the roof of the building. In this way, the MAI provides a large comfortable building for foreign investors in every aspect.

The MAI is an investment agreement with high standards in investment protection, investment liberalization and dispute settlement system. The background for such a high standard agreement is that OECD countries are broadly like-minded countries at similar levels of economic development and where liberalization is already very advanced.[19] Even in such a case, not all developed countries would like to accept the high standards in all respects. In order to offset the heavy obligations resulted from the purpose of high standard, every country takes advantage of the reservation clause of the MAI to "grandfather" those non-conforming measures. In the process

---

[14]   The Preamble Center for Public Policy, "The Multilateral Agreement on Investment: A 'Bill of Rights' for International Investors?", available at http://www.flora.org/library/mai/preamble.html; Aid Watch, "Corporate Bill of Rights on the Ropes", available at http://www.aidwatch.org.au/news/14/02.htm.

[15]   R. Geiger, "Towards a Multilateral Agreement on Investment", 31 *Cornell International Law Journal* (1998), no. 3, pp. 472–473.

[16]   Id., p. 473.

[17]   J. R. Shelton, "Opening Address", *The Multilateral Agreement on Investment: State of Play as of February 1997*, p. 4. The author is Deputy Secretary General of the OECD.

[18]   F. Engering, *supra* note 10, p. 7.

[19]   W. H. Witherell, "The OECD Multilateral Agreement on Investment", 4 *Transnational Corporations*, no. 2 (August 1995), p. 7. The author is Director for Financial, Fiscal and Enterprise Affairs of the OECD.

of the negotiations, about 1000 exceptions (reservations) were raised by different countries.[20] These exceptions and their precautionary purpose in essence weaken the high standards of the MAI. Furthermore, there were many contentions as to the measures allowed to be reserved and the time period of their final cancellation during the negotiations. All these are strong negative evidence to show that developed countries are not satisfied with the high standards of the MAI.

Developing countries neither have the same economic background as developed countries, nor have participated in the MAI negotiations. The high standards of the MAI are unacceptable for them. If developing countries accede to the MAI at the high standards, they do not have the ability to assume the heavy obligations, and the consequences would be too ghastly to contemplate. Take for example, the developing countries are backward in their financial service, and their self regulation capacity in this sector is still weak. If their pre-mature capital market is open too early to foreign investors, their domestic financial order is sure to be disturbed. The Asian Financial Crisis is a case in point and a bitter lesson.

It is suggested that developing countries may also take advantage of the MAI's clauses concerning general exceptions, safeguards and country specific exceptions to relieve their obligations.[21] The author is of the opinion that this is not easy to achieve. According to the MAI, only those countries which are willing and able to undertake their obligations on terms agreed between them and the contracting parties acting through the Parties Group are possible to accede to the MAI.[22] Now that a country is considered by contracting states as able to undertake its obligations, it can not be expected that contracting states will agree with this country to undertake less heavy obligations, or to have too many country specific exceptions proposed by this country. What is more, it is possible that contracting states will ask for high "accession fee" from this country. China's being beset with difficulties in its accession to the WTO is a case in point.

The MAI's dispute settlement mechanism, especially the investor-state system, accords foreign investors the right to challenge host country in international arbitration tribunal when their profits are damaged by the measure taken by a host country. This system enables foreign investors to enjoy too many benefits. However, domestic investors do not have such rights or benefits. This creates another form of discrimination against domestic investors. This mechanism system also gives foreign investors standing to make use of international arbitral tribunal to challenge a sovereign state at random. This is a serious damage to the sovereignty of a state.

The theory behind high standards is that an investment agreement with high standards can have positive effects on investment decisions by foreign firms and thus can attract more foreign investment. This is also the reason

---

[20] P. Ford, "A Pact to Guide Global Investing Promised Jobs—But at What Cost?", *The Christian Science Monitor International*, February 25, 1998, available at http://www.csmonitor.com/durable/1998/02/25/intl.6.html.
[21] E. V. K. FitzGerald, R. Cubero-Brealey & A. Lehmann, "The Development Implications of the Multilateral Agreement on Investment: A Report Commissioned by the UK Department for International Development (21 March 1998)", p. 4.
[22] The MAI, Chapter XII, Accession.

for developed countries to encourage developing countries to join the MAI.[23] However, is it true that acceding to the MAI will absorb more foreign investment? Many past research and facts show that accession to sort of investment agreement can to a certain extent improve the country's investment environment, but it is not the decisive factor for the inflow of investment. There is no direct and positive connection between accession to an agreement and the amount of inflow of foreign investment. Accession to no international investment agreement does not mean no inflow of investment. For instance, for a variety of reasons, there is no bilateral investment agreement between China and the United States, but the United States is the largest source of capital for China, except for Hong Kong and Taiwan. China is the country that absorbs the largest amount of foreign investment among developing countries. Similarly, joining the MAI does not necessarily mean that foreign investment will come in torrents, while non-accession to the MAI does not mean no inflow of foreign investment.

3.4   APPROACHES ADOPTED BY THE MAI

The MAI established high standards for treatment and protection of investment and imposed heavy burden of obligations on governments. But to relieve the commitments, the MAI allows two categories of exceptions. One is the general exceptions to the MAI commitments.[24] They are permanent exceptions applicable to all contracting parties. The other is country-specific exceptions to protect non-conforming measures. These exceptions are subject to review by the other participating countries and the Negotiating Group to ensure an acceptable balance of commitments among contracting parties.[25] Under the regime of country-specific exceptions, the MAI negotiators adopted top-down, standstill and rollback approaches to raise the level of existing liberalization.

3.4.1   The Top-down Approach

The top-down approach is an approach that sets general high standards for almost all economic sectors in one agreement with some specific exceptions as an annex to the agreement. In the case of the MAI, the contracting parties make an overall commitment to the MAI's non-discrimination provisions and absolute standards, then list country-specific exceptions for those areas they do not want to be covered by these obligations.[26] Therefore, the structure of the MAI is that the first several chapters are concerning the general commitments and obligations of the parties and then there is one

---

[23]   F. Engering, "The Multilateral Investment Agreement", 5 *Transnational Corporations*, no. 3 (December 1996), p. 159.
[24]   As to the general exceptions, see Chapter Five of this book.
[25]   R. Geiger, *supra* note 15, p. 470.
[26]   A. Böhmer, "The Struggle for a Multilateral Agreement on Investment—an Assessment of the Negotiation Process in the OECD", 41 *German Yearbook of International Law* (1998), pp. 270–271.

chapter concerning the country-specific exceptions. The latter chapter sets out the conditions and approaches for each party's exceptions. The list of each party's exceptions is to be an annex to the MAI. However, the MAI's provisions on expropriation, general treatment standard and performance requirements can never be covered in the country-specific exceptions. Moreover, the country-specific exceptions are not permanent. They are subject to progressive liberalization. The purpose of the top-down approach is to rapidly raise the level of existing liberalization.

The approach in contrast with the top-down approach is the "bottom-up" approach. The bottom-up approach starts with an initial agreement that contains a few general lower commitments, and provides a benchmark towards which the contracting parties agree to proceed. Each party makes an offer and negotiates the liberalization obligations it will undertake in its "schedules". After the agreement comes into effect, new regular negotiation rounds are conducted to discuss each party's new offers of further advances towards the elimination of restrictive measures. The General Agreement on Trade in Services (GATS) is an example of the bottom-up approach. The GATS requires each party to provide MFN treatment to foreign investors and the investments in all service sectors. Those service sectors where the parties agree to undertake specific commitments of national treatment and market access are listed in the "schedules" as an annex to the Agreement. In the follow-up negotiations, each party offers other sectors to undertake national treatment and market access.[27]

3.4.2 The Standstill Approach

The standstill approach is only used in the case of country-specific exceptions. General exceptions are excluded from the standstill principle. The objective of standstill is to freeze the existing non-conforming measures (*the status quo*) and make them as an irreversible minimum standard for liberalization. Any introduction of new restrictions is not allowed unless this is made possible by other provisions, e.g. (temporary) derogation.[28]

The standstill was first adopted in the European Community Treaty. The treaty provides that member states shall not introduce any new restrictions on the right of establishment in their territories of nationals of other Member States, save as otherwise provided in this treaty.[29] The MAI contains an article in the chapter of Country Specific Exceptions of standstill to "grandfather" existing non-conforming measures and prevent the introduction of more restrictive measures.[30]

For those matters to be standstilled, the MAI requires that: (a) each contracting party should list all non-conforming measures in an annex to the MAI; (b) the reservations should describe the nature and scope of the non-conforming measures so that the reservations are not of a "precautionary" nature; (c) no additional non-conforming measures could be introduced;

---

[27] GATS, Arts. XVI–XXI.
[28] W. H. Witherell, *supra* note 19, p. 11.
[29] Article 53 of the European Community Treaty.
[30] The MAI, Chapter IX, Lodging of Country Specific Exceptions, Part A and its footnote 3.

(d) an amendment to a non-conforming measure would be permitted provided it did not decrease the conformity of the measure.[31]

The standstill approach is used by the MAI to ensure a high minimum standard of treatment for investors and their investments. A violation of standstill rule would be a violation of the underlying MAI obligations, and the dispute settlement provisions would apply to such breaches of the MAI obligations.[32]

3.4.3 The Rollback Approach

The rollback approach in the MAI is also only used in the case of country-specific exceptions. It is designed to reduce over time exceptions to liberalization obligations, with a view to their eventual elimination.[33] According to the Commentary to the MAI, rollback is the liberalization process by which the reduction and eventual elimination of non-conforming measures to the MAI would take place. It is a dynamic element linked with standstill, which provides its starting point. Combined with the standstill rule, it would produce a "ratchet effect", where any new liberalization measures would be "locked in" so they could not be rescinded or nullified over time.[34] In other words, once a certain sector is liberalized, its status is irreversible.

The rollback rule will likely include both initial measures taken during the negotiations and measures taken after the entry into force of the agreement. For the MAI, in the former case, rollback might be achieved through: (a) liberalization commitments by the contracting parties effective on the date of entry into force of the MAI, which implies that not all restrictions currently maintained by the contracting parties would be included in the list of country-specific exceptions; and (b) rollback commitments inscribed in a country-specific exception or description of a non-conforming measure by means of a "phase out" or a "sunset clause" specifying a future date when the non-conforming measure would be removed or made more limited in the future.[35]

In the latter case, rollback might result from: (a) an obligation for a contracting party to adjust its country-specific exceptions to reflect any new liberalization measure (the "ratchet effect"); (b) periodic examinations of non-conforming measures. These examinations could lead to recommendations in favour of the removal or limitations of specific measures. These reviews could be conducted on a country-by-country basis, or on an horizontal or sectoral basis, taking into account the degree of liberalization already achieved; and (c) future rounds of negotiations designed to remove non-conforming measures. The decision to launch future negotiations could

---

[31] Commentary to the MAI , Chapter IX, Standstill and the Listing of Country Specific Reservations, para. 3.
[32] Id., para. 1.
[33] W. H. Witherell, *supra* note 20.
[34] Commentary to the MAI, Chapter IX, Rollback, para. 1; M. W. Sikkel, "Exceptions, Derogations and National Reservations", *The Multilateral Agreement on Investment: State of Play as of February 1997*, pp. 24–25. The author is Head of Division, Investment Policy and International Organisation, Ministry of Economics, Netherlands.
[35] Commentary to the MAI, Chapter IX, Rollback, para. 3; M. W. Sikkel, *supra* note 34, p. 25.

be taken at the conclusion of the MAI negotiations or the MAI could provide a specific date for the first round of such negotiations.[36]

3.5   COMMENTS ON THE FEATURES AND APPROACHES OF THE MAI

The top-down approach, compared with the bottom-up approach, is a more open and broader approach in the market access. The bottom-up approach is a relatively practical and acceptable approach for developing countries, while the top-down approach is radical and overanxious for quick results.

The standstill approach adopted by the MAI is a comparatively strict method. In general, there are two types of exceptions or reservations adopted by one agreement (e.g. the NAFTA): closed reservations to protect the existing law (A-type reservations), and open-ended reservations to enable legislators to adopt new law or strengthen existing law in certain policy (B-type reservations).[37] A-type reservations permit the government to reserve the laws in conflict with the agreement, but do not permit it to extend the law or apply the law to other areas later on. B-type reservations permit the government to continue to make public policy in violation of the agreement in certain area after it signs the agreement. Therefore, B-type reservations are less strict. The reservations allowed by the MAI are A-type reservations, and they need to be eliminated in certain time period, according to the MAI's rollback provisions. As to whether the B-type reservations should be allowed, a lot of controversies arose among negotiators. It was agreed that even if they were permitted, they should be limited in a narrow policy area.[38]

The rollback approach excludes the reservations from traditional protection or the exemption of certain laws. It only postpones the time limit of the effect of these laws which have to be eventually eliminated. The result of rollback is to limit and deprive a state of its legislation power and regulation power for its national economy. That is to say, rollback approach will limit the economic sovereignty of a state.

3.6   CONCLUSION

Although the MAI failed, its high standards and the approaches adopted by it might be regarded as "precedents" by future negotiations for multilateral investment rules. Therefore developing countries should be alert to these tendencies.

---

[36]   Commentary to the MAI, Chapter IX, Rollback, para. 4; M. W. Sikkel, *supra* note 34, pp. 25–26.
[37]   L. Wallach, "For the Multilateral Agreement on Investment", *The NGO Pocket Trade Lawyer*, pp. 4–5, available at http://www.citizen.org/pctrade/mai/What%20is/ngo.htm.
[38]   The MAI, Chapter IX. Part B and footnote 9; M. Sforza, "MAI Provisions and Proposals: An Analysis of the April 1998 Text", *Public Citizen's Global Trade Watch*, July 1998, p. 20.

4. An Analysis of the MAI's Scope of Application

4.1   INTRODUCTION

The object of an international investment agreement's substantive provisions, such as standards of treatment, investment protection and dispute settlement mechanism is investor and investment. To be specific, standards of treatment are accorded to investors and investments, and just as its name implies, investment protection is provided especially for investment. Any treatment or protection will lose its significance without the existence of investors and their investments. Consequently, the problems regarding who can enjoy the rights under the investment agreement, and what kind of commercial activities can be protected by the agreement are the problems concerning the scope of application which should be first solved in formulating an investment agreement.

   The purpose and target of formulating an investment agreement will determine the scope of investor and investment. The scope of investor and investment has significant but different impact on capital-import countries and capital-export countries. Once the scope of investor and investment is determined, the scope of application of an investment agreement is determined. It may be said that the terminologies of investor and investment stands at the center of an international investment agreement. They help to delimit the boundary of an agreement.

   As mentioned above, the MAI was to be an agreement with high standards. One of its facets of high standards is its broadest scope of application. To serve this purpose, it is necessary to define investor and investment in the broadest sense. At the beginning of the negotiations, delegations achieved the consensus that the definition of investor should be as broad as possible.[1] After the definition was drafted, even the MAI delegate had to admit that it would be difficult to make that definition any broader.[2]

---

[1]   M. Schekulín, "Scope of the MAI: Definition of Investor and Investments', *The Multilateral Agreement on Investment: State of Play as of February 1997*, p. 10. The author is Chief Negotiator for the MAI (Austria), Vice-Chairman of the OECD Committee on International Investment and Multinational Enterprises CIME) and Vice-Chairman of the MAI Expert Group on Financial Services Matters.
[2]   X. Musca, "Scope of the MAI", *Proceedings of the Special Session on the Multilateral Agreement on Investment Held in Paris on 17 September 1997*, p. 9. The author is Treasury Directorate, Ministry for the Economy and Finance, France.

4.2   DEFINITION OF INVESTOR

An international investment agreement should define the investor properly so as to safeguard its protection for member states investors and prevent the abuse of the agreement by the investors from non-member states. However, it is not an easy task for an investment agreement to define the investor, the reason being that different countries have their own but different definitions of investor.

Generally speaking, how a country defines its investment subject depends to a large extent on its national economic development. For developing countries, there are more restrictions on the subjects who are allowed by national law to engage in domestic and international economic activities. As a consequence, investors are defined in a comparatively narrow sense. For developed countries, developed and active national and international economy encourages large number of subjects to conduct such economic activities. There are less restrictions by national law on the qualification of investors. The investor is defined in a much broader way.

Even if there exist differences as to the definition and scope of investor in each country, there is one thing in common. The term "investor" usually includes natural persons and artificial or legal person (or juridical entities), the latter is often referred to as "companies".[3]

4.2.1   Definition of Investor in the MAI

Likewise, the MAI defines investor as including natural persons and legal persons. But the MAI defines them in a very broad sense.

The definition of investor in the MAI reads as follows:

Investor means: (i) a natural person having the nationality of, or who is permanently residing in, a Contracting Party in accordance with its applicable law; or (ii) a legal person or any other entity constituted or organised under the applicable law of a Contracting Party, whether or not for profit, and whether private or government owned or controlled, and includes a corporation, trust, partnership, sole proprietorship, joint venture, association or organisation.[4]

The MAI's definition of investor covers natural persons. According to the above definition, any natural person who has the nationality of a contracting party, no matter where he lives, or who is permanently residing in a contracting party, no matter what nationality he has, might be qualified as an investor under the MAI. In other words, both the nationals and permanent residents of one contracting party are covered by the scope of natural persons as investors. So both nationality criterion and residence criterion are

---

[3]   UNCTAD, *Bilateral Investment Treaties in the Mid-1990s*, United Nations, New York and Geneva, 1998, p. 37; UNCTAD, *Scope and Definition*, United Nations, New York and Geneva, 1999, p. 32.
[4]   The MAI, Chapter II, Definitions, para. 1.

adopted by the MAI in defining an investor of natural person. Consequently, the scope of natural persons qualified as investors is very broad.

From the perspective of international investment agreements, the scope of natural persons as investors varies. Some agreements do not deem natural persons as investors. For instance, the bilateral investment agreements (BITs) concluded by Romania exclude natural persons from investors.[5] Some agreements adopt nationality criterion to ascertain the scope of natural persons as investors.[6] Some developing countries which adopt the nationality criterion further require that for a person to be an investor, it should get authorization from the government to make an investment.[7] Some other agreements adopt the residence criterion as an alternative to the nationality criterion. This is in the interest of high immigration countries such as Australia, Canada and the United States, in which a considerable proportion of the economically active population may not yet be full citizens. So these countries regularly extend a special legal status to permanent residents.[8] Because the nationality criterion does not require the natural person to reside in the state of asserted nationality, the link between the person and the state may be in-genuine or loose. As a result, agreement with such a criterion is easy to be abused by those persons who assert to have the nationality of the contracting state but does not reside in the state. In order to avoid such an abuse, many agreements combine the nationality criterion with the residence criterion. They require that such a person should also reside or be domiciled in the country of nationality.[9]

By and large, the national laws of developing countries impose more qualifications on the natural persons to be investors, while developed countries impose less qualifications. Further, developed countries always tend to expand the scope of object to be protected by an investment agreement. There are great conflicts in this regard when the two categories of countries come to conclude bilateral investment agreements. To solve such a problem, the BIT does not give a common definition for both parties. Instead, the BIT gives respective definitions according to respective requirements of two parties.[10] Such a solution is a practical way to solve disagreements between different countries.

Unfortunately, the MAI does not take into account the above differentiated practice of different countries, and defines investor in a broad way to cover almost all natural persons.

The MAI's definition of investor also covers legal persons. The criterion of place of constitution is used to determine the nationality of legal persons.

In general, three different criteria have been used to determine the nationality of companies by international investment agreement in different

[5] UNCTC, *Bilateral Investment Treaties*, United Nations, New York, 1988, p. 22. One example is the bilateral investment agreement concluded between China and Romania.
[6] UNCTC, *supra* note 5, p. 22; UNCTAD, *Bilateral Investment Treaties in the Mid-1990s*, p. 37; UNCTAD, *Scope and Definition*, p. 35.
[7] See, for example, the China's definition of investor in the BIT between China and Sweden.
[8] UNCTAD, *Scope and Definition*, p. 35.
[9] UNCTC, *supra* note 5, p. 22; UNCTAD, *Bilateral Investment Treaties in the Mid-1990s*, p. 38. Examples are the BITs between Germany and Israel (Article I(3)(b)) and between Denmark and Indonesia (Article I(a)).
[10] Examples are the BITs between China and Sweden, and China and Germany.

combinations: the place of incorporation or constitution, the location of the seat (or the principal place of business), and the nationality of ownership or control.[11]

The criterion of place of incorporation is often used in the treaties concluded by some developed countries such as Denmark, the Netherlands, Switzerland, the United Kingdom and the United States, and by some developing countries.[12] This criterion is the easiest to determine but not easily changed.[13] However, such a company may have no other connection with the country where it incorporates. It does not contribute any benefits to this country, either. This criterion is easily made use by foreign nationals who constitute a company according to the laws of a contracting party so as to gain the treaty protection.[14] Therefore, to avoid the above disadvantages, the model BIT used by the United States permits the host country to deny a company of the benefits of the treaty if the company has no substantial business activities in the territory of the country.[15]

The criterion of the location of the company's seat is used in the treaties concluded by Belgium, Germany and Sweden.[16] This criterion is not as easy to determine as the place of incorporation. But it reflects more significant economic links between the company and the country where it is seated.[17]

The criterion of the nationality of ownership or control may well reflect a genuine economic relation between the company and the country. But it is the most difficult to ascertain and the least permanent.[18] It is seldom used alone in investment treaties,[19] but mostly used in conjunction with one of the other criteria.[20]

In some treaties the criteria of place of incorporation and the location of the seat are used in combination with each other.[21] For some other treaties, the three criteria should be met at the same time.[22]

In addition to the above criteria, developing countries have some other restrictions on legal persons, e.g., the investor should have been authorized by the government to make an investment, or should have the legal personality

---

[11]   UNCTAD, *supra* note 9, p. 39.
[12]   For example, the BIT between Singapore and Sri Lanka.
[13]   UNCTAD, *supra* note 9, p. 39; UNCTAD, *supra* note 8, p. 37.
[14]   Id.
[15]   Article XII of the BIT Model (1994) of the United States.
[16]   UNCTAD, *supra* note 9, p. 40.
[17]   UNCTAD, *supra* note 8, pp. 38–39.
[18]   Id., p. 39.
[19]   Article 1 of the Swiss standard draft agreement (1996 version) used this criterion. See UNCTC, *supra* note 5, p. 41.
[20]   One example for the conjunction of ownership or control with the place of incorporation is the definition of "companies" in the Model BIT of the Asian-African Legal Consultative Committee. One example for the conjunction of ownership or control with the location of the seat is Article 17.1 of the Convention Establishing the Inter-Arab Investment Guarantee Corporation. See UNCTAD, *supra* note 8, p. 39.
[21]   One example is the BIT between China and France. Another example is Article I(2) of the ASEAN Agreement for the Promotion and Protection of Investments. See UNCTAD, *supra* note 8, p. 40.
[22]   One example is Article 1 of the Charter on a Regime of Multinational Industrial Enterprises in the Preferential Trade Area for Eastern and Southern African States. See UNCTAD, *supra* note 8, p. 40.

and, under the laws of the contracting party, be entitled to undertake activities of economic cooperation with foreign countries,[23] or should have the legal capacity to invest abroad.[24] Due to their less developed economy, developing countries have to adopt a combination of the criteria and have more and stricter requirements in defining the companies.

Most developed countries adopt one or two of the above criteria in concluding investment agreements. For some developed countries, such phrase as "whether or not for profit, or privately or governmentally owned" or the like is used in defining companies,[25] so as to reduce possible restrictions on the companies.

As far as the MAI is concerned, it adopts the easiest but not the most common criterion in defining legal persons. It also uses the phrase "whether or not for profit, and whether private or government owned or controlled". There is not any restriction on the definition of legal persons.

To make the definition of legal persons more specific, the MAI lists the forms of entities to be investors: corporation, trust, partnership, sole proprietorship, joint venture, association or organisation. The long list shows that the scope of legal persons is very broad. Moreover, the Commentary to the MAI emphasized that the list is only illustrative but not exclusive.[26] It is open-ended so as to cover any other forms of entities not listed in the MAI and any other possible forms in the future.

To sum up, for the MAI, an investor can be anyone, including any natural person and any legal person and any other entity. It is difficult to imagine a broader definition than this.[27]

4.2.2 Arguments in Drafting the Definition of Investor

The MAI's broad definition of investor aroused many controversies during the negotiations. Some delegations tried to widen further the scope of investors, others wanted to give some limits on investors. The controversies mainly focused on the following four points.

4.2.2.1 *Whether Branches could be Considered as Investors*

Branch is not in the MAI's list of the forms of entities. Delegations had a very heated debate on whether branches could be considered as investors.[28] Legislation in most countries regards branches as parts of the corporations

---

[23] One example is the BIT between China and Romania.
[24] One example is the definition given by China in the BIT between China and Sweden.
[25] Examples are Article I of the BIT Model (1994) of the United States and the definition by Germany in the BIT between China and Germany.
[26] Commentary to the MAI, Chapter II, Definitions, Investor, para. 1.
[27] X. Musca, *supra* note 2, p. 9.
[28] M. Schekulin, *supra* note 1, p. 11; F. Engering, "The Multilateral Investment Agreement", 5 *Transnational Corporations*, no. 3 (December 1996), p. 150.

and thus does not confer upon them the appropriate legal capacity to act independently as investors in their own name and on their own account. That was why the reference to branches in the list was deleted.[29] However, according to Switzerland law, branches have the legal capacity to make an investment. This situation made it doubtful that whether branches could be investors under the MAI. The Commentary to the MAI is of the opinion that this situation would be covered by the definition of investor even after the deletion of the word "branch" from the list, the reason being that the list of "legal and other entities" covered by the definition of "investor" is not exclusive.[30] It shows that the MAI not only defines investor in a broad way, but also interprets it widely.

4.2.2.2   *Whether Contracting Parties could be Considered as Investors*

According to the MAI's definition of investor, natural persons, legal persons and other entities could be investors under the MAI. But because contracting parties are neither natural persons, nor legal persons or other entities constituted under the applicable law of a contracting party, they could not be considered as investors. But some delegations tried to widen the scope of investor to cover contracting parties. They argued that the MAI's definition should include all entities with the capacity to invest and a contracting party may itself make an investment without being a legal person.[31] But most delegations held that a contracting party would invest through state-owned entities that are covered by the definition and thus might gain protection under the MAI. In case the contracting party is an economic actor, it does not need to be protected under the MAI, it may be protected by diplomatic processes under international law.[32]

The author is of the opinion that it is inappropriate to include contracting parties in the definition of investors. Otherwise it would lead to confusion and contradiction. According to the MAI, an investor should be accorded national treatment and most-favoured-nation treatment. When a contracting party as a sovereign state makes an investment in another contracting party, should it enjoy national treatment and be subject to the law of the another country, as an investor under the MAI, or can it enjoy the immunity under international law, as a sovereign state? Further, with the state-state dispute settlement procedure and investor–state dispute settlement procedure in the MAI, if a contracting party could be regarded as an investor, when there is any dispute arising under the MAI, which procedure should be followed, the state-state procedure, or the investor–state procedure, or the contracting party might choose either one? Therefore, in view of the definition itself, the substantive norms of the MAI, and the special status of the contracting parties, contracting parties should not be included in the definition of investors.

---

[29]   M. Schekulin, *supra* note 1, p. 11.
[30]   Commentary to the MAI, Chapter II, Definitions, Investor, para. 1.
[31]   Id., para. 3.
[32]   Ib.; M. Schekulin, *supra* note 1, p. 11.

4.2.2.3   Whether the Definition should be Further Restricted

The MAI's definition of investor is the broadest in comparison with the definitions of other developed countries. Some delegations suggested to add the phrase "provided it has the legal capacity to invest" at the end of the definition. But most delegations considered it unnecessary, and if it is added, it would create legal uncertainty.[33]

The author thinks it necessary to add such a phrase since this phrase helps to restrict the broad definition. Such a phrase can rule out the possibility that the entities without the legal capacity to invest to become the investors under the MAI. Thus it reduces the opportunities that the rights accorded to investors by the MAI may be abused by those natural or legal persons or other entities which do not engage in investment in other contracting parties. It can also help to solve the above problem that whether Switzerland branches with the legal capacity to invest could be considered as investors. Most developing countries such as China use such a phrase to restrict the scope of investor.

4.2.2.4   Whether the Definition should Include a Link Between the Investor and the Activity of Investing

Some delegations suggested that the link between the investor and the activity of investing should be clearly stated so as not to give the rights, and especially standing in dispute settlement procedures, to any natural or legal person but only to investors in relation to their present or future investment.[34] The Canadian BIT Model mentions such a link, but the Energy Charter Treaty (ECT) does not. The MAI negotiators decided to follow the example of the ECT because they thought that such a link could be defined from the context of the definition, especially the provision on the treatment of investors.[35]

The author considers that reference to the link is necessary so that the MAI could not be taken advantage by those investors who do not have any investment activities in other contracting parties.

4.2.3   Comments on the MAI's Definition of Investor

The only requirement for investor by the MAI is that natural person should have the nationality of a contracting party, or reside permanently in a contracting party, or legal person should be constituted or organized under the applicable law of a contracting party. Such a requirement is the minimum requirement for an investor. Therefore the scope of investor is so broad that it is possible for any natural person or entity to be an investor under the MAI.

---

[33]   Commentary to the MAI, Chapter II, Definitions, Investor, para. 2.
[34]   M. Schekulin, *supra* note 1, p. 11.
[35]   Id.

The possible result is that almost any natural person and legal person could enjoy the treatment and protection provided by the MAI, and could avail themselves of the dispute settlement procedures, no matter whether they have the legal capacity to make an investment or whether they have any substantial investment in a contracting party. This loophole is easily made use by those lawless persons to gain from the MAI so that the interest of contracting parties might be damaged.

In contrast, most countries, especially the developing countries, have more restrictions on natural persons and legal persons to be investors to engage in international economic activities. So their scope of investors is quite limited. When different countries with different definitions of investor come to conclude BITs or multilateral investment agreements, they tend to define investor in a way agreed by all parties, or give a common definition with reservations by different countries in the annex, or each country gives its own definition according to its domestic law. These approaches respect each country's national law and avoid many debates during negotiations and thus make the definition acceptable by each contracting party. The way the MAI defines investor is not in conformation to the requirements of many countries' national laws. This definition is far beyond the practice of developing countries and thus unacceptable by developing countries. This is one of the main reasons why developing countries protest the MAI.

4.3   DEFINITION OF INVESTMENT

The definition of investment is of great significance for the whole investment agreement. First, it helps to define the object and scope to which the provisions of the agreement apply.[36] Second, the definition of investment interacts with other provisions of the agreement, and then ascertains the scope of application of other provisions and the scope of dispute settlements.[37] For example, as far as the national treatment is concerned, the broader the investment is, the stronger the obligations of a contracting party will be. On the other hand, the according of the national treatment enlarges the scope of investment. Therefore, the definition of investment itself does not mean a lot. Only when the definition is put into the substantive disciplines of the agreement can people see its breadth of scope of application.

So far, the concept of "investment" does not have a generally accepted definition.[38] One reason is that investment is an evolving concept and new forms of investment are constantly created. Another reason is that different treaties with different aims and purposes define investment differently. The other reason is that different countries have different definitions in their national legislations. Generally speaking, home countries tend to define it

---

[36]   UNCTAD, *Existing Regional and Multilateral Investment Agreements and Their Relevance to a Possible Multilateral Framework on Investment: Issues and Questions*, 21 January 1998, TD/B/COM.2/EM.3/2, p. 7.
[37]   UNCTAD, *Report of the Expert Meeting on Existing Regional and Multilateral Investment Agreements and Their Development Dimensions*, 22 April 1998, TD/B/COM.2/EM.3/3, p. 5.
[38]   UNCTAD, *supra* note 9, p. 32.

with the broadest possible coverage and host countries tend to limit it in the scope in compliance with their development aims and priority.[39] It is easy to imagine the complex and difficulties in defining investment in an international investment agreement.

4.3.1   General Categories of Investment in International Investment Agreement

There are two ways to define investment in earlier investment instruments.

For capital movement-oriented instruments, they usually define foreign investment in narrow terms, insisting on an investor's control over the enterprise as a necessary element of the concept.[40] They address investment before it is made—in the past, with a view towards its control, in the current context of liberalization, with a view to removing obstacles to its realization.[41] The definition looks primarily to the act of investing, not the assets in which the investment becomes eventually embodied.[42]

For protection-oriented instruments, they generally define investment broadly and comprehensively to cover not only the capital (or the resources) that has crossed borders with a view towards the creation of an enterprise or the acquisition of control over an existing one, but also most other kinds of assets of the enterprise or of the investor, such as property and property rights of various kinds, etc.[43] They seek to safeguard the interests of the investors. Investment is seen as something that already exists.[44] The broad definition is to cover as many as possible the investors' assets.[45]

There are other categories: "asset-based" definition and "enterprise-based" definition. Asset-based definition is a broad definition that includes all assets, followed by an enumeration of specific assets covered.[46] Enterprise-based definition focuses on the business enterprise or the controlling interests in a business enterprise. It includes the establishment or acquisition of a business enterprise and a share in a business enterprise.[47] The asset-based definition is much broader than the enterprise-based definition.

Nowadays, many international investment agreements try to seek both to liberalize investment regulations and to protect foreign investment. They tend to adopt broad definition to include all assets in the territory of one party owned by investors of another party.[48] But some experts think that from the point of development, it is unnecessary to include portfolio investment and non-commercial assets in the agreements for the purpose of liberalization.

---

[39]   UNCTC, *supra* note 5, p. 16.
[40]   UNCTAD, *supra* note 8, p. 15.
[41]   Id., p. 16; UNCTAD, *International Investment Instruments: A Compendium*, vol. I, United Nations, New York and Geneva, 1996, p. xxvii.
[42]   Id.
[43]   UNCTAD, *supra* note 8, p. 15.
[44]   Id., pp. 16–17.
[45]   UNCTAD, *supra* note 41.
[46]   UNCTAD, *supra* note 8, p. 31.
[47]   Id.
[48]   Id., p. 17.

Some other experts think that in the long run, narrow definition of investment in a multilateral agreement can not provide enough flexibility. To balance the two aspects, they suggest that a broad definition approach is adopted in the agreement and then add some qualifications to some of its substantive disciplines.[49]

4.3.2   Definition of Investment in the MAI

It was a tough task for the MAI negotiators to give a common definition to investment. To be an agreement with high standards of liberalization and protection, the MAI pursues a broad definition of investment. But at the beginning of the negotiations, there were substantial disagreements on the definition of investment. Not until 31 January 1997 was a breakthrough made and a basic consensus found: the MAI should have a single, broad and asset based definition of investment.[50]

"Single" means the one definition should apply to all obligations of the MAI without the distinction between the pre-establishment phase (market access phase) and the post-establishment phase (operation phase).[51] While for most international investment agreements, the agreement obligations only apply to the post-establishment phase. In this way their scope of investments is limited.

"Broad" means the definition will go beyond the traditional concept of foreign direct investment to cover portfolio investment.[52] In tradition, foreign investment refers to direct investment. It does not include indirect investment—portfolio investment.

"Asset based" means the definition is based on the concept of assets instead of the concept of enterprise.[53] Therefore it includes both tangible and intangible assets. Traditionally, the asset-based definition is much broader than the enterprise-based definition.

Such a broad definition is to serve for the two purposes of the MAI: investment protection and liberalization. Just as Mr. F. Engering, Chairperson of the Negotiating Group on the MAI, said, "the definition should be broad enough to ensure that all relevant forms of investment undertaken by foreign investors enjoy the benefits of the MAI".[54]

Finally, investment is defined in the MAI as meaning:

every kind of asset owned or controlled, directly or indirectly, by an investor, including: (1) an enterprise; (2) shares, stocks or other forms of equity participation in an enterprise, and rights derived therefrom; (3) bonds, debentures, loans and other forms of debt, and rights derived therefrom; (4) rights under contracts, including turnkey, construction, management, production or revenue-sharing contracts; (5) claims to money and claims to performance; (6) intellectual property rights; (7) rights

---

[49]   UNCTAD, *supra* note 37.
[50]   M. Schekulin, *supra* note 1, p. 11.
[51]   Id.
[52]   Id.
[53]   Id.
[54]   F. Engering, *supra* note 27, p. 148.

conferred pursuant to law or contract such as concessions, licenses, authorisations, and permits; (8) any other tangible and intangible, movable and immovable property, and any related property rights, such as leases, mortgages, liens and pledges.[55]

The Commentary to the MAI considers that this definition covers all recognised and evolving forms of investment and includes the products of an investment.[56] Such a commentary further widens the scope of investment.

The list of assets is a non-exclusive positive list. There is not any negative list of assets that are considered not an investment, though the negotiators once thought over the approach.[57] Such a broad definition makes it uncertain that whether an asset is the investment under the MAI, because there is not any other requirement such as the link with economic activities to qualify the asset as an investment. To narrow the definition, in the footnote of the definition, negotiators consider it necessary to have an interpretative note to indicate that an asset must have the characteristics of an investment, such as the commitment of capital or other resources, the expectation of gain or profit, or the assumption of risk.[58] But in fact, such an interpretative note does not exist. Further, footnote is only footnote, which does not have the effect of the provisions of an agreement.

Compared with other international investment agreements, the MAI's definition of investment is the broadest. It is broader not only than the definition in earlier investment agreements, but also than that in recent agreements, such as the NAFTA and the ECT. In practice, it is difficult to make this definition any broader.

The NAFTA does not mention that investment means every kind of assets, but only gives both positive and negative lists to ascertain the scope of investment. The positive list includes: (1) an enterprise; (2) an equity security of an enterprise; (3) a debt security of an enterprise; (4) a loan to an enterprise; (5) an interest in an enterprise that entitles the owner to share in the income or profits; (6) an interest in an enterprise that entitles the owner to share in the assets on dissolution; (7) real estate or other property; and (8) interests arising from the commitment of capital or other resources in the territory of a Party to economic activity in such territory.[59]

There are further restrictions on the above items to be investment. For example, for a debt security or a loan to an enterprise to be an investment, the enterprise should be an affiliate of the investor or the maturity of them should be at least three years. Anyway, the debt security of or the loan to a state enterprise can never be an investment.[60] The MAI does not have such restrictions. In the NAFTA, for the real estate or other property, only when they are acquired in the expectation or used for the purpose of economic benefit or other business purposes can they be considered investment.[61] Moreover, Intellectual property rights are not covered in the positive list.

---

[55] The MAI, Chapter II, Definitions, para. 2.
[56] Commentary to the MAI, Chapter II, Definitions, Investment, para. 1.
[57] M. Schekulin, *supra* note 1, p. 12; F. Engering, *supra* note 28, p. 149.
[58] The MAI, Chapter II, Definitions, para. 2, footnote 2.
[59] NAFTA, Article 1138.
[60] Id.
[61] Id.

The negative list includes: (1) claims to money that arise solely from: A. commercial contracts for the sale of goods or services by a national or enterprise in the territory of one party to an enterprise in the territory of another party; B. the extension of credit in connection with a commercial transaction; and (2) any other claims to money, which do not involve the kinds of interests set out in the positive list.[62] The negative list is to exclude certain claims to money from investment. But according to the MAI, any claims to money could be investment.

The above positive and negative lists show that the scope of investment in the NAFTA is narrower than that in the MAI.

The ECT gives the same general definition to investment as the MAI, and its illustrative list of assets is more or less the same as in the MAI. But there are more limitations on the scope of investment. Investment in the ECT includes: (1) tangible and intangible, and movable and immovable, property, and any property rights such as leases, mortgages, liens, and pledges; (2) a company or business enterprise, or shares, stock, or other forms of equity participation in a company or business enterprise, and bonds and other debt of a company or business enterprise; (3) claims to money and claims to performance pursuant to contract having an economic value and associated with an investment; (4) intellectual property; (5) returns; and (6) any right conferred by law or contract or by virtue of any license and permits granted pursuant to law to undertake any economic activity in the energy sector.[63]

The ECT limits the claims to money and claims to performance to be investment to those that are pursuant to contract having an economic value and associated with an investment.[64] Further, any investment should be associated with an economic activity in the energy sector.[65] This general limitation greatly restricts the scope of investment. As a consequence, the scope of the investment in the ECT is narrower than that in the MAI. But the definition of investment in the ECT was regarded by scholars as the widest definition ever found.[66] In contrast, the width of the scope of investment in the MAI can be imagined.

4.3.3   Detailed Analysis on the MAI's Definition of Investment

The MAI does not give further explanation to the meaning of the definition or each asset in the list. But the Commentary to the MAI gives detailed supplement to the definition.

The author tries to further analyze the breadth of the MAI's definition of investment, based on the illustration of the Commentary and the relevant provisions of other investment agreements.

---

[62]   Id.
[63]   ECT, Article 1(6).
[64]   Id.
[65]   Id.
[66]   T. W. Waelde, "International Investment under the 1994 Energy Charter Treaty: Legal, Negotiating and Policy Implications for International Investors within Western and Comonwealth of Independent States/Eastern European Countries", 29 *Journal of World Trade* (1995), no. 5, p. 24.

Controlled. Both the MAI and its Commentary do not interpret what "controlled" means. But since the general definition of the MAI "investment means every kind of asset owned or controlled, directly or indirectly, by an investor" is directly transplanted from the definition of the ECT, the meaning of "controlled" can be deduced from the relevant documents of the ECT.

According to the Understandings of the ECT, "control" on investment means factual control. The considerations whether an investor controls an investment in reality are: the economic interest in the investment, the capacity to impose substantial effect on the operation and management of the investment, and the capacity to impose substantial effect on the election of the board of directors and members of other administration.[67] In practice, it is easy to satisfy one of these considerations to regard an investor as having control in the investment.

Indirectly. There were different views on whether the definition should cover the investment "indirectly" owned or controlled by investors.[68] Covering such investment would offer maximum protection to investors. Some delegations thought that such approach would offer the most flexibility to investors in managing their capital flows.[69] It is not difficult to see that the MAI tries its best to broaden the scope of investment to provide benefits to investors.

There could be four cases as to the investment indirectly owned or controlled by an investor:[70]

(a) investment by an investor established in another MAI party, but owned or controlled by a non-MAI investor;
(b) investment by an investor established in a non-MAI party, but owned or controlled by a MAI party investor;
(c) investment by an investor established in another MAI party, but owned or controlled by an investor of a third MAI party;
(d) investment in a MAI party by an investor there covered by the MAI.

According to the MAI's definition of investment, the above four cases are covered in investment. It is understandable and acceptable that the investment in cases (c) and (d) are covered by the MAI. But covering the investment in case (a) and case (b) in the MAI would greatly widen the scope of investment and lead to a lot of problems.

Possible problems arising from case (a) are: in order to obtain the benefits from the MAI, non-MAI investors might first establish an investment in one MAI party and then through this investment invest in other MAI parties. This is the case concerning the abuse of agreement. The EU member states would be seriously troubled by this case because there are many companies established in the EU but owned or controlled by non-EU investors. Some

---

[67] Final Act of the European Energy Charter Conference, Understandings, 3. With respect to Article 1 (6).
[68] Commentary to the MAI, Chapter II, Definitions, Investment, para. 2.
[69] Id.
[70] Id.

delegations suggested that the MAI might include a denial of benefits clause to exclude the investment when the MAI investor lacks substantial business activity in the MAI party.[71]

Possible problems arising from case (b) are: many companies established in developing countries, especially in the tax havens of developing countries, but owned or controlled by investors from developed countries would be protected by the MAI. In other words, the non-MAI developing countries would bear the MAI obligations to those companies. This is absurd. But some delegations argued that if the investment from those companies could not be covered by the investment under the MAI, the investment flows would be diverted from developing countries.[72] This argument is only an excuse, because there is not positive causation between non-protection of the MAI and the diversion of investment flows. The real purpose of this argument is to offer maximum protection to investors from developed countries.

The MAI gives an illustrative list of assets to be investment and the Commentary to the MAI broadens the scope of each of them.

Enterprise. The Commentary to the MAI explicitly points out that enterprise covers scientific research institutes and universities.[73] Normally scientific research institutes and universities only engage in scientific research and teaching and have nothing to do with economic activities. Including institutes and universities in the definition shows the intention of negotiators to widely interpret enterprise. The cause for this inclusion is that the MAI does not mention the link between assets and economic activities. Moreover, the inclusion shows that the requirement in the footnote of the MAI that an asset must have the characteristics of an investment is ignored. This is an evidence showing that footnote does not have any legal effect and exists only in name. Now let's look at the ECT. The ECT requires an investment to be associated with an economic activity in the energy sector and thus excludes scientific research institutes and universities from investment.[74]

Shares, bonds, etc. These assets include portfolio investment and minority holdings. They also cover an interest in an enterprise that entitles the owner to share in income and profits of an enterprise and its assets. The negotiators also considered to cover in them strategic alliances and other arrangements involving know-how, intellectual property, or technology or the joint conduct of research and development programmes.[75] The tendency to widely interpret investment is obvious.

As mentioned above, loans in the NAFTA cover only the loans and debts of long-term maturity and do not cover any loan or debt of a state enterprise. However, loans in the MAI also cover all maturities and debt securities of a state enterprise.[76] Public debt is also covered in the definition. But the nature and characteristics of public debt are different from private debt. Including

---

[71] Id., para. 3.
[72] Id., para. 2.
[73] Id., para. 7.
[74] T. W. Waelde, *supra* note 66, p. 27.
[75] Commentary to the MAI, Chapter II, Definitions, Investment, para. 8.
[76] Id., para. 9.

public debt in investment would lead to such a problem: the rescheduling of public funds could be considered as expropriation under the MAI.[77]

The inclusion of portfolio investment would also cause problems. Portfolio investment has much shorter duration than direct investment. Developing countries are lack of effective control over short-term capital inflows. When portfolio investment is covered by investment under the MAI and thus enjoy the protection of the MAI (such as the national treatment, most-favoured-nation treatment and free transfer of funds), developing countries would be more powerless to conduct control over them. Maybe another Asian Financial Crisis would be unavoidable. Moreover, the risk of a host country to be involved in investor-state arbitration is increased, since mere portfolio investors could also have standing against the host state.[78]

Rights under contracts. The contracts include turnkey, construction, management, production and revenue-sharing contracts. All rights including economic rights and legal rights under these contracts could be considered as investment. The ambition to define investment in a possibly wide way is clear.

Claims to money and claims to performance. Most BITs include claims to money and claims to performance in investment, but require that the claims should have economic value.[79] Those claims without economic value could not be considered as investment. The NAFTA excludes those claims to money in the negative list from investment. However, the MAI not only imposes no qualification or restriction on the claims to money or claims to performance to be investment, but also consider them to cover bank deposits and derivatives.[80] Although the Commentary points out that the claims arising as a result of a sale of goods or services are not generally considered as investments,[81] the possibility that they are considered as investments in some particular cases still exists.

As a matter of fact, some claims to money, especially bank deposits and derivatives, fall within the areas of trade and finance instead of investment. Although the negotiators stated previously that the definition of investment must not be so broad as to cover trade operations and purely financial transactions that by themselves lack the characteristics of an investment and fall under existing international regimes for cross border trade operations and financial market regulations,[82] the definition was interpreted to be expanded to the areas of trade and finance.

Intellectual property rights. According to the Commentary, all forms of intellectual property are included in the definition of investment, including copyrights and related rights, patents, industrial designs, rights in semiconductor layout designs, technical processes, trade secrets, including know-how and confidential business information, trade and service marks, and

---

[77] M. Schekulin, *supra* note 1, p. 13.
[78] A. Böhmer, "The Struggle for a Multilateral Agreement on Investment—an Assessment of the Negotiation Process in the OECD", 41 *German Yearbook of International Law* (1998), p. 279.
[79] Examples are Article I, 1, (b)(iii) of the BIT Model (1984) of the United States and Article 1, 1(c) of China's BIT Model. See also A. Böhmer, *supra* note 78, p. 277.
[80] Commentary to the MAI, Chapter II, Definitions, Investment, para. 10.
[81] Id., para. 11.
[82] M. Schekulin, *supra* note 1, p. 12.

trade names and goodwill.[83] However, there were different views among delegations. Some think that literary and artistic property rights should not be included. Some hold that only the intellectual property rights acquired in the expectation of economic benefit or other business purposes can be covered by the investment under the MAI.[84] However, these different views were not adopted by the MAI.

In many investment agreements, not all forms of intellectual property rights are considered as investment. As mentioned above, the NAFTA does not include intellectual property rights in investment. In China's BIT Model, only copyrights, industrial property, know-how and technological process are considered as investment.[85] The coverage of intellectual property rights as investment under the MAI is very broad.

Moreover, the issue of intellectual property rights itself is a very complicated issue. There have been many international conventions and agreements concerning this subject ever since 1880s, such as the Paris Convention for the Protection of Industrial Property, the Berne Convention for the Protection of Literary and Artistic Works, the Agreement on Trade-Related Aspects of Intellectual Property Rights (TRIPs) of the WTO, etc. The World Intellectual Property Organization (WIPO) was established in 1974 to promote the protection of intellectual property throughout the world and to administer various multilateral treaties dealing with the legal and administrative aspects of intellectual property. In 1996 the WIPO began to cooperate with the WTO.

As far as the protection of intellectual property rights is concerned, many WTO member states claim that they can not bear any obligations heavier than that in the TRIPs. But the MAI regards all forms of intellectual property as investments and accords to them national treatment, protection against expropriation and free transfer of funds and the right to file the investor-state arbitration against the host state. These obligations are much heavier than those in the TRIPs. On the other hand, the standards of treatment and dispute settlement mechanisms provided for by the MAI are different from those by other conventions and agreements related to intellectual property rights, how to deal with these conflicts? As a consequence, the relationship of the MAI to other conventions needs to be further clarified.

Rights conferred pursuant to law or contract. These rights such as concessions, licenses, authorizations, and permits generally cover the rights to search for, cultivate, extract or exploit natural resources,[86] or cover the rights to build infrastructure. Regarding these rights as investment and expanding the MAI's protection to them will arise two problems.

First, developing countries would gravely oppose this approach. There have been different views on the nature of concession between developing countries and developed countries. Developing countries regard concession contracts as national contracts and thus the contracts should be subject to national law. The host state has absolute jurisdiction over concession contracts.

---

[83] Commentary to the MAI, Chapter II, Definitions, Investment, para. 12.
[84] Id.
[85] Article 1, 1(d) of China's BIT Model. See UNCTAD, *supra* note 9, p. 247.
[86] Commentary to the MAI, Chapter II, Definitions, Investment, para. 14.

Developed countries regard concession contracts as international contracts and they should be subject to international law. The substance of the difference is the fight for jurisdiction over concession contracts. Developed countries try to exclude the contracts from the jurisdiction of host state and strengthen their protection over their investment in developing countries through international law. When this dispute is still in pending, it is not suitable to cover concessions under the protection of the MAI—an international agreement.

Second, some aspects of concessions raised issues related to monopolies and cross-border government procurement.[87] The latter two issues are special issues to be dealt with in the MAI. Conflicts would arise as to the rules concerning concessions and rules concerning monopolies and government procurement.

Due to the above facts, until 1997, there was no consensus among negotiators as to whether the granting of concessions should fall under the discipline of the MAI and therefore be covered by the definition.[88] Unfortunately, in the April 1998 edition of the MAI, concession is included in the definition of investment.

Any other property and rights. This is a general item to cover those assets not in the above list. This general item is open-ended and is easy to be interpreted widely to cover any other assets and new forms of investment. For example, the Commentary thinks the products of an investment are included in the definition.[89] This means that assets to be investment under the MAI could be inexhaustible.

Take for example, Real estate is not in the list of assets in the MAI. But it is still regarded as investment by the footnote to the definition of investment in the MAI and the Commentary to the MAI.[90] Most developing countries do not cover real estate in the definition in the BITs they sign. Neither does the ECT. The United States covered it in the BITs only after 1994.[91] The NAFTA explicitly includes it in investment with the qualification that it should be "acquired in the expectation or used for the purpose of economic benefit or other business purposes".[92] This means that any real estate acquired for personal use can not be regarded as investment. Likewise, the MAI negotiators suggested different ways to limit real estate as investment during the negotiations.[93] But the MAI does not reflect any of the suggestions. The Commentary explicitly mentions real estate as investment, but admits that how to treat summer residences or second homes is a problem.[94]

To sum up, the MAI defines investment very broadly. It gives a positive list of assets to be included in the definition of investment. Such a list is only illustrative and is open-ended. Moreover, the Commentary gives wide

---

[87] Id., para. 16.
[88] M. Schekulin, *supra* note 1, p. 13.
[89] Commentary to the MAI, Chapter II, Definitions, Investment, para. 1.
[90] The MAI, Chapter II, Definitions, footnote 1; Commentary to the MAI, Chapter II, Definitions, Investment, para. 19.
[91] Real estate (property) was not in the list of investment in the BIT Model (1984) of the United States. But it was put on the list in the BIT Model (1994) of the United States.
[92] The NAFTA, Article 1138(g).
[93] M. Schekulin, *supra* note 1, p. 13.
[94] Commentary to the MAI, Chapter II, Definitions, Investment, para. 19.

interpretation to almost every form of asset. The consequence of broad definition and interpretation is that more laws and measures of the contracting parties would be considered as violating the obligations under the MAI and thus governments would have to bear more potential responsibilities.

4.3.4   Features and Restrictions of the MAI's Definition of Investment

4.3.4.1   *Features of the MAI's Definition of Investment*

The above analysis and discussion on the definition of investment show that the MAI gives broad definition to investment. Such a broad definition can be seen from other perspectives:

First, the investment under the MAI covers investment in almost all economic sectors, such as manufacture, agriculture, service, fishery and natural resources.

Second, the investment covers all forms of investment, such as foreign direct investment (establishment of branches and subsidiaries), portfolio investment (shares, stocks), financial investment (bonds, debentures, loans) and intangible property. New forms of investment likely to emerge in the future will also be covered by the MAI.[95]

Third, the investment covers investment at all stages, such as "the establishment, acquisition, expansion, operation, management, maintenance, use, enjoyment and sale or other disposition" of investments.[96] That is to say, both the investment at the stage of making and the investment once made are covered.[97] However, the investment under most international investment agreements does not cover investment at the stage of making.

4.3.4.2   *Restrictions of the MAI's Definition of Investment*

The broader the definition, the more requirements on exceptions and deviations from the MAI will be asked for by contacting states. The Negotiating Group agrees that such a broad definition of investment calls for further work on appropriate safeguard provisions.[98] The main restrictions on the definition are as follows:

Restriction on the assets to be investment.   There is an interpretative note in the footnote of the MAI requiring that an asset must have the characteristics of an investment in order to qualify as an investment under the MAI.[99] Such

---

[95] X. Musca, *supra* note 2, pp. 9–10.

[96] The MAI, Chapter III, National treatment and most favoured nation treatment, paras. 1, 2 and 3.

[97] R. Ley, "the Scope of the MAI", *Multilateral Agreement on Investment: State of Play in April 1997*, p. 16. The author is Head of the Division on Capital Movements, International Investment and Services Division, Directorate for Financial, Fiscal and Enterprise Affairs.

[98] The MAI, Chapter II, Definitions, footnote 1.

[99] Id., footnote 2.

a requirement will exclude those assets without the characteristics of an investment from enjoying the benefits of the MAI. However, only the text of the MAI has legal effect, and footnotes to the text has no legal effect.[100] So this requirement could exist only in name.

Restriction on the treatment that some special investment can enjoy. The MAI covers indirect investment, intellectual property, concessions, public debt and real estate in the definition of investment. Taking into account the special characteristics of these issues, the Negotiating Group admits that further work is needed to determine their appropriate treatment in the MAI.[101] In other words, these investment can not enjoy all the treatment accorded by the MAI.

Making use of the "country specific exceptions" to exclude some investment from the definition. Broad definition of investment is one of the results of the MAI's top down approach. Likewise, each contracting party can list those forms of investment it does not want to be covered in the definition under the MAI in the country specific exceptions so as to exclude them from enjoying the benefits of the MAI.[102]

However, each contracting party's country-specific exceptions should be subject to agreement of all contracting parties. It is not free for any contracting party to list any item in the exceptions. Even if some forms of investment are in the exception list, according to the MAI's rollback approach, they should be eliminated eventually.

Making use of the MAI's "temporary safeguard" clause to restrict portfolio investment. According to the MAI, in the event of serious balance-of-payments and external financial difficulties or threat, and when movements of capital cause or threat to cause serious difficulties for macroeconomic management, a contracting party may adopt or maintain measures inconsistent with its obligations.[103] This temporary safeguard clause might be used to restrict portfolio investment so as to protect the contracting party's financial market.

4.4 CONCLUSION

In summary, the MAI defines both investor and investment in a broad way in order to expand its scope of application and provide as more protection as possible to foreign investors and their investments.

---

[100] L. Wallach, "For the Multilateral Agreement on Investment", *The NGO Pocket Trade Lawyer*, pp. 4–5, available at http://www.citizen.org/pctrade/mai/What%20is/ngo.htm.
[101] The MAI, Chapter II, Definitions, footnote 1.
[102] For example, it is suggested that developing countries can take advantage of the country specific exceptions to exclude concessions and permits in the development sectors such as natural resources and tour from the definition. See E. V. K. FitzGerald, R. Cubero-Brealey & A. Lehmann, "The Development Implications of the Multilateral Agreement on Investment: A report commissioned by the UK Department for International Development" (21 March 1998), p. 18.
[103] The MAI, Chapter VI, Temporary safeguard, 1 (a), (b).

5. The MAI's General Principles for the Treatment of Foreign Investors and Their Investments*

5.1 INTRODUCTION

The OECD's Multilateral Agreement on Investment (MAI) provides broad definitions for investor and investment, the purpose of which is to establish a broad base for the application of the treatment of foreign investors and their investments. The articles concerning the treatment of foreign investors and their investments are the core provisions of the MAI.[1] These articles set up core obligations for contracting parties under the MAI. In general, the treatment of foreign investors and their investments provided by the MAI consists of two categories: general principles of treatment and specific disciplines of treatment for specific matters under the guidance of general principles. The general principles of treatment refer to national treatment, most-favoured-nation (MFN) treatment and transparency. They apply to all aspects of the MAI, including investment protection and investment control. The specific disciplines of treatment are the treatment that contracting parties shall, according to the MAI, accord to foreign investors and their investments in such new issues as performance requirements, investment incentives, privatization, etc. in the field of investment. The standard of the two categories of treatment of foreign investors and their investments provided by the MAI is the minimum standard each contracting party shall accord. Compared with the standard provided by other investment treaties, the MAI's standard is the highest standard so far among existing multilateral frameworks for foreign investment, and represents the trend of treatment of foreign investors and their investments pursued by developed countries.

The general principles of treatment provided by the MAI are discussed in this chapter, and the specific disciplines of treatment on special issues will be discussed in Chapter Six.

---

* This chapter is based on the author's article "Comments on the MAI's General Principles for the Treatment of Foreign Investors and Their Investment. A Chinese Scholar's Perspective" which was published in *Multilateral Regulation of Investment*, E. C. Nieuwenhuys & M. M. T. A. Brus (ed.), Kluwer Law International, 2001.

[1] As to the articles concerning the treatment, see MAI, Chapter III: Treatment of Investors and Investments.

5.2   ANALYSIS OF THE MAI'S GENERAL PRINCIPLES FOR THE TREATMENT OF FOREIGN INVESTORS AND THEIR INVESTMENTS

Generally speaking, from the perspective of the legal regime of international investment, there are three standards of treatment accorded to foreign investors and their investments by investment treaties: national treatment, MFN treatment and non-discriminatory treatment. These three standards of treatment can be defined both broadly and narrowly.[2]

In its narrow definition, national treatment means that the host country shall extend to foreign investors the preferential treatment given to domestic investors. MFN treatment means that the host country shall extend to foreign investors the preferential treatment given to the investors from any third country. Non-discriminatory treatment means that the host country shall not impose any special restrictions on foreign investors which are not imposed on domestic investors, or the investors from any third country.[3] From the above definitions, it becomes clear that national treatment and MFN treatment are treatments provided from a positive perspective, while the non-discriminatory treatment is the treatment provided from a negative perspective.[4] However, their purpose is the same, i.e. to ensure that foreign investors can enjoy in the host country equal legal treatment as domestic investors and the investors from any third country. When national treatment, MFN treatment and non-discriminatory treatment are defined in the narrow sense, they may be used jointly in the same investment treatment.[5]

In its broad definition, national treatment covers the implications of both the narrowly defined national and non-discriminatory treatments concerning domestic investors. MFN treatment broadly defined covers the implications of both MFN treatment and non-discriminatory treatment concerning the investors from any third country in their narrow definitions. Similarly, non-discriminatory treatment covers the treatment in narrow definitions provided both from a positive perspective and from a negative perspective.[6] Therefore, the non-discriminatory treatment in its broad definition covers national treatment and MFN treatment in their broad definitions. It requires of the host country that it treats nationals of other countries in the same way

---

[2]   Xu Chongli, *A Study on Bilateral Investment Treaties* (1996) (Chinese edition, unpublished Ph.D. Dissertation), p. 106. Mr. Xu is professor of law and the supervisor of Ph. D. candidates in Xiamen University, Law School, China. As to the specific analyses of national treatment, MFN treatment and non-discriminatory treatment, see UNCTAD, *National Treatment*, New York and Geneva, 1999; UNCTAD, *Most-Favored-Nation Treatment*, New York and Geneva, 1999; G. Schwarzenberger, "The Most-Favored-Nation Standard in British State Practice", 22 *British Year Book of International Law*, (1945); S. Muhammad, *The Legal Framework of World Trade*, London, Stevens and Sons Ltd., 1958.

[3]   Xu Chongli, *supra* note 2, p. 106.

[4]   S. Mo, "Some Aspects of the Australia-China Investment Protection Treaty", 1 *Journal of World Trade* (1991), p. 52.

[5]   For example, there are articles concerning both MFN treatment and non-discriminatory treatment in the BIT between China and Australia.

[6]   Xu Chongli, *supra* note 2, p. 106.

as its nationals or nationals of a third country.[7] Where national treatment, MFN treatment and non-discriminatory treatment are defined in their broad sense, some bilateral investment treatments (BITs) clearly state that non-discriminatory treatment is national treatment and/or MFN treatment.[8] The North American Free Trade Agreement (NAFTA) regards the better treatment of national treatment and MFN treatment as non-discriminatory treatment.[9] The treatments in their broad definitions can provide better protection to foreign investors and their investments.

In the draft version of February 1997 of the MAI, non-discriminatory treatment is listed together with national treatment and MFN treatment. Although the text does not state that non-discriminatory treatment means national treatment and MFN treatment, as is stated in the BIT between the United States and Russia, this was in effect the intention of the negotiators. In the draft version of April 1998, only national treatment and MFN treatment are stated. But when further analyzing the implications of the MAI's national treatment and MFN treatment, we still find that the MAI defines its national treatment and MFN treatment broadly. In addition, the MAI also requires transparency of all contracting parties' internal law and policies relevant to foreign investment.

5.2.1 Implications of MAI's National Treatment, Most-Favored-Nation Treatment and Transparency Clauses

The MAI's provision on national treatment reads as follows:

Each Contracting Party shall accord to investors of another Contracting Party and to their investments, treatment no less favorable than the treatment it accords [in like circumstances] to its own investors and their investments with respect to the establishment, acquisition, expansion, operation, management, maintenance, use, enjoyment and sale or other disposition of investments."[10]

Its purpose is to ensure that the treatment of foreign investors and their investments is not lower than that of domestic investors and their investments.

The MAI's provision on MFN treatment reads as follows:

Each Contracting Party shall accord to investors of another Contracting Party and to their investments, treatment no less favorable than the treatment it accords [in like circumstances] to investors of any other Contracting Party or of a non-Contracting Party, and to the investments of investors of any other Contracting Party or of a non-Contracting Party, with respect to the establishment, acquisition, expansion,

---

[7]   John S. Mo, *supra* note 4, p. 53.

[8]   For example, in Article 3(2) of the BIT between China and Japan in 1988, non-discriminatory means national treatment; in the APEC Non-binding Investment Principles (1994), non-discriminatory treatment means MFN treatment; in the Article 1(1)(g) of the BIT between the United States and Russia in 1992, non-discriminatory treatment means the mixture of both national treatment and MFN treatment.

[9]   NAFTA, Article 1104.

[10]   MAI, Chapter III, National Treatment of Investors and Investments, para. 1.

operation, management, maintenance, use, enjoyment, and sale or other disposition of investments.[11]

Its purpose is to guarantee that the treatment of foreign investors and their investments is not lower than that of the investors and their investments from any third country.

According to the MAI, the relationship between national treatment and MFN treatment is that "each Contracting Party shall accord to investors of another Contracting Party and to their investments the better of the treatment..., which is the more favorable to those investors or investments."[12] The national treatment and MFN treatment provided by the MAI complement each other, so as to ensure that all foreign investors and their investments and domestic investors and their investments can operate and compete under the same treatment condition.

In order to make sure that the national treatment and MFN treatment are fully extend by all contracting parties, the MAI requires the transparency of their internal laws and policies. To be specific:

Each Contracting Party shall promptly publish, or otherwise make publicly available, its laws, regulations, procedures and administrative rulings and judicial decisions of general application as well as international agreements which may affect the operation of the Agreement. Where a Contracting Party establishes policies which are not expressed in laws or regulations or by other means listed in this paragraph but which may affect the operation of the Agreement, that Contracting Party shall promptly publish them or otherwise make them publicly available.[13]

This obligation requires the contracting host country to provide information that may be useful to foreign investors and other contracting parties. The purpose is to make these rules, regulations, and administrative practices clear and predictable for them.

Although the MAI adopts the same treatment terms as many other investment treaties, the following analysis will show that the MAI gives a broader and richer connotation to these terms. Compared with other international investment treaties, the standard of the treatment of foreign investors and their investments provided for by the MAI are of a relatively high level.

First, in international investment treaties, MFN treatment is by and large generally accepted as general treatment for foreign investors with few specific exceptions, while national treatment is not universally accepted.[14] For example, most developed countries and some developing countries extend national treatment to foreign investors and their investments in their own domestic laws, and for this reason include a clause of national treatment in their bilateral investment treaties with other countries. But most developing countries do not stipulate national treatment; neither in their domestic laws nor in their bilateral investment treaties with other countries. Even those

[11]   Id., para. 2.
[12]   Id., para. 3.
[13]   MAI, Chapter III, Transparency, para. 1.
[14]   UNCTAD, *Trends in International Investment Agreements: An Overview*, New York and Geneva, 1999, p. 61.

countries that have adopted national treatment still impose a variety of exceptions and restrictions.[15]

There are two reasons why national treatment is not universally accepted and fully extended. One is that the standard of national treatment is too high for the host countries to bear its full implications. The other is that many host countries still wish to retain the ability to favor their own domestic firms when needed with respect to the admission and establishment of investment, and in some cases with respect to the treatment of investments after their admission.[16]

The MAI features both national treatment and MFN treatment at the same time and regards them as non-discriminatory treatment. The treatment provided for in the MAI is compulsory for each contracting party. Irrespective the fact that national treatment is not accepted as a universal principle, the MAI still imposes national treatment obligations on each contracting party as "hard-law" obligations.[17] Therefore, it may be said that the general standard of treatment of foreign investors and their investments provided for by the MAI is very high.

Second, according to the original intention of the OECD in drafting the MAI, the phrase "each Contracting Party" shall include all levels of government.[18] Thus, all measures taken by central government, federal government, provincial government or local government shall be applied to both domestic and foreign investors and their investments, in accordance with the requirements of national treatment and MFN treatment of the MAI. As a result, the obligations of contracting parties weigh much heavier than when the "contracting party" would only refer to the central or federal government.

Third, according to the intention of the negotiators, the term "treatment" to be accorded to investors and their investments shall include all policies which have an impact on investment, i.e. economic policy, financial policy, tax policy, and company law, etc. The term "treatment" also includes the measures that will lead to *de jure* or *de facto* discrimination.[19] This means that where measures do not formally constitute discriminatory treatment of a foreign investor, but nonetheless limit the ability of such foreign investor to compete on equal terms, such measures would be incompatible with the MAI.[20] For example, if a law provides that, except for the existing investments no new investments are allowed to flow to an economic sector such as natural resources, and the law is equally applied to both domestic investors and foreign investors, the law itself is non-discriminatory. But if domestic investors made all the existing investments, the law might still be regarded as *de facto* discrimination to foreign investors. This would amount

---

[15]   The exceptions may concern the pre-entry phase, or specific sectors, or other matters. For a general discussion, see UNCTAD, *National Treatment*, pp. 43–51.

[16]   UNCTAD, *supra* note 14, p. 61.

[17]   Because the term "shall" is used in the national treatment clause in the MAI.

[18]   V. Charolles, "National Treatment, Most Favored Nation Treatment and Transparency", *The Multilateral Agreement on Investment: State of Play as of February 1997*, p. 19.

[19]   Id.

[20]   A. Böhmer, "The Struggle for a Multilateral Agreement on Investment—An Assessment of the Negotiation Process in the OECD", 41 *German Yearbook of International Law* (1998), p. 282.

to a violation of the rules of national treatment according to the MAI. One more example: if a law itself does not prohibit the investments of foreign investors in a certain economic sector, but some technical rules in it in effect make it impossible for foreign investors to invest in such an economic sector while this law is in place, such a law might still be regarded as a violation of the MAI's national treatment. In sum, the standard of treatment of foreign investors and investments provided for by the MAI is very high.

Fourth, the Energy Charter Treaty (ECT) and the bilateral investment treaties (BITs) of the United States only grant MFN treatment to the investment.[21] Some BITs accord national treatment only to investment.[22] Some investment agreements provide that the principal beneficiaries of MFN treatment and national treatment are "investors" and "investments". The question of whether the beneficiaries of the standard of treatment are foreign investment only or also include foreign investors can have important practical implications.[23] In the MAI, it is clearly stated that the beneficiaries of national treatment and MFN treatment are both investors and investments. Moreover, the MAI uses broad definitions for both investors and investments,[24] making the scope of application of national treatment and MFN treatment wide and broad.

Fifth, the MAI's national treatment and MFN treatment clauses apply to all activities relevant to investments, such as the establishment, acquisition, expansion, operation, management, maintenance, use, enjoyment and sale of investments. They also apply to different phases of investments, i.e. phase of pre-establishment of investment and phase of post-establishment of investment. The phase of pre-establishment of investment is also called pre-establishment phase, pre-entry phase, admission phase, or market access phase, while the phase of post-establishment of investment is also known as post-establishment phase, post-entry phase, or operation phase. When negotiating the MAI, some delegations preferred separate articles on pre- and post-establishment, while the majority of delegations felt that a single text would better capture the intended coverage of the agreement.[25] So the MAI applies national treatment and MFN treatment not only to post-establishment phase as many investment treaties do, but also to pre-establishment phase. Generally speaking, national treatment only applies to post-establishment phase in those legal regimes which accord national treatment to foreign investors and their investments. The pre-establishment phase is left to the sovereign right of states in terms of deciding on admission of an investment.[26] The reason why national treatment does not apply to the pre-establishment phase is that the obligations that would arise therefrom are too heavy for host countries to bear. The MAI's extension of national treatment from the post- to pre-investment phase means a "revolution" for many countries.[27]

---

[21]   See ECT, Article 10(10); also see UNCTAD, *Most-Favored-Nation Treatment*, p. 6.

[22]   UNCTAD, *supra* note 15, p. 18.

[23]   Id., pp. 9–10.

[24]   As to the broad definitions of investors and investments, see MAI, Chapter II, Definitions, paras. 1 and 2.

[25]   Commentary to the MAI, Chapter III, National Treatment and Most Favored Nation Treatment, para. 1.

[26]   UNCTAD, *supra* note 15, pp. 1 and 4.

[27]   Id., p. 4.

Sixth, there are two different contexts as to the principle of national treatment. One is known as the Calvo doctrine supported by developing countries, which requires that the treatment to foreign investors be "the same as" or "as favorable as" that accorded to national investors. This doctrine emphasizes the equality of treatment between foreign investors and national investors and prevents the accordance of special privileges to foreign investors. The other is that "no less favorable" treatment should be accorded to foreign investors. This means that foreign investors may receive better treatment than national investors where it is deemed appropriate.[28]

In the MAI, the national treatment with the second meaning is stipulated. This means that the treatment to foreign investors and their investments can be more favorable than that to domestic investors and their investments. Therefore, this kind of national treatment is compatible with the preferential treatment accorded to foreign investors by a host country which is more favorable than that accorded to domestic investors. As a consequence, the preferential policies adopted by many developing countries so as to attract more foreign investments would not be considered measures in violation of the MAI's national treatment clause, if these countries were to accede to the MAI. However, some delegations consider preferential treatment as positive discriminatory treatment, which will cause unlimited competition among countries for international investment funds and so distort investment flows. Therefore they proposed the use of terms such as "same" or "comparable" treatment rather than "no less favorable" treatment. But most delegations considered that this would unacceptably weaken the standard of treatment from the investor's viewpoint.[29] These different viewpoints on the "same" or "no less favorable" treatment reflect different contexts of national treatment, as mentioned above.

Seventh, in the MAI the articles concerning the standard of treatment, include the phrase "in like circumstances", marked by square brackets to indicate that consensus had not yet been reached among the negotiating group on whether or not to use the phrase to limit the national treatment and MFN treatment. National treatment and MFN treatment are comparative standards of treatment: the specific content of the treatment is based on a comparison of the different circumstances of domestic investors and their investments and foreign investors and their investments. But in fact, it is in many regards impossible to compare domestic investors and their investments and foreign investors and their investments. Therefore, some delegations considered it necessary to clearly point out that foreign investors and their investments can only enjoy the same treatment as domestic investors and their investments if they are in like circumstances. If the circumstances differ, so may the treatment. On the other hand, some delegations considered that the phrase "in like circumstances" was open to abuse, since the host country could say that foreign investors and their investments and domestic investors and their investments are not in like circumstances, so as

---

[28] UNCTAD, *supra* note 15, pp. 5 and 7; UNCTAD, *Bilateral Investment Treaties in the Mid-1990s*, Geneva, 1998, p. 59.
[29] Commentary to the MAI, Chapter III, National Treatment and Most Favored Nation Treatment, para. 3.

not to have to accord the same treatment. In addition, national treatment and MFN treatment themselves are relative treatments, so their comparative nature is obvious. Therefore, it is not necessary to expressly point this out.[30] Phrases such as "in like circumstances", "in like situations" or "in similar situations" are used to limit national treatment and MFN treatment in most international investment treaties.[31]

Eighth, inside the regional economic integration organization (REIO), members usually confer privileges and benefits on one another. When these member countries sign investment agreements with other countries outside the REIO, they may have a REIO clause to exclude the accordance of these privileges to other countries, as is required under MFN treatment rules. Therefore, the REIO clause exists in many international investment agreements.[32] Similarly, during the MAI negotiating process, the European Union, which is the largest REIO in the world, tried to exclude the REIO from the scope of the MAI. The negotiators could not reach a consensus in this respect. The MAI kept silent on this issue in its articles concerning standard of treatment.

Ninth, the MAI requires each contracting party to accord the better and more favorable treatment arising out of national treatment and MFN treatment to foreign investors and their investments. The utilization of both the MFN and national treatment standards, whichever is more favorable, is a recent trend.[33] In the case when one contracting party accords more favorable treatment to a third country's investors and their investments than to domestic investors and their investments, the more favorable treatment shall also be accorded to any other foreign investors and their investments. As a result, foreign investors and their investments might be in a more favorable position than domestic investors and their investments.

Tenth, most international investment treaties do not contain any articles about transparency.[34] Some recent investment agreements such as the GATS, the ECT and the APEC Non-Binding Investment Principles do carry the transparency clause,[35] but these agreements only require the contracting party to disclose relevant laws, regulations, judicial decisions and measures. The transparency article in the MAI not only requires this of each contracting party, but also requires it to disclose discriminatory measures and all

---

[30] V. Charolles, *supra* note 18, p. 20; W. A. Dymond, "The Main Substantive Provisions of the MAI", *Proceedings of the Special Session on the Multilateral Agreement on Investment Held in Paris on 17 September 1997*, p. 14.

[31] UNCTAD, *supra* note 15, p. 33. Examples can be found in the United States BITs, NAFTA, Canada-Chile Free Trade Agreement and the World Bank Guidelines on the Treatment of Foreign Investment.

[32] For a discussion of the REIO, see UNCTAD, *supra* note 21, pp. 20–22; Article 3 of the Chile-Malaysia BIT, Article 3(3) of the Model BIT of China and Article V of the GATS are examples of the REIO clause.

[33] UNCTAD, *Supra* note 14.

[34] UNCTAD, *supra* note 28, p. 85. The BITs between Malaysia and the United Arab Emirates (1991), Canada and Hungary (1991), and China and Viet Nam (1992) have a transparency clause. The treaties signed by the United States have such a clause.

[35] GATS, Article III; ECT, Article 20, and the APEC Non-Binding Investment Principles under "Transparency".

policies that have an impact on investments, including the established policies.[36] Such a requirement lays a heavy burden on contracting parties.

Last, the obligations of all contracting parties to extend national treatment and MFN treatment under the MAI, are subject to strong dispute settlement mechanisms, including both state–state and investor–state dispute settlement. In contrast, almost all international investment treaties have the state-state dispute settlement provisions, but only some BITs, the NAFTA and the ECT provide for investor–state dispute settlement procedure.[37]

To sum up, the above detailed analysis of the implications of the MAI's national treatment, MFN treatment and transparency clauses shows that the MAI adopts a high standard as to the general treatment of foreign investors and their investments.

5.2.2   The Exceptions and Restrictions to the MAI's National Treatment and Most-Favored-Nation Treatment Rules

Although the MAI sets high standard for the treatment of foreign investors and their investments, there are still some exceptions and restrictions to its national treatment and MFN treatment clauses, as is the case for most other international investment treaties. The two main reasons for this are that, first, national treatment and MFN treatment themselves are relative standards of treatment, and not an absolute standards of treatment. Second, the MAI standards of treatment are so high that they will not be fully and completely accepted by all contracting parties. But compared with other international investment treaties, the MAI's exceptions are rather limited.

The followings are the main exceptions and restrictions to the MAI's national treatment and MFN treatment rules:

General exceptions.   The text of the MAI shall be examined as a whole. On the one hand, it sets out obligations for contracting parties and, on the other hand, it provides for situations when contracting parties may deviate from those obligations. These situations are stipulated in part VI, entitled "Exceptions and Safeguards". This part applies to the entire text of the MAI, thereby including the national treatment and MFN treatment provisions.

According to the MAI's general exceptions, a contracting party may take any action in contravention of the MAI so as to protect its essential security interests, to maintain international peace and security under the United Nations Charter, and to maintain its public order.[38] In such cases, a contracting party may refuse to fulfill their obligations under the MAI to accord to foreign investors and their investments national treatment and MFN

---

[36] V. Charolles, *supra* note 18, p. 19.
[37] For example, the BITs between Lithuania and the Netherlands (1994), and Australia and the Lao People's Democratic Republic (1994) include the investor–state dispute settlement provisions. For a discussion of dispute settlement mechanism, see UNCTAD, *supra* note 28, pp. 87–104; UNCTAD, *supra* note 14, pp. 82–86.
[38] MAI, Chapter VI, General Exceptions, paras. 2 and 3.

treatment. However, such contracting party is under an obligation to notify its according actions or measures to the Parties Group of the MAI.[39] Most international investment treaties contain similar articles of general exceptions, but their scope is broader, including national health exceptions and morality exceptions.[40]

However, the MAI clearly stipulates that the above general exceptions shall not apply to expropriation and compensation and protection from strife.[41] Therefore, a contracting party's obligation to accord national treatment and MFN treatment to foreign investors and their investments remains absolute in case of expropriation and compensation and protection from strife. The reason is that compensation in case of expropriation is considered central to investor protection and investors should be granted an absolute guarantee.[42] But this is not the case for most other international investment treaties.

Subject-specific exception. The MAI excludes taxation, prudential measures in financial services, and temporary macroeconomic safeguards from national treatment and MFN treatment commitments.

Taxation exception. Although taxation is not an important component for international investment, the MAI does provide rules for taxation. However, it is stipulated that national treatment and MFN treatment do not apply to taxation, although the MAI's requirements for transparency do apply to taxation.[43] The reason is that taxation itself is a complicated matter; there have existed many international taxation treaties, such as bilateral agreements for the avoidance of double taxation. Different countries bear different commitments under different treaties; one and the same country even bears different commitments under different treaties. If they would be required to extend national treatment and MFN treatment under the MAI, it is certain that confusion and conflicts will arise.

Prudential measures in financial services exception. Financial services form part of the MAI. However, financial services sector is highly regulated for prudential reasons and therefore calls for specific treatment.[44] So when a country takes prudential measures with respect to financial services, it is allowed to suspend national treatment and MFN treatment under the MAI. Prudential measures include measures for the protection of investors, depositors, policy holders or persons to whom a fiduciary duty is owed by an enterprise providing financial services, or to ensure the integrity and stability of its financial system.[45]

Temporary macroeconomic safeguards exception. It is clearly stated that national treatment, MFN treatment and transparency clauses do not apply to transactions carried out in pursuit of monetary or exchange rate policies by the central bank or monetary authority of a contracting party.[46] This provision in effect excludes such transactions from the MAI. It is also clearly

---

[39]   MAI, Chapter VI, General Exceptions, para. 4.
[40]   Xu Chongli, *supra* note 2, p. 112; UNCTAD, *supra* note 15, p. 44.
[41]   MAI, Chapter VI, General Exceptions, para. 1.
[42]   A. Böhmer, *supra* note 20, p. 284.
[43]   MAI, Chapter VIII, paras. 1 and 3.
[44]   MAI, Chapter VII, footnote 1.
[45]   MAI, Chapter VII, Prudential Measures, paras. 1 and 2.
[46]   MAI, Chapter VI, Transactions in Pursuit of Monetary and Exchange Rate Policies, para. 1.

stated that national treatment may not apply to cross-border capital transactions, if there are serious balance-of-payments and external financial difficulties or threat, or if movements of capital cause or threaten to cause serious difficulties for macroeconomic management, in particular monetary and exchange rate policies.[47]

There are more exceptions in other international investment agreements, for example, the intellectual property rights guaranteed under international intellectual property conventions (as in the United States BIT model, Article 11(2)(b)), incentives (as in NAFTA, Article 1108.7(a)), public procurement (as in NAFTA, Article 1108.7(b)), cultural industries (as in NAFTA, Annex 2106).[48] These exceptions are not covered by the MAI.

Country-specific exceptions. The OECD adopted the top-down approach in drafting the MAI text to enable the adoption of high standards. However, in a supplement to the MAI, each contracting party is allowed to set out specific exceptions to its obligations under the MAI. There are two types of country specific exceptions. One is that national treatment and MFN treatment do not apply to any existing non-conforming measures or to amendments of non-conforming measures as set out by a contracting party in the annex to the MAI.[49] The other is that national treatment and MFN treatment do not apply to measures in specific sectors, sub-sectors or activities that a contracting party sets out in the annex to the MAI.[50]

Country-specific exceptions were taken advantage of by many negotiating parties to exclude those sectors to which they do not want to apply national treatment. Therefore there are many pages of exceptions raised by negotiating parties. EU itself also issued several pages of proposed exceptions during the negotiations.[51] As far as the specific exceptions raised by contracting parties during the negotiations are concerned, most exceptions focus on the application of national treatment to admission phase in such service sectors as transportation and communication.[52] According to the domestic laws of many contracting parties, these service sectors are generally not open to foreign investors and their investments. Another sector, which is specifically excepted by many contracting parties, is the culture industry. For many countries, the culture industry is also excepted from the application of national treatment in their domestic laws. During the negotiations on the MAI, the culture industry was a key issue of disagreement. Some countries suggested treating it as an exception, others, such as France and Canada, suggested its total exclusion from the MAI.

As mentioned before, the MAI's national treatment rules apply both to access phase and to the operation phase. This is not the case in most domestic laws and most other international investment agreements. The latter always regard the access phase as an except from the application of national treatment.

---

[47] MAI, Chapter VI, Temporary Safeguard, para. 1.
[48] UNCTAD, *supra* note 15, p. 45.
[49] MAI, Chapter IX, Lodging of Country Specific Exceptions, para. A.
[50] Id., para. B.
[51] A. Böhmer, *supra* note 20, p. 286.
[52] W. A. Dymond, *supra* note 30, p. 15.

5.3 IMPACTS OF MAI'S NATIONAL TREATMENT AND MOST-FAVOURED-NATION TREATMENT RULES ON INTERNATIONAL INVESTMENT LIBERALIZATION

There are two main purposes for the MAI's high standards of general treatment of foreign investors and their investments. One is to ensure that foreign investors and their investments are accorded equal legal treatment as domestic and third country investors and their investments. The other is to promote the realization of international investment liberalization.

5.3.1 The Extension of National Treatment will Promote International Investment Liberalization

In international agreements, the principle of national treatment has been used in two different contexts[53]: national treatment can mean that no less favorable treatment is to be accorded to aliens and their property than is accorded to nationals and their property. In this context, preferential treatment of foreign investors is allowed. The national treatment principle in the MAI carries this meaning. National treatment may also mean that the same and equal treatment is accorded to aliens and their property as is accorded to nationals and their property. In this context, no more favorable treatment of aliens is allowed. This doctrine is known as the Calvo doctrine and is supported and applied by some developing countries. This is the main reason why some developing countries include national treatment in their own investment codes. So national treatment acts like a double-edged sword. On one hand, if the treatment of foreign investors is less favorable than that of domestic investors in a host country, it may be improved by invoking national treatment. On the other hand, if the treatment of foreign investors is more favorable than that of domestic investors in a host country, it may also be lowered by invoking national treatment so as to prevent privileges from being enjoyed by foreign investors in the host country. Unfortunately, the first meaning and function of national treatment is underlined in modern international investment agreements.

To extend national treatment and MFN treatment is to remove discriminatory treatment; to accord foreign investors and their investments national treatment and MFN treatment is to make sure that they can enjoy equal legal treatment and the same treatment as domestic and third country investors and their investments. Through the two standards of general treatment, foreign investors and their investments obtain the opportunity of equal competition with all other investors and their investments.[54] Therefore, if bilateral investment treaties and multilateral investment treaties accord national treatment and MFN treatment at the same time, it is very probable that investors from one contracting party become "world citizens" in other

---

[53]   UNCTAD, *supra* note 28, p. 59.
[54]   UNCTC, *Bilateral Investment Treaties*, New York, 1988, pp. 33–39.

contracting parties.[55] Therefore they can freely carry out their investments almost everywhere and thus international investment liberalization is realized.

However, countries do not have the obligation to accord national treatment and MFN treatment to foreign investors and their investments.[56] Pursuant to customary international law, what kind of treatment a foreign investor and his investment may enjoy in the host country depends completely on domestic laws of the host country and the international treaties to which the host country has acceded. Whether to accord national treatment to foreign investors is an issue of state sovereignty entirely. Most developed countries usually accord national treatment with some exceptions to foreign investors and their investments, and some developing countries such as Egypt, Philippine, Bulgaria and Argentina also provide for national treatment in their domestic laws and BITs.[57] Most developing countries strongly oppose the inclusion of national treatment in their domestic laws or BITs, due to the fact that their domestic economy lags behind and their national industry is not yet competitive. However, even those countries that do extend national treatment include exceptions and specific reservations in their domestic laws or treaties, and thus weaken the fundamental implications of national treatment. To sum up, the principle of national treatment has not yet become a generally applied principle.[58]

The United States is the strongest proponent of the application of national treatment. Due to the fact that the United States is the most developed country in the world and has the strongest national economy, there is great amount of surplus capital in its national market seeking its way into the international market. Therefore, it is a matter of urgency for the United States to promote the realization of international investment liberalization, so that the domestic markets of other countries may be easily accessed. One of the measures to be taken to this end is the universal application of national treatment. As a first step, the United States always requires a national treatment clause to be included in all its bilateral investment protection agreements with other countries.[59] The national treatment standard included in these agreements will, together with "the multiplier effect" of MFN treatment, automatically apply to any other country that concludes bilateral treaties with countries which have entered into BITs with the United States. As a second step, the United States promotes the inclusion of national treatment clauses in both regional and multilateral investment agreements. In consequence, the North American Free Trade Agreement (NAFTA) and

---

[55]   Xu Chongli, *supra* note 2, p. 111.

[56]   K. S. Gudgeon, "United States Bilateral Investment Treaties: Comments on the Origins, Purpose and General Treatment Standard", 4 *International Tax and Business Lawyer* (1986), p. 117.

[57]   A. R. Parra, "The Principles Governing Foreign Investment, as Reflected in National Investment Codes", 7 *ICSID Review—Foreign Investment Law Journal* (1992), no. 2, p. 436.

[58]   UNCTAD, *supra* note 14, p. 61.

[59]   Article II of the U.S. BIT Model (1984) only provided that "Each Party *shall permit and treat* investment, ... on a basis no less favorable than ... of its own nationals or ...", but Article II of the 1994 Model clearly provided that "... each Party *shall accord* treatment no less favorable than ... its own nationals ..." (emphasis added). Thus the obligation of according national treatment to foreign investment is greatly strengthened.

Energy Charter Treaty (ECT) both include national treatment and MFN treat-ment.[60] The MAI's national treatment and MFN treatment clauses are mainly copies of the corresponding clauses in the NAFTA.[61] If the MAI had suc-ceeded, its national treatment clause would have made it possible for all investors of all contracting parties to invest freely in all other contracting parties.

5.3.2   Extending National Treatment and Most-Favored-Nation Treatment to the Admission of Foreign Investment is an Important Measure to Realize International Investment Liberalization

Pursuant to customary international law, the host country has the right to regulate or prohibit the admission of aliens and their property into its terri-tory. This right derives from the principle of the territorial sovereignty of states.[62] So far, no country offers absolute and unconditional rights of entry and establishment.[63] Most countries, developing countries in particular, according to their specific situations, provide for legal control or restrictions to a differing extent on the admission of foreign investment in their domes-tic laws.[64] The admission of foreign investment was not an issue in BITs and other international investment agreements before the 1990s.

However, in 1990s, the United States applies national treatment to the admission of foreign investments when it signs BITs with other countries.[65] With the impact of such bilateral treaties, many international investment treaties concluded in the 1990s include the clause of national treatment, and apply the national treatment and MFN treatment to the admission of foreign investments. For example, the GATS, NAFTA, ECT and APEC's Non-binding Investment Principles all contain such a clause.[66] But exceptions or reservations are still possible.[67] Moreover, the obligation to apply national treatment rules in the admission of foreign investments is mostly "soft-law".[68] For example, the ECT requires that contracting parties "shall endeavor to" accord national treatment to foreign investors.[69] Just because of

---

[60]   NAFTA, Article 1102; ECT, Article 10(2)(3).
[61]   Compare the MAI, Chapter III, the clauses concerning national treatment and most-favored-nation treatment, with the NAFTA, Articles 1102 and 1103.
[62]   A. A. Fatouros, *Government Guarantees to Foreign Investors*, Columbia University Press, 1962, pp. 40–41; UNCTAD, *supra* note 28, p. 46; UNCTAD, *supra* note 14, p. 39.
[63]   UNCTAD, *Admission and Establishment*, New York and Geneva, 1999, pp. 1, 16 and 32.
[64]   For a discussion of admission, see UNCTAD, *supra* note 63; UNCTAD, *supra* note 14, p. 63–66; UNCTAD, *supra* note 28, pp. 46–50.
[65]   Article II of the U.S. BIT Model (1994) specifically mentions that "With respect to the *estab-lishment*, ... each Party shall accord treatment no less favorable that ..." (emphasis added).
[66]   GATS, Article XVI(1); NAFTA, Articles 1102(1), 1103(1); ECT, Article 10(2), (3); APEC's Non-Binding Investment Principles under "Non-Discrimination between Source Economies" and "National Treatment".
[67]   UNCTAD, *supra* note 63, p. 32.
[68]   A "soft-law" obligation is unenforceable, while a "hard-law" obligation is enforceable.
[69]   ECT, Article 10(2) and (3).

this, the United States refused to ratify the ECT.[70] The APEC's Non-binding Investment Principles are, as their name suggests, non-binding, so any obligation to apply national treatment and MFN treatment to the admission of foreign investment is unenforceable.

There are some reasons why the admission of investment became an issue in the legal regimes of international investment in the 1990s. From the end of the Second World War to the 1970s, most newly founded independent developing countries cherished their hard-earned political sovereignty and economic sovereignty very much, causing them to impose restrictive control over the admission of foreign investment. In the meantime, the economic progress of the developed countries was limited too and the admission of investment to these countries was also restricted. As a consequence, the issue of admission of investment was not touched in BITs or other international investment regimes concluded during that period. Instead, the focus of those investment treaties was investment protection.[71]

In the 1980s, the power of developing countries had been consolidated and stabilized. Great economic progress had been made. To further the progress of national economic growth, capital and advanced technology were in great demand. To this end, attracting foreign investments became an effective solution. Accordingly, these countries eventually relaxed their screening system of foreign investment, broadened the economic sectors in which foreign investment was allowed, softened the conditions for admission and even worked out some preferential policies and measures so as to absorb more foreign investments.

At the same time, developed countries had shown great economic development and their control over the admission of foreign investment became rather loose. A large amount of surplus capital had been accumulated in these countries. The great demand for foreign investments and the relaxation of control over the admission of foreign investment by developing countries, plus the economic development of the developed countries and the surplus of capitals: all these factors stimulated the rising tide of international investment liberalisation in the world. In turn, the international investment liberalisation required all countries to further loosen their control over the admission of foreign investment and thus led to further liberalization.

In theory, there are four approaches to phrase the admission of foreign investment in international investment regimes.[72] First is "an unconditional right to invest". This was a purely theoretical notion that was not reflected in any existing agreement. Second is the "right of establishment". This is a narrower concept that referred to the setting up of enterprises or the

---

[70] T. W. Waelde, "International Investment under the 1994 Energy Charter Treaty: Legal, Negotiating and Policy Implications for International Investors within Western and Commonwealth of Independent States/Eastern European Countries", 29 *Journal of World Trade* (1995), no. 5, p. 34; ECT, Preamble, Principle No. 6; Article 10 (4).
[71] UNCTAD, *World Investment Report 1996*, pp. 154–156; UNCTAD, *Existing Regional and Multilateral Investment Agreements and Their Relevance to a Possible Multilateral Framework on Investment: Issues and Questions*, Note by the UNCTAD Secretariat, TD/B/COM.2/EM.3/2, pp. 4–5.
[72] WTO, *Report of the Working Group on the Relationship between Trade and Investment to the General Council* (1998), pp. 44–45.

provision of services by a natural person in another country. This concept existed only in a small number of agreements that aimed at far-reaching economic integration in a regional context. The third approach involved the application of non-discrimination standards to the pre-establishment phase. The application of the standards of national treatment and MFN treatment to the admission of investment was typically associated with a top–down approach that provided for general application of non-discrimination standards, subject to country-specific exceptions. NAFTA and the MAI are examples. The fourth approach is the "market access, bottom up" approach. It was exemplified by the GATS, in which member states had obligations regarding the admission of investment only to the extent that a specific sector had been inscribed in their schedules of commitments, although the GATS also contained some obligations of a general nature, such as MFN. The scope of application of these various standards depended crucially on the definition of the term investment. Various types of exceptions qualified each of the above-mentioned approaches to the admission of investment.

The scope of the admission of foreign investment under the MAI is the broadest and widest. Almost all economic sectors of the host countries shall be open to other contracting parties. Moreover, the obligation to accord national treatment to foreign investments in the admission phase is regarded by the MAI as a "hard-law" obligation.

When foreign investors and their investments enjoy the same legal treatment as domestic investors and their investments with respect to the admission of investment, the purpose of investment liberalization is realised. Of course, there are still some limits for such investment liberalisation. For example, national treatment does not apply to those sectors listed in the country-specific exceptions. However, if one of the sectors listed in the country-specific exceptions is open to any other countries through BITs or other investment treaties, this sector should be open to all other contracting parties, as a result of the fact that MFN treatment also applies to the admission of foreign investments.

5.4   IMPACTS OF NATIONAL TREATMENT AND INTERNATIONAL INVESTMENT LIBERALIZATION ON DEVELOPING COUNTRIES

The MAI was to be open for accession by all countries, especially to developing countries. During the MAI negotiations, some developing countries such as China, Brazil and Chile were invited to participate as observers. Therefore, it is necessary to analyse the impact on developing countries if national treatment is extended and international investment liberalization is realized.

In general, the standard for the treatment of foreign investors and their investments set by the MAI is too high and unacceptable to developing countries at the present stage. As mentioned before, most developing countries have not included national treatment in either their domestic laws or international investment treaties, let alone that they apply national treatment to the admission of foreign investment. In those circumstances, if they accede to the MAI, they will need to change their entire current domestic legal regimes on foreign investment. This is not different from requesting them to reach the sky in a single bound. There is a famous saying that "Rome was not built in a day". When developed countries were in their developing stage, they did not extend national treatment either, and also made many reservations with respect to the admission of foreign investment.

In order to accomplish their national development targets, most developing countries take measures to select and guide foreign investment to those areas that are in great need. In order to protect their national economy and national investors, especially these countries' "infant industries" and national industries, they prohibit foreign investments in some industries and sectors, which are left for domestic investors. According to the MAI, all such measures are prohibited. If these countries accede to the MAI, they have to eliminate all measures inconsistent with the MAI and open up almost all industries to foreign investors.

When developing countries open their doors to foreign investors, foreign investments from developed countries may flow straight in without any conditions. The domestic capital in developing countries is thin on the ground and weak; the national industries lag behind those of the developed countries. The developing countries' national investors are not able to compete with foreign investors. The possible result is that the national industries and "infant industries" such as the financial sector, service sector and public utility sector of the host developing countries would be ferociously attacked or monopolised by foreign investors. It is politically dangerous if foreign investors control a country's domestic economy.

Moreover, the MAI's national treatment not only accords to foreign investors and their investments the same treatment as it does to domestic investors and their investments, but also enables foreign investors and their investments to enjoy more favorable treatment than domestic investors and their investments. At the same time, the MAI's investment dispute settlement mechanism bestows on foreign investors the right to sue host government in international arbitration tribunal, which is not a possibility for domestic investors. As a result, foreign investors in effect could enjoy so-called" supra-national treatment" in a host contracting country.

As far as natural persons are concerned, the immigration laws of all over the world never guarantee foreign natural persons the right of completely free entry into their countries. This "discriminatory" practice is not condemned by international society, but regarded as an established principle. In contrast, the MAI requires contracting parties to allow free access of foreign investments through the application of national treatment rules.

On the other hand, the requirements of the MAI constitute a restriction on the state sovereignty of developing countries.[73] The MAI prohibits host contracting parties to adopt special laws or policies on foreign investment in order to accomplish the national economic growth target. Although the

---

[73] A. Böhmer, *supra* note 20, pp. 273–274; C. Baumgartner, "The Demise of the Multilateral Agreement on Investment", *Colorado Journal of International Environmental Law & Policy Yearbook* (1998), p. 46.

state's existing non-conforming policies or measures on foreign investment can be remained as country-specific exceptions, according to the MAI, they shall be eliminated eventually in accordance with the MAI's rules of stand-still and rollback. Moreover, they are not allowed to adopt such policies or measures after accession. All this constitutes a serious restriction on and infringement of the national right to adopt economic laws and policy.

As far as China is concerned, it does not in its domestic legislation accord national treatment to foreign investors and their investments in the phase of operation. The Chinese government is only prepared to "gradually extend national treatment to foreign-invested enterprises in China", according to one of its official report.[74] Most BITs concluded between China and other countries do not mention national treatment. But in the BIT between China and the United Kingdom, the Chinese government agreed to accord national treatment "to the extent possible."[75]

There are two main reasons for China's refusal to extend national treatment at present and in the near future. One is that the reform from a planned econ-omy system to a market economy system is still in progress. In a planned economy system, state-owned enterprises are under more obligations and contribute more to the government and therefore enjoy more favourable treatment from the government. For instance, the government will guarantee the supply of raw materials or the sale of products, and they can invest in almost all economic areas. Privately owned enterprises account for only a small portion of the national economy. The government imposes more restric-tions with regard to the areas where they can invest. They can not enjoy the same treatment as the state-owned enterprises. So discriminatory treatment exists even among Chinese enterprises themselves. The other reason is that the technology and management of domestic enterprises still lag behind the international level and so domestic enterprises are less competitive than foreign enterprises. Therefore it is necessary to provide special treatment for the protection of domestic enterprises. Given these circumstances, it is not possible for China to extend national treatment to foreign enterprises.

In China, national treatment does not apply to the phase of operation, let alone to the phase of admission. According to China's BIT Model, the admis-sion of foreign investment should take place in accordance with China's laws and regulations.[76] The Chinese government draws up a Catalogue for the Guidance of Foreign Investment Industries.[77] In this Catalogue, four categories of industries open to foreign investment are listed. Each category is made up of a long, detailed list of industries. The four categories are as follows: (1) encouraged foreign investment industries (high-tech industry is an example); (2) restricted foreign investment industries (domestic com-merce and foreign trade are examples); (3) prohibited foreign investment

---

[74]   Li Peng (former Prime Minister of China), *A Report on "the Ninth Five Plan" of National Economy and Social Development and the Compendium of Expecting Targets by 2010* (1995) (Chinese edition).

[75]   The BIT between China and the United Kingdom, Article 3 (3).

[76]   Article 2 of China's BIT Model stipulates that "Each Contracting Party shall ... and admit such investment in accordance with its laws and regulations".

[77]   This Catalogue was jointly published by the State Plan Committee, the State Economy and Trade Committee and the Ministry of Foreign Trade and Economic Cooperation of China in 1995 in Chinese, and was revised in 1997.

industries (agriculture and forestry are examples); and (4) permitted foreign investment industries (all those industries not covered by the above categories). This Catalogue only applies to foreign investment in China. So national treatment is not extended to the phase of admission of foreign investments. The purpose of the Chinese government in drawing up such a Catalogue is to direct the foreign investment to those areas where China is in great need of them so as to achieve the social development target and protect national industry. If China acceded to the MAI, according to national treatment rules, China would have to abolish its Catalogue. Then foreign investment would be allowed into all areas of industry, except for those listed in the country-specific exceptions.

China is so large a country that the economic development between different districts is uneven and unbalance. This makes it necessary to carry out different economic policies to stimulate even and balance development. The Chinese government carries out such different economic policies and grant investment incentives with respect to foreign investment in different administrative districts. This is also not allowed under the MAI's national treatment rules.

The Chinese industries of financial service, communication, transportation, automobiles manufacture, etc., are less competitive in the international market. If foreign investments are allowed into such areas without any conditions, these national industries will soon be occupied by foreign investment.

In all of the above circumstances, the ability of the Chinese government to formulate foreign policies would be greatly limited. Therefore, the economic sovereignty of China would be seriously infringed.

5.5 CONCLUSION

The MAI's general treatment principles for foreign investors and their investments are national treatment, MFN treatment and transparency. From the implications of these treatment rules and in comparison with other, similar treatment rules in other investment regimes, we may conclude that the MAI's minimum standard of treatment is the highest. The main characteristic of the MAI's standard of treatment is the adoption of national treatment and its application to the admission of foreign investment with the purpose of promoting and realizing international investment liberalization. However, this will greatly damage developing countries' national economic growth and their state sovereignty over the economy, if they accede to the MAI.

Imposing high standards of treatment on developing countries by developed countries in a single investment treaty will inevitably give rise to disputes over international investment regimes between the two worlds, and therefore result in the difficulty in concluding an effective multilateral legal investment agreement. To avoid and resolve such disputes, and to conclude a worldwide legal investment agreement, the developed countries need to fully take into account and respect the right to their own administration of the developing countries in the field of foreign investment and to balance the interest of the two worlds, while at the same time promoting and pursuing international investment liberalization.

6. The MAI's Specific Disciplines on Special Investment Issues

6.1   INTRODUCTION

As aforesaid, the comprehensive application of national treatment and MFN treatment and the transparency requirement of domestic laws and regulations are basic principles of the treatment of foreign investors and their investments. They become the general obligations of contracting parties. However, these obligations are considered in sufficient to guarantee the realization of the MAI's targets of drawing up an open investment regime and promoting investment liberalization. It is deemed necessary to further remove those alleged obstacles to investment such as temporary entry and stay of investors and key personnel, performance requirements, investment incentives, privatization, monopolies and state enterprises. Therefore the MAI negotiators decided to make specific disciplines for the above issues in addition to the general standards of treatment of foreign investors and their investment, so as to strengthen investment liberalization in these areas. The obligations under the specific disciplines are also compulsory for contracting parties, just as those under the general standards of treatment.

The issues of key personnel, performance requirements, investment incentives, privatization, monopolies and state enterprises are new and special issues in the investment field which are rarely touched upon by international investment agreements. Normally international investment agreements only provide for general rules for the treatment of foreign investor and investment, and the application of the general rules to the specific issues of investment are left to national regulations of each contracting party. Therefore, there are almost no existing rules or disciplines for the special issues which could be found in existing international investment agreements, nor in the OECD instruments on investment.

The MAI negotiators constituted an expert group on special topics to study such issues and to draft strict specific disciplines for the special issues on the basis of non-discrimination. In this way the restrictive measures of the host countries in foreign investment could be eliminated, and the so-called equal competition opportunities could thus be created. The treatment of foreign investors provided for by such disciplines is absolute rather than relative, and then foreign investors could enjoy such absolute rights. Meanwhile, to extend the treatment is also a compulsory obligation for contracting parties. If any law or regulation of the host country is not in conformity with the disciplines therein, the foreign investors can invoke the MAI's dispute settlement mechanism to challenge the country of its law or regulation.

However, it is a very complex and difficult matter to create specific disciplines for the special issues. First, these issues are quite new in the area of international investment, so there are few existing rules or provisions which could be reference. Therefore it is technically difficult to create new disciplines. Second, these issues are always subject to domestic laws and regulations concerning the country's political and economical policies and social development target. It would be politically sensitive, if specific, uniform and universal disciplines on these issues are imposed on countries.

Due to the above reasons, there are a lot of bargains and disputes on these issues during the negotiations. The final provisions on these issues in the Negotiating Text of the MAI are not at all final: the wording of many provisions needs to be further decided, a lot of footnotes are used to explain the connotations of certain provisions, and the Commentary to the MAI contains many paragraphs to express different viewpoints and opinions of certain countries. Nevertheless, certain general rules have been agreed for the purpose of investment liberalization.

The general agreed disciplines for investors and key personnel, performance requirements, investment incentives, privatization and monopolies, state enterprises and concession will be discussed in detail in the following sections.

6.2   MAI'S DISCIPLINES ON INVESTORS AND KEY PERSONNEL

The issue of investors and key personnel deals with the temporary entry, stay and work of investors and key personnel. It is greatly related to the immigration law and labor law of the country where they intend to enter, stay and work.

6.2.1   Relevant Provisions on Investors and Key Personnel in the BITs and Other International Investment Agreements

Generally speaking, one country has absolute sovereignty to decide on whether foreigners are allowed to enter and stay and who is permitted to enter and stay. Normally, there are few restrictions, or even encouragement, on the entry of foreign tourists by the immigration law, the reason being that the inflow of foreign tourists helps facilitate the development of travel industry and bring more foreign currencies. However, the entry, stay and work of foreigners in one country is strictly restricted by the country's immigration law and labour law, the reason being that the employment of domestic nationals would be affected and thus their benefits and interests would be infringed. Therefore, most countries wish to retain an unrestricted right to exclude foreign nationals from their territory.[1]

From the perspective of foreign investment, the entry and presence of foreign investors and key personnel in the host country might have significant effect on their investment decision and efficient control and operation of investment. So business considers the possibility of bringing their key personnel with them as an indicator of a liberal business climate in host countries.[2] As a result, strict restrictions on the entry, stay and work would cause negative effect on the inflow of foreign investment.

Consequently, host countries need to find a proper balance between their right to exclude aliens and their desire to attract more foreign investment.[3] But anyway, the entry and sojourn of foreign investors and key personnel are strictly subject to domestic laws and regulations. They are not touched upon by most bilateral investment treaties (BITs) and other international investment agreements.[4]

Only some BITs recently concluded by the United States, Germany, France and Canada, and some BITS between some developing countries contain a provision on the question of entry and stay of foreign investors.[5]

For the United States, this question was first addressed in the new BIT Model (1994). In this model it is stipulated that "subject to its laws relating to the entry and sojourn of aliens, each Party shall permit to enter and to remain in its territory nationals of the other Party ...".[6] It is clear that the foreigner's right to entry is subordinate to the domestic laws of the parties to the BIT. However, the model further stipulates that "Neither Party shall, in granting entry ..., require a labor certification test or other procedures of similar effect, or apply any numerical restriction".[7] This provision constitutes a partial exemption from the application of national rules.

The BITs concluded by France and Germany require of each contracting party to, within the framework of their national legislations, give sympathetic consideration to applications for the entry and sojourn in its territory of persons of the other contracting party in connection with an investment.[8] It is self-evident that the entry and stay of aliens are entirely subordinate to national rules. Therefore, contracting parties do not bear any "hard-law" obligation to grant entry and stay to foreign investors or key personnel.

The Energy Charter Treaty (ECT) contains a similar provision of the France and Germany approach which states that "a Contracting Party shall, subject to its laws and regulations relating to the entry, stay and work of natural persons, examine in good faith requests ... to enter and remain

---

[1] UNCTAD, *Bilateral Investment Treaties in the Mid-1990s*, United Nations, New York and Geneva, 1998, p. 83.
[2] M. Grau, "Temporary Stay and Work of Investors and Key Personnel", *Multilateral Agreement on Investment: State of Play in April 1997*, p. 25. The author is Counselor, International Investment & Multinational Enterprises, German Permanent Delegation to the OECD.
[3] UNCTAD, *supra* note 1.
[4] Id.
[5] Id.
[6] The BIT Model (1994) of the united states, Article VII, 1(a).
[7] Id, Article VII, 1(b).
[8] UNCTAD, *supra* note 1.

temporarily in its Area ...".[9] This provision also shows that national rules are respected with regard to the entry and stay of aliens. Furthermore, the obligation of host country to admit entry and stay of foreign investors and key personnel is only a "soft-law" obligation.[10]

6.2.2   MAI's Disciplines on Investors and Key Personnel

During the MAI negotiations, business community expressed their desire that the MAI develop rules to give basic guarantees for the entry and stay of key personnel.[11] Since it is impossible for foreigners to enjoy the same right as domestic nationals in regard to the entry, stay and work, the MAI has to develop its own specific rules. But the relationship between the MAI rules and the domestic immigration and labour laws of host countries was greatly debated. A number of delegations indicated that they were neither willing nor able to waive their national regulations for key personnel. Finally, it was decided that the national immigration law and labour law would be kept untouched in the MAI.[12]

In drawing up disciplines for investors and key personnel, the MAI negotiators referred to the existing two solutions: a "best efforts clause", and the "partial exemption from the application of national rules".[13] Eventually, the latter solution was adopted because it "offers stronger rights to foreign business".[14] In effect, the MAI's rules in this regard go much further than this solution.

The MAI's disciplines on a foreign investors and key personnel consist of two basic elements: general rule and its exception.

The general rule reads as follows:

Subject to the application of Contracting Parties' national laws, regulations and procedures affecting the entry, stay and work of natural persons, each Contracting Party shall grant temporary entry, stay and authorization to work ... to a natural person of another Contracting Party...[15]

The exception to the general rules reads as follows:

No Contracting Party may deny entry and stay ..., or authorization to work ..., for reasons relating to labour market or other economic needs tests or numerical restrictions in national laws, regulations, and procedures.[16]

---

[9]   ECT, Article 1(1).
[10]   C. P. Andrews-Speed & T. W. Waelde, "Will the Energy Charter Treaty help international energy investors?", 5 *Transnational Corporations*, no. 3 (December 1996), p. 51. See also T. W. Waelde, "International Investment under the 1994 Energy Charter Treaty: Legal, Negotiating and Policy Implications for International Investors within Western and Commonwealth of Independent states/Eastern European Countries", 29 *Journal of World Trade* (1995), no. 5, p. 50.
[11]   A. Ahnlid, "Special Topics", *The Multilateral Agreement on Investment: State of Play as of February 1997*, p. 27. The author is Deputy Permanent Representative, Swedish Delegation to the OECD and Chairman of MAI Expert Group on Special Topics.
[12]   Id.
[13]   M. Grau, *supra* note 2.
[14]   Id.
[15]   The MAI, Chapter III, Temporary Entry, Stay and Work of Investors and Key Personnel, para. 1.
[16]   Id., para. 2.

The MAI's general rule still respects the application of national rules in this regard. But the MAI uses the word "shall" to make compulsory the obligation of contracting parties to grant entry and stay to aliens. This compulsory obligation in effect renders the application of national rules unfeasible. Moreover, the contracting parties are required to grant not only the entry and stay but also the authorization to work to aliens, including investors in both establishment and operation phases and key personnel. If any of the people could not get permission from a host country to enter and stay, he could invoke the MAI's investor–state dispute settlement mechanism to sue the host state.

Normally, in order to guarantee the employment of domestic labour forces, countries, and developing countries in particular, have numerical restrictions on the maximum number of foreign natural persons who can enter, stay and work in its territory. Foreigners are permitted to enter and work only when it is proved that some special demands or needs in domestic market for certain special personnel could not be satisfied by domestic labour, and foreign human resources have to be relied on. However, according to the exception rule, contracting parties are not allowed to restrict the entry, stay and work of investors and key personnel for the reasons of economic needs tests or numerical restrictions. The intention of the exception rule is to remove the barrier and to ensure the free entry and work of investors and key personnel, and the final end is to pave a smooth way for the liberalization of foreign investment.

Because this exception clause is legally binding, with regard to these two measures of economic needs tests or numerical restrictions, the national legislation does not precede over the MAI.[17] In other words, the MAI prevails national legislation. As is well known, economic needs tests and numerical restrictions are two major measures in national legislation to restrict the work of aliens. Although the MAI negotiators indicated in drafting the MAI that they were not willing to let the MAI override national legislation in this field,[18] in essence, this exception rule makes the above general rule of the application of national rules a mere figurehead. Fortunately, this exception rule does not cover those restrictions of national labour law based on health, safety and criminal law considerations.[19]

The rationality and acceptability of the MAI's above disciplines on aliens are greatly challenged. Unsatisfied with the MAI's relevant rules, the Consumer Unity & Trust Society (CUTS) proposed an equitable alternative reading as follows: "A Contracting Party, shall, subject to its laws applicable from time to time relating to the entry and sojourn of non citizens, permit natural persons ... to enter and remain in the territory ...".[20] In this clause, contracting parties only have the obligation of permitting entry and stay of

---

[17] M. Grau, *supra* note 2.
[18] A. Ahnlid, "New Disciplines," *Proceedings of the Special Session on the Multilateral Agreement on Investment Held in Paris on 17 September 1997*, p. 23.
[19] M. Grau, *supra* note 2.
[20] International Agreement on Investment, Chapter III, Special Topics—Key Personnel—A Temporary Entry and Stay, *International Investment Instruments: A Compendium*, vol. V, United Nations, 2000. This Agreement was prepared by the CUTS for discussion at the UNCTAD Round Table in 1998.

aliens. They don't have the obligation of granting authorization to work. Moreover, there is not any exception to the application of national laws.

In order to avoid the abuse of this clause by street traders, the MAI requires that only those natural persons who have committed or are in the process of committing a substantial amount of capital to the enterprise may invoke this clause. The MAI also stipulates that key personnel consist of executive, manager, specialist, and those who are essential to the enterprise.

In addition, all contracting parties also have compulsory obligation to grant entry and stay to the spouses and minor children of investors and key personnel.[21] They are encouraged to grant authorization to work to the spouses of investors and key personnel,[22] which is not a compulsory obligation.

6.2.3   Related Issue

The discipline on key personnel is related to the issue of the hiring of local personnel. Most host countries, especially developing countries, have laws requiring foreign investors to hire local personnel so as to ensure that domestic nationals receive employment, technical training and managerial experience.[23] They also require certain members of the board of directors to be local people so as to guarantee the power balance in the enterprise. For example, China requires in its Joint Venture Law and Co-operative Enterprise Law that if the president of the board of directors is from one party, the vice-president should be from the other party; and the positions of general manager and deputy manager of the enterprise should be held by each party respectively.[24] But foreign investors prefer to employ as they like members of board of directors, managers, executives, and other personnel without considering their nationalities.

The United States is the first to include a clause in its BITs to remove nationality restriction on key personnel. It added a new article in its Model BIT (1994) stating that "each Party shall permit covered investments to engage top managerial personnel of their choice, regardless of nationality".[25] The MAI goes even further than this, which stipulates that contracting parties can not have any nationality requirements for executives, managers or members of board of directors,[26] and each contracting party shall permit foreign investors to employ any natural persons of the investor's or the investment's choice regardless of nationality and citizenship.[27] The enforcement of the

---

[21]   The MAI, Chapter III, Temporary Entry, Stay and Work of Investors and Key Personnel, para. 1(b)(i).

[22]   Id., para. 1(b)(ii).

[23]   UNCTAD, *supra* note 1, p. 84.

[24]   China-foreign Co-operative Enterprise Law of People's Republic of China (Chinese edition), Article 12; China-foreign Joint Venture Law of People's Republic of China (Chinese edition), Article 6.

[25]   The Model BIT (1994) of the United States , Article VII, 2.

[26]   The MAI, Chapter III, Nationality Requirements for Executives, Managers and Members of Boards of Directors.

[27]   The MAI, Chapter III, Employment Requirements.

above two articles could be strongly ensured by the former discipline on the movement of key personnel.

6.3   MAI'S DISCIPLINES ON PERFORMANCE REQUIREMENTS

6.3.1   The Issue

Performance requirements, or conditions on investment, are requirements or measures that governments impose on investors/enterprises in order to achieve perceived economic benefits for the country as a whole or for a particular region.[28] Performance requirements may take forms of local content requirements, local sourcing requirements, product export requirements, trade balancing requirements, foreign exchange balancing requirements, domestic sale requirements, local equity requirements, local employment requirements, etc. Local content and local sourcing requirements are the most prominent forms of performance requirements. A same performance requirement could be imposed on investors as a condition for allowing various phases such as establishment and operation of an investment, which is called "straight performance requirement", or could be imposed on investors as a condition for receiving an advantage offered by host government, which is called "performance requirement linked to an advantage".[29] The former could also be called "restrictive performance requirement"; while the latter could be called "encouraging performance requirement". The latter is therefore related to investment incentives. Performance requirements could be imposed on both domestic and foreign investors. But generally speaking, most performance requirements are imposed on foreign investors.

Host countries include performance requirements in their national or regional laws, regulations, or economic or social policies in connection with investment, with the hope that they could create employment, increase exports, generate foreign exchange and improve the balance of payments.[30] Hence performance requirements exist in both developed and developing countries, though they are more frequent in developing countries.[31]

In developed countries, performance requirements linked to an advantage are more often used. They are closely related to politically sensitive targets, such as creating jobs in poor districts, community reinvestment against discrimination in bank loans, environmental protection, etc.[32]

---

[28]   A. Ahnlid, "Performance Requirements and Investment Incentives," *Multilateral Agreement on Investment: state of Play in April 1997*, p. 28; A. Böhmer, "The Struggle for a Multilateral Agreement on Investment—an Assessment of the Negotiation Process in the OECD", 41 *German Yearbook of International Law* (1998), p. 293.
[29]   J. Brooks, "Performance Requirements," *Proceedings of the Special Session on the Multilateral Agreement on Investment Held in Paris on 17 September 1997*, p. 26.
[30]   UNCTAD, *supra* note 1, p. 81.
[31]   T. H. Moran, "The impact of TRIMs on trade and development," 1 *Transnational Corporations*, no. 1 (February 1992), p. 56.
[32]   M. Sforza, "MAI Provisions and Proposals: an Analysis of the April 1998 Text", *Public Citizen's Global Trade Watch*, July 1998, p. 20.

In developing countries, performance requirements are often used to guide and control the direction of foreign investment so as to realize the countries' economic or social targets. Therefore, performance requirements are imposed as requirements for entry and operation of investment and for obtaining advantages from the governments. Take China for example. One of its performance requirements for admission and operation of foreign investment is to require foreign-related enterprises to keep foreign exchange balance by themselves.[33] The typical performance requirement linked to an advantage is to apply reduced income tax rate or exempt income tax to royalties if foreign patented technology is provided for scientific research, energy exploration, transportation, agriculture, forestry and stock raising.[34]

6.3.2   Existing Disciplines on Performance Requirements

According to the theory of sovereignty of state, a state has an absolute right to the control and management of foreign investment, including the right to decide whether to impose performance requirements and what performance requirements to impose. This right can not be intervened by any other country. This is the main reason for the fact that so far there are few existing international regulations on the removal of performance requirements. Neither BITs nor multilateral investment frameworks before 1980 touched this area. But from 1980s, some BITs and international treaties began to develop rules for performance requirements.

6.3.2.1   *United States BIT Model*

Ever since 1980, the United States considered performance requirements as a most serious but rapidly developed issue in international investment.[35] Therefore it "innovated" a clause in its BIT Model (1984) to eliminate performance requirements. This clause reads as follows: "Neither Party shall impose performance requirements as a condition of establishment, expansion or maintenance of investments, which require or enforce commitments to export goods produced, or which specify that goods or services must be purchased locally, or which impose any other similar requirements."[36] This clause prohibits only those performance requirements used as conditions for admission and operation of investment, not those performance requirements linked to an advantage. In the BIT Model (1994), the scope of performance requirements to be prohibited is extended to import limitation requirements, local sales limitation requirements, technology transfer requirements and

---

[33]   China-foreign Co-operative Enterprise Law of People's Republic of China, Article 20; Foreign-owned Enterprise Law of People's Republic of China (Chinese edition), Article 18. These two articles were abolished in 2001.
[34]   China's Income Tax Law for Foreign-invested Enterprises and Foreign Enterprises (Chinese edition), Article 19(4).
[35]   Cited from Xu Chongli, *A Study on Bilateral Investment Treaties* (1996), p. 89.
[36]   The BIT Model (1984) of the United Sates, Article II(5).

research and development requirements. But it still explicitly states that the requirements linked to the receipt of an advantage are not included.[37]

However, the process of including this standard clause in the BITs with other countries was not successful at the beginning. Some countries accepted the standard clause as it was, while others accepted it with some changes from "shall" to "shall seek to" or "shall endeavor to".[38] Since 1988, more developing countries have accepted this standard clause in their BITs with the United States, the reason being that many developing countries took some liberal investment policies.[39]

Following the precedent of the United States, France and Canada include such clauses in some of their BITs with other countries.[40]

6.3.2.2   WTO TRIMs Agreement

The United States sought to remove performance requirements from the areas of international investment and trade. In the Uruguay Round of negotiations, a list of 14 trade-related investment measures (TRIMs) was produced by developed countries for discussion.[41] This aroused strong contentions between developed countries and developing countries. The developed countries argued that TRIMs would cause distortions in patterns of trade and investment because business decisions on the part of TNCs come to be made on the basis of considerations other than market forces. Developing countries argued that TRIMs could be useful policy tools to promote development objectives and strengthen trade balances.[42] As a compromise, the final WTO Agreement on Trade-related Investment Measures (TRIMs Agreement) in 1994 prohibits only four forms of performance requirements: local content requirements, trade-balancing requirements, foreign exchange requirements and export requirements.[43] The reason for the prohibition of the above four TRIMs is that they are inconsistent with the obligation of national treatment and general elimination of quantitative restrictions under the GATT. The four TRIMs will also be prohibited if they are linked to an advantage.[44] This is the first time that the performance requirements linked to an advantage are prohibited.

For the rules on performance requirements under the TRIMS Agreement, attention should be paid to the following points. Firstly, the TRIMs Agreement only applies to the performance requirements related to trade in goods, not in service.[45] Secondly, all other performance requirements except

---

[37]   The BIT Model (1994) of the United Sates, Article VI.
[38]   Xu Chongli, *supra* note 35.
[39]   Id., p. 91.
[40]   UNCTAD, *International Investment Instruments: A Compendium*, vol. 1, 1996, p. xxxiii; UNCTAD, *supra*, note 1, p. 81.
[41]   T. H. Moran, "The Impact of TRIMs on Trade and Development", *Transnational Corporations*, vol. 1, no. 1 (February 1992), p. 55.
[42]   Id.
[43]   WTO Agreement on Trade-related Investment Measures, Annex, Illustrative List.
[44]   Id.
[45]   WTO Agreement on Trade-related Investment Measures, Article 1.

for the four TRIMs are permitted. Thirdly, there is an exception that a developing country member can deviate temporarily from the obligation to remove TRIMs if they are confronted with balance-of-payments problems.[46] Fourthly, the performance requirements prohibited by the TRIMs Agreement do not have to be removed immediately after the Agreement comes into effect. Transitional arrangements are provided for developed countries to eliminate their TRIMs within two years, developing countries within five years and least developed countries within seven years.[47] In 2000, the TRIMs Agreement was under review in the Council of Trade in Goods. Eight developing countries had produced requests for extension of the time limit to eliminate their TRIMs.[48]

6.3.2.3   Energy Charter Treaty

According to the ECT, the four TRIMs prohibited by the WTO TRIMs Agreement are prohibited, too. Those TRIMs linked to an advantage are prohibited by the ECT as well.[49] However, compared with the TRIMs Agreement, the ECT includes more exceptions: TRIMs are allowed as a condition of eligibility of export promotion, foreign aid, government procurement or preferential tariff and quota programmes.[50] Furthermore, a dispute between contracting parties with respect to the application or interpretation of the TRIMs is not subject to the dispute settlement mechanism of the ECT.[51]

6.3.2.4   North American Free Trade Agreement (NAFTA)

The draft of the NAFTA was greatly influenced by the United States. With regard to performance requirements, the NAFTA contains broader coverage than the United States BIT Model and the TRIMs Agreement. The NAFTA not only gives a longer list of prohibited performance requirements, but also extends them to investment area and to service sector. The NAFTA explicitly distinguishes two categories of performance requirements: prohibited and permitted performance requirements.

The prohibited performance requirements include: (1) export requirements, local content requirements, local purchase requirements, trade-balancing requirements, local sale requirements, transfer-of-technology requirements, and exclusive supplier requirements, when they are used as straight performance requirements;[52] and (2) Local purchase requirements, local content requirements, foreign exchange requirements, trade-balancing

---

[46]   Id., Article 4.
[47]   Id., Article 5.
[48]   C. Raghavan, "TRIMs Review", *Extensions Before Goods Committee*, available at http://www.twnside.org.sg/title/goods-cn.htm.
[49]   ECT, Article 5.
[50]   ECT, Article 5(3).
[51]   ECT, Article 28.
[52]   NAFTA, Article 1106(1).

requirement, when they are used as performance requirements linked to an advantage.[53]

The permitted performance requirements include: (1) transfer-of-technology requirements as straight performance requirements, when an enterprise is required to use a technology to meet generally applicable health, safety or environmental standards-related measures;[54] and (2) Local production requirements, service-providing requirements, worker-training or -employing requirements, facility-construction or expansion requirements and research and development requirements, when they are used as performance requirements linked to an advantage.[55] (3) All those performance requirements not explicitly prohibited by the NAFTA are permitted.[56]

6.3.2.5   APEC Non-Binding Investment Principles

The APEC Non-binding Investment Principles (1994) only address that the use of performance requirements will be minimized by member countries.[57] Therefore performance requirements are not prohibited. Such a principle is appropriate for the APEC as a regional organization among developed countries such as United States and Australia and developing countries such as China and Malaysia, for the purpose of promoting open trade and practical economic cooperation.

6.3.3   Arguments on Performance Requirements in the MAI Negotiations

During the negotiations of the MAI, some delegations were of the opinion that performance requirements would interfere in the decision-making process within individual enterprises and thus lead to market distortions,[58] and have been major burdens on investors and thus would impair the competitiveness of their investments.[59] They claimed that such distortions could not be sufficiently overcome by the application of the MAI's principles of national treatment and most-favoured-nation treatment,[60] though the requirements imposed merely on foreign investors could partly be removed by the invocation of the MAI's non-discrimination principle. Therefore the delegations were thinking of making disciplines on performance requirements.

However, there were varied opinions as to the necessity to make new disciplines on performance requirements in the MAI. Some delegations doubted the value of covering performance requirements in the MAI in view of the TRIMs Agreement and the different characters of performance

---

[53]   NAFTA, Article 1106(3).
[54]   NAFTA, Article 1106(2).
[55]   NAFTA, Article 1106(4).
[56]   NAFTA, Article 1106(5).
[57]   APEC Non-Binding Investment Principles, Performance Requirements.
[58]   A. Ahnlid, *supra* note 28, p. 28.
[59]   J. Brooks, *supra* note 29, p. 26.
[60]   A. Ahnlid, *supra* note 11, p. 28.

requirements of "developed-developing" countries.[61] Some delegations insisted that no more obligations than those in the TRIMs Agreement and the ECT should be imposed on contracting parties.[62] Some delegations held that the MAI should include applicable disciplines on performance require-ments, though the "developed-developing" country differences on perform-ance requirements were important.[63] Finally, the last proposition won. New disciplines would be created to go beyond the relevant provisions in both the TRIMs Agreement and the NAFTA. The MAI's disciplines would deal with investment related measures and cover both goods and services.[64] It would intend to prohibit all performance requirements.[65]

Two possible solutions were proposed at the beginning of the negotiations as to how to address the performance requirements issue in the MAI: a clear prohibition of a number of defined performance requirements with a roll-back mechanism (similar to, but more ambitious than, the TRIMs Agreement), or a standstill of existing performance requirements (with agreed exceptions which could be reduced over time) combined with a list of prohibited per-formances).[66] However, it turned out to be that the final disciplines in the MAI are stronger than the two proposed solutions.

6.3.4   MAI's Disciplines on Performance Requirements

Firstly, 12 performance requirements in connection with all phases of invest-ment and used as straight performance requirements are prohibited by the MAI, which is a "hard-law" obligation on contracting parties. These 12 pro-hibited performance requirements include: export requirements, local content requirements, local purchase requirements, trade-balancing requirements, local sale requirements, transfer-of-technology requirements, headquarter location requirements, exclusive supplier requirements, employment require-ments, joint venture establishing requirements, and minimum domestic equity participation requirements.[67] Such a prohibitive list is so far the longest and broadest ever found for performance requirements. It covers almost all the existing forms of performance requirement.

Secondly, the MAI explicitly states that the last seven items in the above-mentioned list are permitted to be used as performance requirements linked to an advantage.[68] Of course, the MAI's non-discrimination principle should still be observed in imposing these performance requirements. On the other hand, the above stipulation implies that the first five items are

---

[61]   OECD, "New Issues: Report by Working Group B", *Towards Multilateral Investment Rules*, p. 129.
[62]   The MAI, Chapter III, Performance Requirements, footnote 15.
[63]   OECD, *supra* note 61, pp. 129–130.
[64]   A. Ahnlid, *supra* note 11, OECD, p. 28.
[65]   F. Engering, "The Multilateral Investment Agreement", 5 *Transnational Corporations*, no. 3 (December 1996), p. 153.
[66]   OECD, *supra* note 61.
[67]   The MAI, Chapter III, Performance Requirements, para. 1.
[68]   Id., para. 2.

prohibited even when they are used as performance requirements linked to an advantage.

Thirdly, the MAI does not state whether the performance requirements not on the list are permitted or not; while the NAFTA does state that they are permitted. However, there are not many performance requirements left outside the MAI's list.

Fourthly, the phrase "an investor of a Contracting Party or of a non-Contracting Party"[69] shows that the investor might include any investor, e.g., a domestic investor, a foreign investor coming from a contracting party, or a foreign investor coming from a non-contracting party. Such a wording has significant effect on the prohibition of performance requirements. That is to say, the above prohibition rules should be extended to any requirements imposed on any investors, including domestic investors and all foreign investors. In other words, performance requirements can be imposed neither on foreign investors coming from contracting parties, nor on domestic investors and foreign investors coming from non-contracting parties. This is a powerful provision.[70] All in all, the MAI intends to remove all performance requirements in all respects.

Fifthly, the phrase "Each contracting Party" includes all levels of government, as has been is shown in Chapter Five. Therefore, performance requirements include all performance requirements imposed by central government, federal government, provincial government or local government. The scope of performance requirements to be prohibited in this sense is thus much broader than those constrained only to central or federal government.

Sixthly, although the MAI includes some clauses concerning the exceptions to the above rules, these clauses are marked by square brackets and followed by a number of footnotes stating delegations' different opinions. The proposed exceptions in the MAI include: (1) environmental requirements and other requirements necessary for the compliance of national laws and regulations, necessary to protect human, animal or plant life or health, and necessary for the conservation of living or non-living exhaustible natural resources;[71] (2) qualification requirements with respect to export promotion and foreign aid programs, government procurement, and qualification requirements for preferential tariffs or preferential quotas.[72] Certainly, the country-specific exception principle is also applicable in this regard.

6.3.5 Comments on the MAI's Disciplines

According to the MAI's disciplines, the first five items of requirements, e.g., export requirements, local content requirements, local purchase requirements, trade-balancing requirements and local sale requirements are absolutely prohibited in all circumstances, whether as straight requirements or as requirements linked to an advantage. The claimed reason for this

---

[69] Id., para. 1.
[70] J. Brooks, *supra* note 29, p. 27.
[71] The MAI, Chapter III, Performance Requirements, para. 4.
[72] Id., para. 5.

prohibition is that they are the most likely requirements to distort patterns of trade and investment.[73] Indeed, it is important to remove negative measures to keep normal trade and investment for the benefit of foreign investors. On the other hand, it is equally important to respect the host countries' right to regulate the activities of foreign investment. As mentioned in 6.3.1, these requirements are frequently used by developing countries as an effective tool to control and guide the direction of foreign investment and to realize their social and economic targets. The requirements linked to an advantage are often used by host state to compensate for the weakness and disadvantage of the country and thus the country can be in a more competitive position in attracting foreign investment. Therefore, the balancing of the interests and benefits of both investors and host governments is an important issue. We can not sacrifice the interests and benefits of one party (the host country) to satisfy the interests and benefits of the other party (the investors). In essence, prohibiting host government from imposing any performance requirements, is prohibiting host government from realizing its social and economic goals with the help of performance requirements, and thus deprives the host government of its right to make strategies for its economic development and limits its power to impose control on foreign investment. Moreover, in order to avoid the negative effect of the clause of prohibiting performance requirements, host countries may make use of the MAI's country-specific exception rule to reserve some frequently used requirements and thus the list of country-specific exception would be longer and longer.

Even if it is excusable for the MAI to prohibit the use of straight performance requirements because these requirements would directly hinder the admission and interfere in the operation of an investment and thus go against the liberalization target of the MAI, it is unreasonable to prohibit the performance requirements linked to an advantage, the reason being that these requirements would not affect the admission or operation of investment. Moreover, these requirements constitute a kind of "win-win" scheme from which both investors and host countries will benefit. Therefore, it is unreasonable to prohibit such requirements. Therefore, there were divided opinions on this issue during the MAI negotiations.[74]

The MAI does not mention whether the prohibited performance requirements cover only mandatory requirements or also cover voluntary requirements. Mandatory performance requirements are compulsory requirements imposed, enforced, or maintained by laws, rules or regulations. Voluntary performance requirements are optional requirements stipulated in an agreement or a contract, especially in a concession agreement, as a condition on the investor to exchange for the admission or an advantage from the host government after negotiations. At the beginning of the negotiations, negotiators distinguished these two types of performance requirements and considered whether to cover the latter in the MAI.[75] However, the 1997 Text of the MAI made a distinction between them and thus it could be interpreted that both mandatory and voluntary requirements are prohibited. The author

---

[73] J. Brooks, *supra* note 29.
[74] F. Engering, *supra* note 65, p. 154.
[75] OECD, *supra* note 61, pp. 129–130.

is of the opinion that voluntary requirements are voluntarily accepted by investors and thus could not be prohibited.

With the prohibition of the five major performance requirements, host countries have to rely more on those performance requirements linked to an advantage which are permitted by the MAI. As a result, host governments have to pay foreign investors in return for the realization of their economic targets, because the straight performance requirements which are free can not be used.

The powerful provision on the prohibition of performance requirements on any investor has exceeded the boundary of the MAI's non-discrimination principle because host countries are not allowed to use performance requirements even if these requirements are imposed equally on both domestic investors and foreign investors. The consideration for this rule is that if host countries are not permitted to impose performance requirements on those investors from contracting parties, they would impose requirements on investors from non-contracting parties or on domestic investors. Thus the MAI's prohibition of performance requirements could be made used by host government as an excuse to be biased toward domestic investors and the foreign investors from non-contracting parties. Thus these investors may enter into certain investment areas or gain some specific advantages from the host government through the performance of some requirements. The investors from contracting parties will thus be put into a comparatively disadvantageous position. Therefore, the purpose of the powerful provision of the MAI is to make sure that performance requirements do not end up causing a detriment, rather than a benefit, for the investor of MAI parties.[76]

As far as the exception rule is concerned, although the MAI includes a number of concrete exceptions, they are far from finally decided. Furthermore, neither rollback provision nor standstill provision is covered as proposed at the beginning of the discussion of the issue. Nor is any transitional arrangement set up in the MAI; while the WTO TRIMs Agreement does.

To sum up, the purpose of the MAI's disciplines on performance requirements is to remove and eliminate almost all performance requirements imposed on investors so that they can act as they please in host country without any restraints or constraints. The prohibition of performance requirements, together with the extension of national treatment is used by developed countries as two sharp swords to fight for the liberalization of investment.

6.4 MAI'S DISCIPLINES ON INVESTMENT INCENTIVES

6.4.1 General Issues on Investment Incentives[77]

Investment incentives came into existence in the 1930s and have been frequently used in Western world (developed countries) since the Second

---

[76] J. Brooks, *supra* note 29, p. 27.
[77] For a full discussion of investment incentives, see B. Bracewell-Milnes & J. C. L. Huiskamp, *Investment Incentives: A Comparative Analysis of the Systems in the EEC, the USA and Sweden*, 1977 Kluwer, Deventer, The Netherlands; UNCTAD, *World Investment Report 1995*, pp. 288–305; UNCTAD, *Incentives and Foreign Direct Investment*, United Nations, 1996.

World War.[78] The range of incentives and the number of countries and local authorities who offer incentives have increased quickly since the mid-1980s.[79] Not only developed countries, but also developing countries, frequently employ investment incentives to achieve their economic policy and plan. In particular, many developing countries commenced from the end of 1970s to carry out "open-up" policy to absorb foreign investment so as to develop their economy. In order to make themselves competitive in international capital market, the developing countries have to sacrifice some of their countries' financial interests through the use of investment incentives such as tax exemption and tax holiday as an instrument to attract foreign investment. That is why nowadays investment incentives are more widely and frequently used by developing countries.

6.4.1.1   Definition of Investment Incentive

To make disciplines for investment incentives, the first thing is to define investment incentives properly. But so far, there is not a generally accepted definition of investment incentive in the world. Economists define it as any measure conditional on new investment taking place which is designed to increase the prospective net-of-tax return from the investment relatively to its cost at the time of the investment decision.[80] The UNCTAD defines it as "any measurable economic advantage afforded to specific enterprises or categories of enterprise by (or at the direction of) a government, in order to encourage them to behave in a certain manner".[81] An investment incentive could include any measure either to increase the rate of return of a particular FDI undertaking, or to reduce (or redistribute) its cost or risks.[82] The UNCTAD further points out that an incentive should be distinctive from a subsidy, which is the "financial aid granted by a government or other organization to an individual or legal entity for something that is considered to be of some advantage to the public",[83] but it also admits that most incentives have a subsidy component.[84] Another opinion with respect to investment incentive is that it can be defined both narrowly and broadly.[85] The narrowly defined incentive covers only those subsidies that are most easily measured and readily available, i.e. cash grants. The broadly defined incentive includes both tax and non-tax incentives. Incentive and subsidy are used interchangeably.[86] In this sense, incentive and subsidy are different terms with the same meaning, which is different from the above opinion of the UNCTAD. Furthermore, incentives can be classified into conditional

[78]   B. Bracewell-Milnes & J. C. L. Huiskamp, *supra* note 77, p. 23.
[79]   UNCTAD, *World Investment Report 1998*, p. 102.
[80]   B. Bracewell-Milnes & J. C. L. Huiskamp, *supra* note 77, p. 11.
[81]   UNCTAD, *supra* note 79, p. 102; UNCTAD, *Incentives and Foreign Direct Investment*, p. 3.
[82]   Id.
[83]   UNCTAD, *Incentives and Foreign Direct Investment*, p. 8.
[84]   Id.
[85]   M. Daiy, "Investment Incentives and the Multilateral Agreement on Investment", 32 *Journal of World Trade* (1998), no. 2, p. 7.
[86]   Id.

incentives and unconditional incentives, and the former may be linked to performance requirements.[87] In this sense, investment incentives overlap performance requirements.

Different opinions of the definition of incentive will lead to disagreements and disputes over whether certain measures constitute incentives. However, it is not easy to come to a universally accepted definition. In such a case, it is quite difficult to formulate proper and effective disciplines on incentives. Moreover, the inter-linkage between incentives and performance requirements increases the complexity of the making of incentive disciplines.

6.4.1.2 *Different Incentives Used by Different Countries*

As mentioned above, both developed and developing countries adopt investment incentives in their national policy. But the types and purposes of their application of incentives are not the same.

It is generally agreed that there are three types of incentives: fiscal incentives, financial incentives and other incentives.[88] Generally speaking, developed countries tend to use more fiscal incentives such as accelerated depreciation and specific deductions for corporate income tax purposes; while developing countries tend to use fiscal incentives such as the reduction of the standard corporate income tax rate, tax holidays, the exemption from import duties and duty drawbacks.[89] Developed countries use much more frequently than developing countries financial incentives, such as government grant, subsidized loans and loans guarantees.[90] Developing countries, on the other hand, employ more often than developed countries other incentives: subsidized infrastructure and services, technical support, protection from import competition, and preferential allocation of foreign exchange.[91]

As to the purpose of the application of incentives, developed countries use incentives mainly to guide investment to their backward regions and priority industries, to encourage pollution prevention and recycling, and to support innovation and research and development. Developing countries use incentives to promote the whole country's economic development, especially the development of priority industries, to encourage export so as to earn more foreign exchanges, and to increase employment and employee training.

Ever since the 1980s, in the whole world, the types and range of incentives afforded to investors have been growing fast, and the number of countries adopting incentives has been increased. Very frequently, in one country, not only the central governments, but also provincial governments and local authorities provide incentives. The purposes for different countries to adopt incentives vary. The resulted competition of incentives in the field of investment makes more countries offer more favorable incentives to foreign investors. The alluded reason is that more favorable incentives have to be

---

[87] UNCTAD, *supra* note 83, p. 5.
[88] Ib.; UNCTAD, *World Investment Report 1995*, pp. 291–298.
[89] UNCTAD, *World Investment Report 1995*, p. 291.
[90] Id., p. 294.
[91] Id., p. 298.

used to offset those offered by other countries, and to compensate for the higher risk of investing in some countries outside the OECD area.[92]

To sum up, different incentives serve for different purposes for different countries. Such background makes it politically sensitive to regulate incentives with the same disciplines, especially when the disciplines are to be used to limit the use of incentives.

6.4.1.3   *How to Evaluate Investment Incentives*

Investment incentives are of help for host countries to direct foreign investment and to realize social development target, and therefore they have positive effect on the country as a whole. Individual investors could also benefit from the incentives. Therefore, in choosing where to make an investment, investors would depend partly on the incentives offered by host countries. But generally speaking, incentive is a minor factor in the location decisions for transnational corporations. More important factors are market size, political and economic stability and so on.[93] On the other hand, hosting governments have to sacrifice for their offering of incentives by the reduction of financial revenues. There is also the tendency of competition of incentives among different countries. As a result, it is quite difficult and complex to measure the gain and loss, advantages and disadvantages, of the offering of investment incentives. Then how to evaluate incentives, whether incentives should be prohibited, and what extent and scope of incentives should be allowed, are questions to be answered before the disciplines of incentives are made.

The above issues explain most of the reasons for the fact that there were only limited but not uniform disciplines on investment incentives in international investment instruments before the MAI. Another reason is that incentives do not have a long history in contrast with other issues such as investment treatment and investment protection in the field of international investment, and thus it is merely a new issue to be regulated.

6.4.2   An Overview of Existing International Disciplines on Investment Incentives

Investment incentive issue is not a subject of bilateral investment treaties. Some regional and multilateral trade or investment agreements contain some provisions on the disciplines on investment incentives, though limited and not concrete. These agreements are chronologically as follows: Treaty of Rome (Treaty Establishing the European Community (now European Union)) (1957), Agreement on the Harmonization of Fiscal Incentives to

---

[92] "Opening to Non-Members for Investment Agreement", *OECD Letter*, vol. 5/5, June 1996, available at http://www.oecd.org//publications/letter/0505.html.
[93] M. A. Wiss, "Book Review and Note: World Investment Report 1995," *90 The American Journal of International Law* (1996), p. 713.

Industry agreed by the Caribbean Community (CARICOM) (1973), OECD International Investment Incentives and Disincentives (1976), NAFTA (1992), APEC Non-Binding Investment Principles (1994), Energy Charter Treaty (1994) and the Uruguay Round Agreements including TRIMs Agreement and the Agreement on Subsidies and Countervailing Measures.[94] A brief overview of the provisions on incentives of the above agreements will help to understand and evaluate the MAI's corresponding clauses.

6.4.2.1   The Treaty of Rome

The Treaty of Rome contains a subsection addressing Aids Granted by States.[95] But this subsection does not deal with investment incentives *per se*, but deals with the state aid to industry.[96] The general principle is that any aid granted by the states which distorts or threatens to distort competition l is incompatible with the Common Market,[97] and thus is prohibited.[98] The absolute exception to the general principle is that some aids listed **shall** be allowed,[99] and the relative exception is that some other categories of aids listed **may** be allowed (emphasis added).[100] The above rules do not make any distinction between foreign-owned and domestic enterprises.[101]

---

[94]   As for a brief discussion of these agreements, see UNCTAD, *supra* note 83, pp. 55–73.

[95]   The Treaty of Rome was adopted on 25 March 1957 and entered into force on 1 January 1958. It was subsequently amended by the Single European Act and by the Treaty on European Union. The subsection concerning state aid is from Arts. 92 to 94.

[96]   According to the definition of incentive, the state aid falls within the scope of incentive.

[97]   Treaty of Rome, Article 92, para. 1. This paragraph reads: "Save as otherwise provided in this Treaty, any aid granted by a Member State or through State resources in any form whatsoever which distorts or threatens to distort competition by favoring certain undertakings or the production of certain goods shall, in so far as it affects trade between Member States, be incompatible with the common market."

[98]   UNCTAD, *supra* note 83, p. 63.

[99]   Treaty of Rome, Article 92, para. 2. This paragraph reads: "The following **shall** be compatible with the common market: (a) aid having a social character, granted to individual consumers, provided that such aid is granted without discrimination related to the origin of the products concerned; (b) aid to make good the damage caused by natural disasters or other exceptional occurrences; (c) aid granted to the economy of certain areas of the Federal Republic of Germany affected by the division of Germany, in so far as such aid is required in order to compensate for the economic disadvantages caused by that division."

[100]   Treaty of Rome, Article 92, para. 3. This paragraph reads: "The following **may** be considered to be compatible with the common market: (a) aid to promote the economic development of areas where the standard of living is abnormally low or where there is serious underemployment; (b) aid to promote the execution of an important project of common European interest or to remedy a serious disturbance in the economy of a Member State; (c) aid to facilitate the development of certain economic activities or of certain economic areas, where such aid does not adversely affect trading conditions to an extent contrary to the common interest. However, the aids granted to shipbuilding as of 1 January 1957 shall, in so far as they serve only to compensate for the absence of customs protection, be progressively reduced under the same conditions as apply to the elimination of customs duties, subject to the provisions of this Treaty concerning common commercial policy towards third countries; (d) aid to promote culture and heritage conservation where such aid does not affect trading conditions and competition in the Community to an extent that is contrary to the common interest; (e) such other categories of aid as may be specified by decision of the Council acting by a qualified majority on a proposal from the Commission.

[101]   UNCTAD, *supra* note 83, p. 62.

6.4.2.2   The Agreement on the Harmonization of Fiscal Incentives to Industry[102]

This Harmonization Agreement established a Harmonization of Fiscal Incentives to Industry Scheme in 1973. The Scheme sets forth the types of fiscal concessions that could be granted to approved enterprises, sets ceilings on the percentage rates of benefits, and sets limits on the duration of the benefits.[103] The Scheme does not make distinction between foreign- and domestic-owned enterprises, either.[104]

6.4.2.3   The OECD's International Investment Incentives and Disincentives[105]

This OECD instrument only provides for consultations when the significant official incentives and disincentives to international investment of one member country have adverse effects on another member country. The purpose of the consultations is to reduce the effects to a minimum. The transparency principle is addressed by this document, but the document does not intend to prohibit, eliminate or even limit the use of investment incentives.

6.4.2.4   NAFTA

NAFTA addresses investment incentives indirectly. It provides that it is inappropriate to encourage investment by relaxing domestic health, safety or environmental measures. If one party offers such an encouragement, any other party may request consultations with a view to avoiding such an encouragement.[106]

6.4.2.5   APEC Non-Binding Investment Principles

This APEC instrument addresses investment incentives as an important subject of it but contains almost the same provision as NAFTA: "member economies will not relax health, safety, and environmental regulations as an incentive to encourage foreign investment."

---

[102]   Source: UNCTAD, *International Investment Instruments: A Compendium*, vol. II, Regional Instruments, pp. 161–174.
[103]   Articles 4 to 14 of this Agreement; UNCTAD, *supra* note 83, pp. 67–68.
[104]   UNCTAD, *supra* note 83, pp. 67–68.
[105]   The OECD Instrument on Investment Incentives and Disincentives was first adopted in 1976 and then revised in 1979 and 1984 respectively. Source: http://www.oecd.org/daf/investment/guidelines/incent.htm.
[106]   NAFTA, Article 1114, para. 2.

6.4.2.6 *Energy Charter Treaty*

ECT does not deal with incentives directly. According to its provision, each contracting party may grant exclusive or special privileges to any entity, but the way to do it shall be consistent with its obligations under the treaty.[107] It provides that the modalities of application of national treatment and MFN to grants or other financial assistance provided by contracting parties shall be reserved for the supplementary treaty of ECT.[108] In other words, each contracting party may offer incentives to investors, but whether national treatment and MFN shall be applied thereto will be discussed separately.

6.4.2.7 *WTO Agreement on Subsidies and Countervailing Measures*[109]

The WTO Subsidies Agreement is an agreement dealing with subsidy measures with respect to goods trade, rather than investment subsidies directly. This Agreement divides subsidies into three categories: prohibited subsidies, actionable subsidies and non-actionable subsidies.[110] There are different rules and remedies for different categories of subsidies. Non-agricultural subsidies that are contingent upon export performance and subsidies that are contingent upon the use of domestic over imported goods are prohibited subsidies.[111] No member countries are allowed to grant or maintain such subsidies in their domestic laws, regulations or policies.

If the use of any subsidy by one member country will cause adverse effects to the interests of other members, such subsidy falls within the scope of actionable subsidy.[112] The corresponding remedy is that the member whose interests are adversely affected may request consultations with the affecting member.[113] Actional subsidies could include, in principle, any of the FDI incentive types.[114]

Subsidies which are not specific within the meaning of Article 2 of this Agreement, assistance for some research activities, assistance to some disadvantaged regions within the territory of a member country, and assistance to meet new environmental requirements, are non-actionable subsidies.[115] The use of the latter three assistances shall be notified to the Committee by the using member.[116] This is the requirement of transparency rule.

In view of the fact that subsidies may play an important role in economic development programs of developing country members, the Agreement

---

[107] ECT, Article 22(4).
[108] ECT, Article 10(8).
[109] This Agreement was first adopted in 1979 and then incorporated in the Uruguay Round Agreements in 1994.
[110] Agreement on Subsidies and Countervailing Measures, Sections I, II and III.
[111] Id., Article 3.1.
[112] Id., Article 5.
[113] Id., Article 7.1.
[114] UNCTAD, *supra* note 83, p. 61.
[115] Agreement on Subsidies and Countervailing Measures, Articles 8.1 and 8.2.
[116] Id., Articles. 8.3 and 25.1.

adopts exceptional rules for some developing countries. The most important two exceptional rules are as follows: (1) the prohibition of subsidies that are contingent upon export performance shall not apply to some specific developing country members referred to in Annex VII to the Agreement, and other developing country members for eight years from the date of entry into force of the WTO Agreement;[117] (2) the prohibition of subsidies that are contingent upon the use of domestic over imported goods shall not apply to developing country members for a period of five years, from the date of entry into force of the WTO Agreement.[118]

The above brief description of the subsidy rules shows three points: first, although the subsidy rules are addressed in the context of trade of goods, they could apply to certain types of investment incentives, such as investment-linked export incentives. Second, the prohibited subsidies such as investment-linked export incentives and local content requirements, are used mainly by developing countries. But the incentives mainly used by developed countries to stimulate investment, such as measures relating to regional subsidies and research-and-development support, are not prohibited.[119] Third, notwithstanding the above, the different circumstances of developed country members and developing country members concerning incentives in trade are taken into consideration in the draft of the Agreement.

6.4.2.8   TRIMs Agreement

As mentioned before, the TRIMs Agreement is recognized as an agreement dealing with those trade-related investment measures, i.e. the performance requirements in investment. Performance requirements could overlap investment incentives, when the incentives are granted conditionally. In this sense, the TRIMs Agreement also applies to investment incentives. To be specific, the TRIMs Agreement prohibits WTO members from conditioning subsidies on local content requirements or conditioning a firm's ability to import goods on its export performance.[120]

6.4.3   Main Arguments in the Drafting Process of the MAI

The main reasons for the OECD to decide to make rules for investment incentives in the MAI negotiations are: investment incentives have distorted effects on the capital flow and investment decisions;[121] and the competition between countries for foreign investment by means of investment incentives is too costly for host countries.[122] The distorted effects and the costly competition become obstacles to the liberalization of international investment.

---

[117]   Id., Article 27.2.
[118]   Id., Article 27.3.
[119]   UNCTAD, *supra* note 83, p. 62.
[120]   Id., p. 59; Annex to the TRIMs Agreement.
[121]   The MAI, Investment Incentives, footnote 97.
[122]   A. Ahnlid, *supra* note 11, p. 28; A. Ahnlid, *supra* note 28, p. 30.

However, it is technically difficult to make rules for incentives, because, just as mentioned before, there is no uniform view on the definition, scope and nature of investment incentives; and there are varied opinions as to how to measure the advantages and disadvantages of investment incentives. It is also politically sensitive to make such rules, the reasons being that developed and developing countries are using incentives in different ways. The most difficult thing was that the OECD was going to formulate additional ambitious disciplines, in addition to the MAI's several principles of non-discrimination, and not merely repeating the existing relaxable rules in other instruments. Therefore, the investment incentive issue was the most difficult one among the five special topics.[123]

In the drafting process, even the negotiating delegations themselves could not come to a consensus. Three considerably differing positions were raised among them.

The first position was that MAI should not seek to discipline investment incentives.[124] Many OECD countries preferred to maintain the *status quo*,[125] and claimed that no specific rules were needed.[126] This argument was based on the following grounds: (1) many countries view incentives as a legitimate and useful policy tool for the promotion of economic development through new investment;[127] (2) the problems concerning the nature and impact of incentives, and the nature and extent of any disciplines needed to be clearly identified prior to the draft of disciplines on investment incentives;[128] (3) the MAI's national and MFN treatment would be a sufficient outcome to cover incentives and constitute a step forward to the present situation;[129] (4) any additional disciplines on incentives in the MAI would divert foreign investment to non-members and place MAI contracting parties at a disadvantage relative to non-members in their ability to retain or attract investment;[130] and (5) such disciplines could constitute an obstacle to the accession to the MAI by non-members.[131] This position would be acceptable for developing countries.

The second position was that additional disciplines on incentives should be introduced.[132] The supporters argued that such disciplines would be an important element of the MAI.[133] They suggested that the additional disciplines could include the following rules: (1) a ban on "positive discrimination", i.e. better treatment for foreign investors than for domestic investors;[134] (2) caps on the magnitude of certain investment incentives;[135]

---

[123] A. Ahnlid, *supra* note 11, p. 28.
[124] A. Ahnlid, *supra* note 28, p. 30; A. Ahnlid, *supra* note 11, p. 29; MAI, Investment Incentives, Provisions, Alternative 1; Commentary to the MAI, Investment Incentives, para. 4.
[125] A. Ahnlid, *supra* note 11, p. 28.
[126] A. Ahnlid, *supra* note 28, p. 30.
[127] Id.
[128] Commentary to the MAI, Investment Incentives, para. 4; A. Ahnlid, *supra* note 11, p. 29.
[129] A. Ahnlid, *supra* note 28, p. 30.
[130] Commentary to the MAI, Investment Incentives, para. 7.
[131] Id.
[132] A. Ahnlid, *supra* note 28, p. 31; The MAI, Investment Incentives, Provisions, Alternative 2.
[133] A. Ahnlid, *supra* note 28, p. 31.
[134] Ib.; A. Ahnlid, *supra* note 11, p. 28;
[135] Id.

(3) notification and transparency requirements for investment incentives;[136]
(4) consultations upon adverse effects of incentives.[137] However, they also
argued that the additional disciplines would not interfere with some legitimate policies for the promotion of the regional, social, environmental and
R & D objectives in which investment incentives are often used mainly by
developed countries.[138]

The second position is, in essence completely unfavourable to developing
countries because: most investment incentives used by developing countries
are favourable treatment to foreign investors so as to attract more foreign
investment, but these incentives are banned in accordance with the second
position. However, most incentives used by developed countries are mainly
aimed at regional, social, environmental and R & D objectives, which could
be an exception to the additional rules, in accordance with the second position. Obviously, such additional rules would place developing countries in a
more disadvantageous position, if they join the MAI. This is a main reason
for developing countries to protest the MAI.

The third position is a compromise between the above two positions. The
additional disciplines on incentives would not be made during the MAI
negotiations, but be taken up in the following negotiations after the entry
into force of the MAI, as part of a "build-in-agenda" for further work.[139]
Moreover, the mandate and the terms and reference for future negotiations
would be worked out before the finalization of the MAI.[140]

On surface, this position seems like a neutral one without new rules for
incentives during the negotiations of the MAI. But in effect, this is also
a dangerous position because the additional disciplines would be put in the
"built-in-agenda" which could be discussed within a specific period of time
and with clear-cut mandate and terms. It would be a trap for developing
countries in that they might join the MAI without the additional rules on
incentives, but after they join in, the additional rules would be formulated
and it is very possible that the rules proposed by the second position would
be included.

After an intense discussion, the clauses of incentives were drafted, which
are similar but not limited to the third position.

6.4.4   MAI's Disciplines on Investment Incentives

Because of the complexities, difficulties and controversies in formulating
new disciplines for investment incentives, no consensus was reached during
the negotiations. So the present clauses of investment incentives are proposed articles and also contain different alternatives. In these articles, some
terms, phrases and sentences are marked with square brackets to show their

---

[136]   A. Ahnlid, *supra* note 28, p. 31.
[137]   Id.
[138]   Id.
[139]   Ib.; p. 31; MAI, Investment Incentives, Provisions, Alternative 2.
[140]   Id.

uncertainty. Many footnotes and commentaries are also included to explain the background of the articles or to show varied attitudes of delegations.

The MAI's disciplines on investment incentives are based largely on the existing disciplines on incentives, but with great development and innovation. The relevant clauses cover the definition of investment incentives, the treatment of these incentives, remedy for those incentives with distorted effects, and the "built-in-agenda" for additional disciplines. In addition, some separate rules under the paralleling subtitle of "Not Lowering Standards (Labour and Environment)"[141] are related to incentives and will be discussed here. A brief introduction and some comments would be made on all these articles, together with their corresponding footnotes and commentaries.

6.4.4.1   Definition of Investment Incentives

According to one delegation's argument that a definition of investment incentives is a necessary prerequisite for increased transparency and disciplines regarding such measures,[142] the MAI defines investment incentives as "the grant of a specific advantage arising from public expenditure [a financial contribution] in connection with the establishment, acquisition, expansion, management, operation or conduct of an investment of a contracting party or a non-counteracting party in its territory".[143]

Such a definition is mainly borrowed from the definition of subsidy adopted by the WTO Subsidies Agreement,[144] but is more general than the latter. The former confers broader implications to investment incentives. Since the MAI only limits the advantage to specific advantage without any other qualifications, just as the definition given by the UNCTAD,[145] the advantage could cover almost every kind of advantage. So the scope of advantage could be very broad. According to the MAI's definition, the grant of any specific advantage could be regarded as incentives. Therefore, the scope of incentives in the context of the MAI is much broader than that in the context of the definition of the UNCTAD. Furthermore, the definition relates incentives to all phases of investment, including the establishment, acquisition, expansion, management, operation and conduct of an investment. As a consequence, any advantage granted in any phase of investment could be regarded as incentives. The broad definition of investment incentives of the MAI coincides with the ambition that the MAI was intended to be a high standards agreement.

6.4.4.2   MAI's Disciplines for Investment Incentives

The MAI's disciplines on investment incentives consist of two articles. The first article is concerning the treatment of investment incentives. It provides

---

141   The MAI, Chapter III, Treatment of Investors and Investments, Not Lowering Standards.
142   Commentary to the MAI, Investment Incentives, para. 3.
143   The MAI, Investment Incentives, Article 4.
144   Please compare the MAI's definition with the WTO's definition of subsidy (Article 1 of the WTO Agreement on Subsidies and Countervailing Measures).
145   Please refer to 6.4.1.1 of this book.

that the principles of national treatment, MFN treatment and the transparency rule should apply to investment incentives.[146] In other words, investment incentives may be used by contracting countries if they are used on a non-discriminatory basis and in compliance with transparency requirement. This is a restatement of the application of national treatment, MFN treatment and transparency rule stipulated by the MAI because these principles are fundamental principles of the MAI which should extend to every aspect of the MAI, surely including the investment incentives.

The requirement of the MAI that national treatment and MFN treatment should extend to investment incentives is an innovation compared with other investment instruments and will cause great difficulties and problems for countries and thus is protested by many countries and their citizens.

The MAI is the only agreement who applies national treatment to investment incentives. Many investment agreements do not adopt national treatment as its treatment principle, some agreements which adopt national treatment do not cover the issue of investment incentives, and even some agreements expressly exclude the application of national treatment to investment incentives. For instance, according to the OECD's National Treatment Instrument, "official aids and subsidies" and "fiscal incentives" are generally treated as exceptions to national treatment for transparency, consultation and review purposes.[147]

The imposition of national treatment and MFN treatment obligations on investment incentives would tend to increase contracting parties' budgetary cost and thereby possibly discourage their use.[148] Secondly, according to this rule, both the investment incentives conferred by developed countries particularly to their less developed areas and the investment incentives granted by developing countries specifically to attract foreign investment would be in violation of the MAI and thus forbidden. That is why this constraining rule is opposed by people from both developed countries and developing countries.

As far as China is concerned, for the time being and in the predictable future, investment incentive is still one of the main measures taken by central and local governments to absorb foreign investment. Although Chinese People's Congress has revised its foreign investment laws and abolished some performance requirements so as to comply with the WTO TRIMs Agreement, the WTO agreements themselves do not restrain the use of investment incentives. Even if China becomes a member of the WTO, China is still allowed to use some investment incentives. For the present time, China still uses different investment incentives to absorb foreign investment and domestic investment to consolidate the economy of coastal areas and to develop the western part of the country. Any such restricting discipline for investment incentives in any international investment agreement will harm the development of China.

The second article of the MAI further points out that investment incentives, even if applied on a non-discriminatory basis, may still have distorting

---

[146]   The MAI, Investment Incentives, Article 1.
[147]   OECD, *supra* note 61, p. 131.
[148]   M. Daiy, *supra* note 85, p. 7.

effects on the flow of capital and investment decisions. So any contracting country may request consultations with the other country if the former's investor is adversely affected by the investment incentives with distorting effect adopted by the latter country. The former country may also bring the incentive before the Parties Group for its consideration.[149] This consultation article is very similar to the articles concerning actionable subsidies and their remedies in the WTO Subsidies Agreement.

Because the distorting or adverse effect of investment incentives is hard to measure or prove, disputes as to whether an incentive adopted by one country distorts or affects investment of another country are easy to arise. History shows that consultation is a time-consuming and costly process, and developing countries are normally put in a disadvantageous position in such a process.

The WTO Subsidies Agreement stipulates that if consultation does not result in a mutually agreed solution, any member party to the consultation may refer the matter to the Dispute Settlement Body for the establishment of a panel.[150] Similarly, the MAI's dispute settlement mechanism would also be applicable for investment incentive disputes. But the MAI does not say whether the incentive disputes should first go through the consultation process and then, if they are not satisfactorily settled, can be submitted for settlement by invoking either the state–state dispute settlement system or the investor–state dispute settlement system, or, the country or its investor may select either channel to settle the dispute. Since the MAI dispute settlement mechanism consists of state–state procedure and investor–state procedure, both the country and its investor may refer respectively to the two procedures for the settlement of the incentive disputes. The MAI only stipulates that the consultation should be brought by the country, and thus it could be inferred that the country may invoke the state–state procedure when the consultation does not produce any result. But the MAI does not say the investor who is adversely affected by the incentive should first go to its home country to raise the consultation, or may directly invoke the investor–state procedure. The ambiguous stipulation and the two different dispute settlement procedures add to the difficulty and complication of the issue of investment incentives.

As many agreements do, the MAI also addresses the issue of encouragement of investment which is related to investment incentives. This issue is not mentioned under the subtitle of "Investment Incentives", but under the subtitle of "Not Lowering Standards". The core stipulation of the four different alternatives provided by the MAI is not to forbid contracting parties to encourage investment by lowering health, safety or environmental standards, but to point out that this practice is inappropriate.[151]

6.4.4.3   Built-In Agenda for Additional Disciplines

As a compromise of the above-mentioned three positions, the MAI, in addition to the present disciplines discussed above, makes a built-in agenda

---

[149]   The MAI, Investment Incentives, Article 2.
[150]   WTO Agreement on Subsidies and Countervailing Measures, Article 7.4.
[151]   The MAI, Chapter III Treatment of Investors and Investments, Not Lowering Standards.

for the establishment of additional disciplines. The negotiations to establish additional disciplines would commence within three years after the signature of the MAI agreement, with the purpose to further avoid and minimize the distorting effects and to avoid undue competition between contracting parties in order to attract or retain investments. The additional disciplines would cover the issues of positive discrimination, transparency, standstill and rollback, with the full recognition of the role of investment incentives with regard to the aims of policies, such as regional, structural, social, environmental or R&D policies of the contracting parties.[152]

The possible additional discipline for positive discrimination would prohibit the existence of positive discrimination, according to the suggestion of some delegations.[153] This is a supplementary rule to the principle of national treatment, under which any foreign investors could not enjoy more favourable treatment than domestic investors in the granting of investment incentives.

Because the MAI has died, its built-in agenda would not come into effect and no additional disciplines would be formulated.

6.4.5 Conclusion

Investment incentive is a new issue in the field of foreign direct investment and therefore there are few existing strict disciplines for it. The MAI delegations had three different positions as to the making of new disciplines and the present MAI disciplines for investment incentives are a compromise of the three positions. Even so, the MAI's disciplines for investment incentives are still on the high level in comparison with the counterparts in other existing agreements.

6.5   MAI'S DISCIPLINES ON PRIVATIZATION

6.5.1 Introduction to Privatization

Privatization is the process that state-owned or controlled enterprises are fully or partly transferred to private sectors.[154] Privatization is therefore interrelated with the issues of monopoly and state-owned enterprise. Privatization is an important instrument of economic policy in both developed countries and developing countries.[155] The primary objective of privatization is to promote

---

[152]   The MAI, Investment Incentives, Article 3.
[153]   Id., Article 3, footnote 102.
[154]   Scholars differ on the precise definition of privatization, but there are not many differences as to its general meaning. For a discussion of the issue of privatization, see UNCTAD, *Comparative Experiences with Privatization: Policy Insights and Lessons Learned*, United Nations, 1995; F. Sader, *Privatization and Foreign Investment in the Developing World*, 1988–92, Working Papers of International Economics Department, the World Bank, October 1993; Y. Mitrofanskaya, "Privatization as an International Phenomenon: Kazakhstan", 14 *American University International Law Review* (1999), p. 1399.
[155]   UNCTAD, *supra* note 154, p. xvii.

economic efficiency through the establishment of well-functioning markets and competition.[156] For developing countries, privatization is also a necessary means to create market economy and to absorb private investment, including foreign investment.[157] It is also a measure moving toward the liberalization of the world economy. Privatization started in many countries during the mid-1980s, but has grown very quickly ever since, especially in developing countries.[158] According to World Bank data, privatization has become increasingly popular in developing countries over the past 10 years.[159]

Privatization is an important measure of a country's economic policy and therefore falls within the scope of state economic sovereignty. But since privatization becomes a common phenomenon for only twenty years, there lack of special and systematic rules to regulate privatization even in domestic law, let alone in international investment regulations. In fact, there is not any rule in international agreements covering the issue of privatization fully.[160]

6.5.2 Arguments in the MAI Negotiations

The fact that privatization is always regulated by domestic law and thus is lack of international rules makes it politically sensitive for the MAI to develop privatization disciplines. During negotiations, most MAI delegations agreed that the issue of privatization was within the state's discretionary competence and thus fell outside the scope of regulation and interference from international bodies.[161] They also stated that it was unsuitable for any international organization to make rules for privatization,[162] and thus the MAI's provisions on this issue would contradict this statement.[163]

But some other delegations asserted that the MAI should create disciplines for privatization for the following two reasons: the first reason was that the particular process of privatization in each country could give origin to preferential treatment distinguishing between local and foreign potential acquirers of shares or assets, and thus might directly affect the goals of the OECD.[164] The second reason was that according to the MAI's definition of investment, the acquisition of shares in a company to be privatized was considered as investment operation, and therefore must be covered by the MAI.[165]

---

[156] Id., p. 2.
[157] Y. Mitrofanskaya, *supra* note 154.
[158] F. Sader, *supra* note 154, pp. 3 and 11.
[159] P. Young, "The Lessons of Privatization," and M. M. Shirley, "Trends in Privatization," 1 *Economic Reform Today* (1998), available at http://www.ncpa.org/pd/private/oct98b.html. There are more detailed data regarding the privatization trends in developing countries available at this web site.
[160] A. Ahnlid, *supra* note 18, p. 24; M. O. Silva, "Privatisation and Monopolies," *Multilateral Agreement on Investment: State of Play in April 1997*, p. 34. The author is Deputy Director, Investment, Trade and Tourism, Portugal.
[161] M. O. Silva, *supra* note 160, pp. 33–34.
[162] Id., p. 34.
[163] Id., p. 33.
[164] Id., p. 34.
[165] Id.

In effect, none of the above arguments are tenable. Any country has sovereignty to make its own economic policies related to privatization. Whether to privatize and how to privatize a public sector or a state-owned enterprise, and what treatment to be accorded to local and foreign investors in the process of privatization, are in the hands of the government. The OECD has no right to interfere with this sovereignty just because other countries' privatization practice would directly affect its goals. Has the OECD ever considered that its regulatory oversight on privatization will also directly affect the economic interests and economic sovereignty of other countries?

It is true that the disposal of the assets or shares of a company to be privatized is a kind of investment operation, but not all investment operations should be regulated by the MAI. Moreover, investment operation is the second phase of investment which should be subject to the first phase of investment—investment access. For most countries, public sectors are restrictive areas for foreign investors to access. Accordingly, the privatization of such areas should not be open to foreign investors.

Disregarding these different arguments, the MAI still proposed disciplines on privatization, including the definition of privatization, the treatment of privatization, rules for special share arrangements and the transparency rule. But some delegations still reserved their position on the MAI's making rules for privatization.[166]

6.5.3   MAI's Disciplines on Privatization

6.5.3.1   MAI's Definition of Privatization

In order to make clear the object of the privatization obligations imposed by the MAI, MAI gave a uniform definition to privatization which means "the sale by a Contracting Party, in part or in full, of its equity interests in any entity or other disposal having substantially the same effect."[167] Because this definition does not attach any qualification to "entity", the scope of the entity is so broad to cover not only the entities owned or controlled by the contracting party, but also any entity in which the contracting party has more or less equity interests. Thus the entity here is not equivalent to state enterprise which will be discussed in 6.6. Therefore a delegation proposed that the word "entity" should be qualified by the addition of "it owns or controls through ownership interests".[168]

According to this definition, the sale of part of the party's equity interests in any entity, i.e. the sale of a division of the entity or a certain percentage of its equity interests, no matter how much percentage of equity interests it owns in the entity, is considered as privatization. Moreover, any other disposal of the party's equity interests which has substantially the same effect is also covered by the definition. This would widen the scope of privatization and thus one delegation reserved on this phrase.[169]

---

[166]   The MAI, Chapter III, Privatization, footnote 41.
[167]   Id., Para. 5.
[168]   Id., footnote 55.
[169]   Id., footnote 54.

Obviously, the MAI's definition of privatization is very broad even if it explicitly excludes transactions between different levels or entities of the same contracting party, and transactions in the normal conduct of business.[170] The broad definition is an inevitable outcome of the ambition to make MAI a high standard agreement.

6.5.3.2 Right to Privatization

It should be made clear that the MAI's disciplines on privatization would apply only when privatization happens. It does not mean that any country has the obligation to privatize its state enterprises.[171] This statement shows respect for the right of each country to decide whether to privatize. Any decision to privatize is in the hands of the government.[172] Any other country or organization does not have the right to direct or to force a country to privatize.

6.5.3.3 Treatment of Privatization

Generally, when a country privatizes its state enterprise, it will normally tend to transfer its equity to domestic investor and put restrictions on the acquisition of this equity by foreign investors. The MAI hopes to eliminate such differential treatment through the imposition of the obligation of national treatment and MFN treatment. Therefore, the MAI provides that each contracting party should accord national treatment and MFN treatment to any investor in the process of privatization.[173] But because national treatment and MFN treatment are the essential principles for the whole MAI, one delegation questioned the need for a separate article confirming the application of them to privatization.[174]

With the application of national treatment in privatization, it should be understood that the exceptions to national treatment discussed in Chapter Five of this book also apply to privatization which is a kind of investment operation. When a certain public sector is prohibited by one country from foreign access by means of country specific exceptions, it is sure that national treatment and MFN treatment do not apply to the privatization of the enterprise in such a sector.

According to the MAI, the application of national treatment and MFN treatment is extended to all phases of the privatization process, i.e. both the initial sales of publicly owned assets and the subsequent sales of the privatized assets.[175] Initial sales include all kinds of privatization, irrespective of the method of privatization (whether by public offering, direct sale or other

---

[170] Id., Para. 5.
[171] Id., Para. 2.
[172] A. Ahnlid, *supra* note 11, p. 29.
[173] The MAI, Chapter III, Privatization, Para. 1.
[174] Commentary to the MAI, Privatization, General.
[175] The MAI, Chapter III, Privatization, Para. 1, 1(a), (b); A. Ahnlid, *supra* note 18, p. 24.

method).[176] The purpose of extending national treatment and MFN treatment to subsequent sales of the privatized assets is to prevent contracting parties from imposing on secondary transactions rules which are inconsistent with national treatment and MFN treatment.[177] However, the subsequent transactions actually go beyond the scope of privatization and thus such a provision is opposed by some delegations.[178] The author is of the opinion that any transaction of private entities including the subsequent transactions involving privatized assets should be governed by domestic law including company law, property law, etc.

6.5.3.4   *Special Share Arrangements for Privatization*

Special share arrangements are some special methods and rules made as regards the allocation of ownership, management or control of the assets to be privatized. There are a variety of such arrangements, such as: (1) the retention of "golden shares" by contracting parties or any persons; (2) stable shareholder groups assembled by a contracting party; (3) management/employee buyouts; (4) voucher schemes for members of the public; (5) maintaining shares for a certain period of time; and (6) special treatment concerning acquisition to locals.[179] Under such arrangements, certain categories of shareholders might be given rights that exceed those of other shareholders.[180]

As to whether national treatment and MFN treatment should apply to special share arrangements for privatization, or, whether the measures of special share arrangements comply with the requirements of national treatment and MFN treatment, there were critically different proposals from the MAI delegations, and one delegation clearly opposed to the inclusion of the issue of special share arrangements in the privatization rules.[181] Under such a circumstance, the MAI could not reach generally accepted rules on special share arrangements, but had to list four alternatives proposed by delegations.

The first alternative is to state that special share arrangements should not be considered to be inconsistent with national treatment or MFN treatment, irrespective whether they led to *de facto* discrimination or not, unless they explicitly or internationally favoured investors or investments of a contracting party or discriminated against investors or investments of another contracting party on the grounds of their nationality or permanent residency.[182] This statement does not imply that any special share arrangement is necessarily compatible with national treatment and MFN treatment, but admits that some arrangements could be contrary to national treatment and MFN

---

[176]   The MAI, Chapter III, Privatization, Para. 1, 1 (a).
[177]   The MAI, Chapter III, Privatization, footnote 43.
[178]   Id.
[179]   The MAI, Chapter III, Privatization, Para. 3, Alternatives 2 and 4.
[180]   A. Ahnlid, *supra* note 11, p. 29.
[181]   The MAI, Chapter III, Privatization, footnote 46.
[182]   The MAI, Chapter III, Privatization, Para. 3, Alternative 1, and footnote 46; Commentary to the MAI, Privatization, para. 3; A. Ahnlid, *supra* note 11, p. 29.

treatment. Therefore, one delegation proposed an illustrative list of the consistent special share arrangements.[183] This alternative gained support from a large number of delegations.

The second alternative states that special share arrangements would allow a contracting party or a domestic person to retain control on the privatized enterprise and thus held strong potential for discrimination against foreign investors and, were in fact inconsistent with national treatment and MFN treatment obligations in many instances.[184] This alternative was proposed by one delegation and he further proposed that any country who wished to maintain or adopted the use of special share arrangements should subject them to their country-specific exceptions.[185]

The third alternative is a compromise that the first alternative is acceptable in principle, but those special share arrangements which explicitly discriminate (i.e. *de jure*) against foreign investors and their investments, or whose application would cause *de facto* discrimination should be regarded as contrary to national treatment and MFN treatment.[186]

The fourth alternative states that special share arrangements should be allowed except that they are against the rules of national treatment and MFN treatment.

The MAI tended to adopt the first alternative which was supported by most delegations.[187] It was also agreed that countries might make reservations on those sectors in which special share arrangements are used in their country-specific exceptions.[188]

6.5.3.5   Transparency Rule

For foreign investors, because obtaining in time any information with respect to privatization so as to make sure that they are not put in a more disadvantageous position than domestic investors is basic for their participation in privatization, they attached particular importance to transparency.[189] The MAI reaffirms the transparency rule in the issue of privatization by requiring each country to publish promptly the essential features and procedures for participation in each prospective privatization,[190] notwithstanding the fact that transparency has been an essential obligation for each contracting state of the MAI. For them, transparency requirement is also necessary for the supervision of the application of national treatment and MFN treatment during the process of privatization.

---

[183]   The MAI, Chapter III, Privatization, Para. 3, Alternative 4.
[184]   The MAI, Chapter III, Privatization, Para. 3, Alternative 2 and footnote 46; Commentary to the MAI, Privatization, Paragraph 3.
[185]   The MAI, Chapter III, Privatization, footnote 49; Commentary to the MAI, Privatization, Para. 3.
[186]   The MAI, Chapter III, Privatization, Para. 3, Alternative 3, and footnote 50.
[187] The MAI, Chapter III, Privatization, footnote 46.
[188]   A. Ahnlid, *supra* note 18, p. 24.
[189]   Commentary to the MAI, Privatization, General.
[190]   The MAI, Chapter III, Privatization, Para. 4.

6.5.4   Conclusion

Although privatization is within the competence of a sovereignty state, the MAI still developed rules for it which requires the application of national treatment, MFN treatment and transparency principles. Under these disciplines, foreign investors could easily get access to such public sectors and state enterprises as to be privatized and the purpose of liberalization of international investment could be eventually effectuated.

6.6   MAI'S DISCIPLINES ON MONOPOLIES, STATE ENTERPRISES AND CONCESSION

6.6.1   Introduction

Monopoly, state enterprise and concession are interrelated issues. State enterprises constitute monopolies in some instances, and the granting of concession by a state usually causes the creation of monopolies or state enterprises. These three issues are also related to privatization since what are often privatized are the state enterprises which are previously monopolies.[191] As stated in the issue of privatization, every state has its own right to choose its own economic policies and thus the creation, maintaining and elimination of monopolies and state enterprises and the granting of concession originate from the state's discretionary competence and are in the hands of the government. That explains why the three issues are outside the regulatory framework covered by international organizations.[192]

OECD considered that domestic provisions concerning monopolies, state enterprises and concession could restrain foreign and domestic investment opportunities in the areas monopolized and thus constitute informal barriers to foreign and domestic investment,[193] and moreover, monopolies and state enterprises often acted in a manner which inhibited or discriminated against foreign investment.[194] OECD then decided that the MAI should make rules on the three issues based on non-discriminatory treatment so as to abolish possible barriers to foreign investment and promote liberalization of international investment.

However, since there were few existing rules for these issues in international agreements, and the making of new rules would limit or detriment state's economic sovereignty, the MAI delegations had heated debates as to the necessity of new rules and the contents of new rules. Finally, the MAI drafted preliminary disciplines on monopolies, state enterprises and concession respectively, but these disciplines were far from consensus and subject to further discussion.

---

[191]   OECD, *supra* note 61, p. 127.
[192]   M. O. Silva, *supra* note 160, p. 34.
[193]   OECD, *supra* note 61, p. 127.
[194]   Id.

6.6.2 MAI's Disciplines on Monopolies

6.6.2.1 Existing Rules on Monopolies

So far, only GATS and NAFTA provide rules for monopolies. GATS requires that any monopoly supplier of a service does not, in the supply of the monopoly service in the relevant market, act in a manner inconsistent with the obligations of MFN treatment and the specific commitments of its country in market access and national treatment.[195] It further requires that when a monopoly supplier competes in the supply of a service outside the scope of its monopoly rights, it should not abuse its monopoly position.[196]

NAFTA provides very detailed rules for monopolies which include:[197] (1) the right of contracting party to designate a monopoly is not challenged; (2) the party shall provide prior written notification of the designation and endeavor to introduce conditions on the operation of the monopoly; (3) any monopoly shall, in principle, act in a manner that is not inconsistent with its state's obligations under NAFTA, provide non-discriminatory treatment to investments in its purchase or sale of the monopoly good or service, and does not use its monopoly position to engage in anticompetitive practices; and (4) procurement by governmental agencies can be an exception to Rule (3). These rules become a model of the counterpart of the MAI.

6.6.2.2 MAI's Definition of Monopoly

The MAI defines monopoly as "any person or entity designated by a Contracting Party as the sole supplier or buyer of a good or service in a relevant market in the territory of a Contracting Party".[198] There were different views on this definition. Most delegations considered that the MAI disciplines on monopolies should apply to all levels of government and thus all monopolies designated by a contracting party (including its central, provincial and local governments) should be covered.[199] One delegation favored a definition to be limited to monopolies designated only by national government and suggested to substitute "Contracting Party" for "national government authority" in the above definition.[200] All delegations agreed that monopolies derived from an exclusive intellectual property right should be excluded from the definition.[201] Therefore, the MAI stipulates that monopoly "does not include a person or entity that has an exclusive intellectual property right solely by reason of such right or the excercise of such right".[202]

---

[195] GATS, Article VIII, para. 1.
[196] GATS, Article VIII, para. 2.
[197] NAFTA, Article 1502.
[198] The MAI, Chapter III, Monopolies/State enterprises/Concession, C. Definitions Related to Articles on Monopolies [and State Enterprises], para. 3.
[199] The MAI, Chapter III, Monopolies/State enterprises/Concession, footnote 79.
[200] Id.
[201] Id., footnote 80.
[202]The MAI, Chapter III, Monopolies/State enterprises/Concession, C. Definitions Related to Articles on Monopolies [and State Enterprises], para. 3.

According to this definition, monopoly can be categorized as monopoly for the supply of good or service, and monopoly for the purchase of good or service. Monopoly can also be devided into privately-owned monopoly and publicly-owned monopoly.[203] Publicly-owned monopoly includes government monopoly and state monopoly.[204] The MAI provides for some slightly different rules for these different types of monopoly.

6.6.2.3   MAI's Rules on Monopolies

The MAI developed separate disciplines respectively for the creation and removal of monopolies and the act of the monopolies maintained or designated by contracting parties.

The MAI first confirms the sovereign right of each contracting party to create, maintain and abolish a monopoly by stipulating that the MAI's rules shall not be construed to prevent a contracting party from maintaining, designating and eliminating a monopoly.[205] This is a basic point of departure for the MAI's monopolies rules. The wording of this article is similar to that of the NAFTA.

For the creation or designation of a monopoly by a contracting party, the MAI provides that each Contracting Party shall [endeavor to] accord non-discriminatory treatment (i.e. national treatment and MFN treatment) to both domestic and foreign investors when designating a monopoly.[206] But there was a debate on the nature of the obligation to accord non-discriminatory treatment. Some delegations maintained that the obligation should be hard-law obligation and thus held that the phrase "endeavor to" in square brackets be removed.[207] Some delegations, pointing out that it was difficult to apply such obligation to every situation, contended that the obligation should be soft-law obligation and insisted on keeping the phrase "endeavor to".[208] More delegations supposed that different obligations should be imposed on different types of monopoly. In other words, when designating a publicly-owned monopoly, the state can bear a best endeavor undertaking; when designating a privately-owned monopoly, the state shall bear hard-law obligation.[209]

The MAI's specific rules on monopolies are as follows. As for the act of a monopoly maintained or designated by contracting parties, regardless of privately-owned monopoly or publicly-owned monopoly, the monopoly shall provide non-discriminatory treatment to investments of foreign

---

[203] The MAI, Chapter III, Monopolies/State enterprises/Concession, footnote 59; MAI, Chapter III, Monopolies/State enterprises/Concession, A. Article on Monopolies, para. 3.
[204] The MAI, Chapter III, Monopolies/State enterprises/Concession, footnote 59.
[205] The MAI, Chapter III, Monopolies/State enterprises/Concession, A. Article on Monopolies, para. 1.
[206] Id., para. 2.
[207] The MAI, Chapter III, Monopolies/State enterprises/Concession, footnote 59; Commentary to the MAI, Chapter III, Monopolies/State Enterprises/Concessions, A. Article on Monopolies, para. 2.
[208] Id.
[209] The MAI, Chapter III, Monopolies/State enterprises/Concession, footnote 59.

investors in its supply or purchase of the monopoly good or service.[210] Government procurement can be an exception to this rule.[211] Further, such monopoly can not abuse its monopoly position to engage in anti-competitive practices and shall act solely in accordance with commercial considerations in its purchase or sale of the monopoly good or service in the relevant market.[212] For these provisions, the MAI provides that neither investors nor their investments of another contracting party may have recourse to the MAI's investor–state dispute settlement mechanism for any matter arising therefrom.[213] The reason is that most governments do not allow private "antitrust" actions in their own courts by their citizens. Moreover, the proposed provisions on monopoly are novel and complex and thus the dispute settlement should be limited only to state–state disputes.[214] But many delegations objected to such a fragmentation of the dispute settlement system.[215]

As for demonopoly (elimination of monopoly), the MAI provides that each party should be given the right to lodge new country-specific exceptions under the MAI when demonopoly situations occur.[216] This means that each country may deviate from the obligation of according national treatment and MFN treatment when it abolishes monopoly. The reason for such a rule is that demonopolization operations are generally favourable to investment liberalization since they open up new investment activities, and would have the effect of extending the obligations of the MAI to a new area.[217] It is sure that such country-specific exceptions should also be subject to the MAI's standstill principle. But some delegations were opposed to the principle of lodging country exceptions after the entry into force of the MAI.[218] Some delegations prefer that each country lodged precautionary country exceptions in case of demonopoly at the time of the entry into force of the MAI.[219] Some other delegations were of the view that in the absence of country exceptions, the non-discriminatory obligations would apply to demonopolization operations.[220]

The MAI also requires of each party to notify to the Parties Group any existing designated monopoly, any newly designated monopoly and any elimination of a designated monopoly.[221]

---

[210] The MAI, Chapter III, Monopolies/State enterprises/Concession, A. Article on Monopolies, para. 2(a) and (b).
[211] Id., para. 2 (b).
[212] Id., para. 2(c) and (d).
[213] Id., para. 6.
[214] The MAI, Chapter III, Monopolies/State enterprises/Concession, footnote 73.
[215] A. Ahnlid, *supra* note 11, p. 30.
[216] Ib., the MAI, Chapter III, Monopolies/State enterprises/Concession, A. Article on Monopolies, para. 4.
[217] Commentary to the MAI, Chapter III, Monopolies/State Enterprises/Concessions, A. Article on Monopolies, Para. 4, 1.
[218] The MAI, Chapter III, Monopolies/State enterprises/Concession, footnote 69.
[219] Commentary to the MAI, Chapter III, Monopolies/State Enterprises/Concessions, A. Article on Monopolies, Para. 4, 1.
[220] Id., Para. 4, 2.
[221] The MAI, Chapter III, Monopolies/State enterprises/Concession, A. Article on Monopolies, para. 5.

6.6.3   MAI's Disciplines on State Enterprises

State enterprises are also called entities with which a government has a specific relationship.[222] They are different from private entities because of their links with governmental authorities.[223] During the MAI negotiations, disciplines on state enterprises were also subject to considerable debate.[224] Therefore the relating provisions in the MAI text were marked with square brackets, which means that they were only proposals instead of the final text.

The definition of state enterprise given by the MAI is "an enterprise owned or controlled through ownership interest by a contracting party",[225] even though many delegations thought such a definition unnecessary .[226]

A large majority of delegations questioned the need for specific provisions on state enterprises because the anti-circumvention clause of the MAI was intended to cover all enterprises, including both state enterprises and private enterprises.[227] They thought state enterprises operating in the competitive sector should be treated no differently than private enterprises and it was better to submit state enterprises to the same rights and obligations as private enterprises.[228]

But some delegations still proposed additional provisions for state enterprises which were similar to those of the NAFTA.[229] The first proposed rule was that state enterprises should accord non-discriminatory treatment to foreign investors and investment in the sale of their goods or services.[230] The second proposed rule was that the MAI's investor–state arbitration did not apply to any matters arising out of the provisions in relation to state enterprises.[231] However, some delegations considered that any additional disciplines should be subject to both state–state and investor–state dispute settlement.[232] The compromised rule was an anti-abuse clause which requires state enterprises not to act in a manner inconsistent with the MAI's obligations when exercising regulatory authority.[233]

Although it was not specifically mentioned by the MAI, the government's right to create state enterprises were still well recognized.[234]

---

[222]   The MAI, Chapter III, Monopolies/State enterprises/Concession, B. Article on State Enterprises.
[223]   The MAI, Chapter III, Monopolies/State enterprises/Concession, footnote 75.
[224]   A. Ahnlid, *supra* note 11, p. 30.
[225]   The MAI, Chapter III, Monopolies/State enterprises/Concession, C. Definitions Related to Articles on Monopolies [and State Enterprises], para. 6.
[226]   The MAI, Chapter III, Monopolies/State enterprises/Concession, footnote 84.
[227]   Id., footnote 74; Commentary to the MAI, Chapter III, Monopolies/State Enterprises/Concessions, B. Article on [State enterprises].
[228]   Commentary to the MAI, Chapter III, Monopolies/State Enterprises/Concessions, B. Article on [State enterprises].
[229]   Compare the MAI's additional provisions with Article 1503 of the NAFTA.
[230]   The MAI, Chapter III, Monopolies/State enterprises/Concession, B. Article on [State enterprises], (ii) Additional provisions, a. Proposal by two delegations, para. 1.
[231]   Id., para. 2.
[232]   The MAI, Chapter III, Monopolies/State enterprises/Concession, footnote 76.
[233]   The MAI, Chapter III, Monopolies/State enterprises/Concession, B. Article on [State enterprises], (ii) Additional provisions, b. Proposal by one delegation, para. 1; The MAI, Chapter III, Monopolies/State enterprises/Concession, footnote 77; A. Ahnlid, *supra* note 18, p. 24.
[234]   OECD, *supra* note 61, p. 128.

6.6.4   MAI's Disciplines on Concession

The purpose for the MAI to develop new disciplines on concession is to ensure that concessions do not prevent or significantly impede foreign investment, i.e. that they apply in the same manner to foreign investors as to domestic investors.[235] During the negotiating process, the Negotiating Group admitted that the subject of concessions needed more technical work before it could be decided whether specific rules for concessions were required or not.[236] But until the last minute, many delegations were still opposed to the inclusion of any article on concessions.[237]

Since in national legislations the concept of concession had different coverage, it was a difficult task to elaborate a definition for concession.[238] Some delegations argued that if the MAI intended to make special transparency provisions for concessions, it was necessary to define concessions properly.[239] The proposed definition of concessions is "any delegation, direct or indirect, which entails a transferring of operation of activities, carried out by a government authority, national or subnational, or any public or para-public authority, to a distinct and independent legal entity."[240] The delegation here shall be realized either by any laws, regulations, administrative rulings or established policies, or by any private or public contract.[241]

For concession, the MAI provides special transparency rule which requires of government to disclose, in granting a concession, all relevant information about the purpose and nature of the activity subject to concession, its conditions and deadline.[242] This rule applies to any form of granting a concession, including granting a concession through tender as well as non-tender.[243] Still, there were many delegations who objected to this additional article to the general transparency article of the MAI.[244]

6.7   CONCLUSION

For the new topics of investors and key personnel, performance requirements, investment incentives, privatization and monopolies, state enterprises and concession in the field of international investment, the MAI still emphasizes the application of its principles of national treatment, MFN treatment and transparency. Through these additional rules, the MAI intends to limit the government's right to regulate foreign investment and thus paves the way for the realization of liberalization of international investment.

---

[235]   Id.
[236]   A. Ahnlid, *supra* note 18, p. 25.
[237]   The MAI, Chapter III, Monopolies/State enterprises/Concession, footnote 85.
[238]   Id., footnote 88.
[239]   Id.
[240]   The MAI, Chapter III, Monopolies/State enterprises/Concession, D. Article on Concessions, Definition, para. 1.
[241]   Id., para. 2.
[242]   The MAI, Chapter III, Monopolies/State enterprises/Concession, D. Article on Concessions, Transparency.
[243]   The MAI, Chapter III, Monopolies/State enterprises/Concession, footnote 85.
[244]   Id.

7. Investment Protection System of the MAI

7.1   INTRODUCTION

The aim of investment protection system of international investment treaties is to provide protection for investment of foreign investors against host government measures unduly detrimental to their interests. Protection became an important topic in international investment regimes ever since the end of the Second World War.[1] In the post-war decolonization movements, many newly independent countries carried out nationalization policy to take over foreign investment so as to strengthen their political power. Government takings were one of the results of large-scale sociopolitical reforms by some other countries. Foreign exchange control was another policy adopted by both developed and developing countries which would affect the free transfer of funds of foreign investment. Therefore, investment protection is one of the most critical subjects of both bilateral investment treaties (BITs), regional and multilateral investment instruments.

Investment protection system normally covers general treatment standards which apply to all aspects of foreign investments, and specific treatment standards which address particular issues such as expropriation, transfer of funds, etc.[2] This practice is similar to the method in the MAI's treatment of foreign investment discussed in Chapter Five and Six of this book which include general principles and specific principles. The general treatment standards of investment protection mainly refer to fair and equitable treatment and other treatment, while the general principles for the treatment of foreign investment mainly refer to national treatment (NT) and MFN treatment. The three kinds of treatment are put together in one article by some agreements or treaties, such as the Energy Charter Treaty (ECT).[3] The MAI seperates them to be provided in two different headings: "Treatment of Investors and Investment" and "Investment Protection". Such an arrangement is an elaboration of the MAI negotiators.

In the first place, NT/MFN treatment and fair and equitable treatment are two categories of treatment standards with different nature.

---

[1]   UNCTAD, *Trends in International Investment Agreements: An Overview*, New York and Geneva, 1999, p. 73.
[2]   UNCTAD, *Bilateral Investment Treaties in the Mid-1990s*, New York and Geneva, 1998, p. 53.
[3]   ECT, Art. 10 (1) and (3).

National treatment and MFN treatment are relative or contingent treatment whose content is ascertained by reference to national law of the host state or international treaties concluded by the host state.[4] Fair and equitable treatment is absolute or non-contingent standard whose content is generally stable though vague and does not vary according to how other investments or entities are treated.[5] Just because of the above differentiation, the MAI negotiators agreed that it was justified to separate NT/MFN treatment and fair and equitable treatment respectively in two different headings.[6]

In the second place, NT/MFN treatment are treatments accorded to both foreign investors and their investments, which is a characteristic of the MAI's treatment system with respect to foreign investment. They apply to all phases of foreign investment, including pre-establishment and post-establishment.[7] According to the MAI, NT and MFN treatment are general principles of treatment for foreign investors and their investments which run through the whole MAI. Of course, they also apply to all matters of investment protection. Meanwhile, fair and equitable treatment is accorded to foreign investments in the territory of a contracting party.[8] In other words, this treatment only applies to foreign investments having established—post-establishment phase. The requirement in the MAI that host government shall not impair the operation, management, maintenance, ... of foreign investments varifies that only those foreign investments in the post-establishment phase are protected.[9] Protection against measures of host country does not extend to foreign investment before its admission. The use of fair and equitable treatment is to ensure that foreign investment can obtain minimum protection and help to interpret and clarify how more specific provisions should be applied in particular situation.[10]

Therefore, the relative standards of NT/MFN treatment applying to the whole MAI and the absolute standard of fair and equitable treatment applying to only investment protection jointly constitute complete and full protection to foreign established investment.

As a comprehensive investment instrument, the MAI provides general treatment standards of fair and equitable treatment, full and constant protection and security, etc., and specific treatment standards on the issues of expropriation and compensation, civil strife, transfer of funds, subrogation, etc.

The goal of providing absolute standards of both general and specific treatment standards is to impose strong and strict obligations on host governments to afford full protection to foreign investment, and to provide levels of investment promotion and protection which are at least as strong as those in other investment treaties.[11] The MAI's provisions of investment

---

[4]   Id.; UNCTAD, *Fair and Equitable Treatment*, New York and Geneva, 1999, pp. 15–16.
[5]   UNCTAD, *supra* note 4.
[6]   Commentary to the MAI, Chapter IV, 1. General Treatment, para. 4.
[7]   MAI, Chapter III, National Treatment and Most Favoured Nation Treatment, paras. 1 and 2.
[8]   MAI, Chapter IV, 1. General Treatment, para. 1.1.
[9]   Id., para. 1.2.
[10]   UNCTAD, *supra* note 2, p. 53; K. S. Gudgeon, "United States Bilateral Investment Treaties: Comments on their Origin, Purpose, and General Treatment Standards," 4 *International Tax & Business Lawyer* (1986), p. 125.
[11]   R. Morgan, "Treatment and Protection of Investors and Investments," *Multilateral Agreement on Investment: State of Play in April 1997*, p. 20.

protection have many similarities with those of most BITs and other international instruments. However, they also have their own "innovation". Just as the MAI negotiators argued, they did not intend to "re-invent the wheel", but rather to add some more spokes in order to strengthen the whole vehicle.[12]

By the way, there were less debates on protection provisions during the MAI negotiations, the reason being fact that the long history of investment protection has piled abundant precedents and experience and thus makes it easier to come to consensus. The investment protection articles of the MAI are therefore clear with very few square brackets.

7.2   GENERAL TREATMENT STANDARDS

7.2.1   Background

General treatment standards have longer history than NT/MFN treatment. In order to protect their own private investors and investment, capital-exporting countries required capital-importing countries to guarantee minimum protection to foreign investment through the general treatment clause in international investment instruments. The general treatment is an absolute standard and thus imposes absolute commitments on host state and confers absolute rights to foreign investors. Even if the treatment to domestic investors accorded by the host state's national law is lower than the general treatment, the host state should still offer the general treatment to foreign investments. In recent decades, general treatment is incorporated with NT/MFN treatment in international treaties concluded by capital-exporting countries. When the treatment to domestic investment by national law, or the treatment to other foreign investment conferred by BITs or other international treaties, is lower than general treatment standard, the general treatment standards prevail. When the treatment foreign investments can obtain according to NT/MFN treatment is higher than general treatment, the NT/MFN treatment prevails. In this sense, and in the context of investment protection, general treatment is a baseline, and NT/MFN treatment is functioning as a supplement and elevation upon the baseline.

General treatment standards vary in different international investment treaties. At least four models exist: (1) fair and equitable treatment; (2) reference to existing international obligations as a minimum standard; (3) full protection and security; and (4) no discrimination (prohibition of unreasonable and/or discriminatory measures).[13] Many BITs and international agreements use one of the above models or combine some models. For example, the BITs concluded by China with other countries adopt fair and equitable treatment;[14] the BITs concluded by developed countries mostly use the

---

[12]   J. Karl, "Investment Protection," *the Multilateral Agreement on Investment: State of Play as of February 1997*, p. 14.

[13]   OECD, "Investment Protection: Report by Working Group C," *Towards Multilateral Investment Rules*, p. 134.

[14]   The BIT Model of China, Art. 3(1).

models in a combined form; NAFTA requires the first three models;[15] the Energy Charter Treaty and the United States prototype BIT adopt the above four models in one article.[16]

For the MAI, negotiators argued that only a mixed solution of the four models would avoid shortcomings resulting from any partial adoption of one particular model.[17] The ambition of the MAI to provide full protection to foreign investments is self-evident. For the convenience of the following comments and discussion, the articles of the MAI on general treatment are cited as follows:

1.1 Each Contracting Party shall accord to investments in its territory of investors of another Contracting Party fair and equitable treatment and full and constant protection and security. In no case shall a Contracting Party accord treatment less favourable than that required by international law.

1.2 A Contracting Pary shall not impair by [unreasonable or discriminatory] [unreasonable and discriminatory] measures the operation, management, maintenance, use, enjoyment or disposal of investments in its territory of investors of another Contracting Party.[18]

The above provisions are borrowed almost directly and exactly from the ECT and the United States prototype BIT.

7.2.2 Fair and Equitable Treatment[19]

The first general treatment standard provided by the MAI is fair and equitable treatment. Although fair and equitable treatment is an absolute treatment and is used by some international investment instruments earlier than NT/MFN treatment, its connotation and extension is far from consensus and clearness in international community.

Fair and equitable treatment is mainly adopted in BITs and some international treaties concluded or proposed by capital-exporting countries except Japan.[20] The perspective of developing countries, very few developing country (capital-importing country) codes employ this treatment.[21] In BITs, this treatment is rejected by most of developing countries, such as Romania and some Asian and African countries. Only some developing countries such as China and Sri Lanka accept this treatment in some of their BITs.[22]

It was the differences among developed and developing countries con-cerning the fair and equitable treatment clause that significantly led to the failure of the United Nations Code of Conduct on Transnational Corporations.[23]

---

[15] NAFTA, Art. 1105(1).
[16] ECT, Art. 10 (1); the BIT Model (1994) of the United States, Art. II (3).
[17] OECD, *supra* note 13, p. 134.
[18] The MAI, Chapter IV, 1. General Treatment, paras. 1.1 & 1.2.
[19] For a full discussion of fair and equitable treatment, see UNCTAD, *supra* note 4.
[20] UNCTAD, *supra* note 4, p. 4; Xu Chongli, *A Study on Bilateral Investment Treaties*, p. 123.
[21] A. R. Parra, "Principles Governing Foreign Investment, as Reflected in National Investment Codes", 7 *ICSID Review—Foreign Investment Law Journal* (1992), no. 2, p. 435.
[22] UNCTAD, *supra* note 2, p. 54; UNCTC, Bilateral Investment Treaties, pp. 32–33.
[23] UNCTAD, *supra* note 4, p. 9.

To date, at the multilateral level, no comprehensive treaty on foreign investment in effect contains such a treatment clause.[24]

Even among those countries who adopt fair and equitable treatment, there are three different viewpoints as to its contents.

The first view is that fair and equitable treatment is equivalent to international minimum standard in international law.[25] This view is questionable. If the two terms are synonymous, why there is no international treaty which expressly indicates this link, and why the two terms are sometimes incorporated into one international treaty? Fair and equitable treatment and international minimum standard are mostly supported by developed countries,[26] but international minimum standard is always questioned by a number of developing countries,[27] even though fair and equitable treatment is accepted by some developing countries such as China. Moreover, there is no consensus as to the content of international minimum standard.

The second view is that fair and equitable treatment is a separate and self-contained treatment parallel with the duty of full protection and security, international minimum standard, and the standard of non-discrimination.[28] The United States prototype BIT and the MAI takes this position.

The third view is that fair and equitable treatment is a comprehensive treatment standard including the duty of full protection and security, international minimum standard, and the standard of non-discrimination.[29]

In addition, western countries have different opinions as to the relationship between fair and equitable treatment and the NT/MFN treatment when the three terms are combined in one treaty. The Netherlands and Switzerland clearly state in their BITs that fair and equitable treatment shall not be less favourable than NT or MFN treatment.[30] The BIT between Finland and Chile has the same clause.[31] This is to say that fair and equitable treatment shall be at least the same as or better than NT/MFN treatment, whichever is more favourable. In this sense, the fair and equitable treatment can elevate the treatment that foreign investment may obtain according to NT/MFN treatment. But the MAI itself, among many others, does not mention the link between fair and equitable treatment and NT/MFN treatment. One scholar in his assessment of the MAI considers that fair and equitable treatment provides a "floor", while the NT/MFN treatment establishes a "ceiling" for the treatment of foreign investment.[32] The implied meaning is that MT/MFN treatment is the treatment better than fair and equitable treatment. The MAI

---

[24]   Id.
[25]   Id., p. 12; UNCTAD, *supra* note 2, p. 53; Xu Chongli, *supra* note 20, p. 127.
[26]   UNCTAD, *supra* note 4, p. 13.
[27]   Id., UNCTAD, *supra* note 2, p. 53.
[28]   K. S. Gudgeon, *supra* note 10, pp. 124–125; Xu Chongli, *supra* note 20, p. 127.
[29]   UNCTAD, *supra* note 22, p. 30; Xu Chongli, *supra* note 20, p. 127.
[30]   G. Sacerdoti, "Bilateral Treaties and Multilateral Instruments on Investment Protection," *Recueil Des Cours: Collected Courses of the Hague Academy of International Law* (1997), Martinus Nijhhoff Publishers, 1998, p. 346; UNCTC, *supra* note 22, p. 32.
[31]   The BIT between Finland and Chile (1993), Art. 3 (2).
[32]   A. Böhmer, "The Struggle for a Multilateral Agreement on Investment—An Assessment of the Negotiation Process in the OECD," 41 *German Yearbook of International Law* (1998), pp. 286–287.

negotiators are of the opinion that fair and equitable treatment is supplemented by NT/MFN treatment and they also admit that in practice there may be some overlap among them.[33]

All in all, as opinions vary, no unanimous conclusion can be drawn as to the exact meaning of the fair and equitable treatment. However, almost all scholars and countries admit that this principle is not precisely defined and needs to be interpreted in each individual case.[34] For the fair and equitable treatment in the context of the MAI, it is the same case.

In the MAI, since this principle is a free-standing standard, the problem is how to determine the meaning of this principle. Neither the text of the MAI nor the MAI Commentary gives any hint. We can get some inference from the approach used to the principle of the United States prototype BIT which can be deemed as a model of the counterpart of the MAI. In consideration of the separation of this standard from other standards in the United States prototype BIT, it is contended that plain meaning of fairness and equity shall be followed.[35] The plain meaning approach is that the terms of "fair" and "equitable" should be understood in their plain, or literal, sense.[36] According to the dictionary definition, treatment is fair when it is "free from bias, fraud, or injustice; equitable, legitimate … not taking undue advantage; disposed to concede every reasonable claim".[37] Equitable treatment is that which is "characterized by equity or fairness … fair, just, reasonable."[38] According to this approach, under the principle of fair and equitable treatment, any particular treatment afforded to foreign investment by host state should be both "fair" and "equitable". Then difficulties arise: (1) the words "fair" and "equitable" themselves are vague and lack of precision, and (2) frequently, a particular treatment to foreign investment considered by capital-importing country as satisfying the standard of fair and equitable treatment fails to do so from the point of view of foreign investors or capital-exporting countries.[39] So how to judge what is fair and equitable is the key disputed issue among developed and developing countries. Developing countries hold that this principle should be determined by their domestic law of host state, while developed countries contend that it should be interpreted by international law.[40] The MAI's provision that general treatment should not be "less favourable than that required by international law" shows that the MAI takes the same position as that of developed countries.

In judicial practice, so far, only one of the international tribunal awards addresses the principle of fair and equitable treatment. In Rankin v. Iran, the Iran-United States Claims Tribunal found that anti-American statements by Iranian government officials in unstable revolutionary conditions were

---

[33]   R. Morgan, *supra* note 11, pp. 20–22.
[34]   K. J. Vandevelde, *United States Investment Treaties: Policy and Practice*, Kluwer Law and Taxation Publishers, Deventer, the Netherlands, 1992, p. 76; UNCTC, *supra* note 22, p. 30; UNCTAD, *supra* note 4, pp. 4–5.
[35]   UNCTAD, *supra* note 4, p. 35.
[36]   Id., p. 10.
[37]   The Oxford English Dictionary, 2nd ed. 1989, cited form UNCTAD, *supra* note 4, p. 19.
[38]   Id.
[39]   UNCTAD, *supra* note 4, p. 11.
[40]   Xu Chongli, *supra* note 20, p. 128.

inconsistent with the requirement of fair and equitable treatment.[41] The finding shows that standard of fair and equitable treatment could be broadly interpreted in a dispute to be in favour of developed countries.

The principle of fair and equitable treatment of the MAI has all the above difficulties and complexities.

7.2.3 Full and Constant Protection and Security

The concept of full protection and security, or constant protection and security was used alone in some BITs before the standard of fair and equitable treatment was introduced.[42] Only in recent decades is the concept of full and constant protection and security used in BITs and other international treaties such as the ECT and the MAI. This concept is not generally accepted, but is supported mostly by capital-exporting countries. The principle requires that the host government protect foreign investment from injurious activities by the government or private persons.[43] Although the protection and security from host government should be full or constant, it is never considered that such protection and security is obsolute, unlimited and unconditional. For example, you can not expect Chinese government to guarantee foreign investors against criminal act, or the United States to promise safety from personnal violence. Host government only has the duty to exercise reasonable care or due diligence to protect foreign investment under the circumstances.[44] Some arbitral tribunals also ruled to the effect that the states have "due diligence" with regard to the obligation to provide protection and security, such as the case of AAPK v. Sri Lanka.[45]

It is debatable whether host states are obligated to give special protection to foreign investors and their investment, or to apply the same protection standards to nationals and foreigners.[46] It is also well recognized that host state is not subject to strict liability of state for injury suffered by foreign investors.[47] Whether the protection and security is full and constant, or whether the host state has exercised due diligence, can not be measured by the law and order of developed countries or by international standards, as contended by developed countries, but must be determined by domestic law and the particular situation of the host state.[48] For instance, in some BITs

---

[41]   World Bank, *Legal Framework for the Treatment of Foreign Investment*, Volume I: Survey of Existing Instruments, 1992, p. 154.
[42]   UNCTAD, *supra* note 2, p. 55.
[43]   K. J. Vandevelde, *supra* note 34, p. 77; UNCTAD, *supra* note 2, p. 55.
[44]   T. W. Waelde, "International Investment under the 1994 Energy Charter Treaty: Legal, Negotiating and Policy Implications for International Investors within Western and Commonwealth of Independent States/Eastern European Countries," 29 *Journal of World Trade* (1995), no. 5, p. 41; K. J. Vandevelde, *supra* note 34, p. 77; UNCTC, *supra* note 22, p. 31.
[45]   World Bank, *supra* note 41, p. 154. For the case of AAPL v. Sri Lanka, see 6 *ICSID Review—Foreign Investment Law Journal* (1991), p. 526
[46]   UNCTC, *supra* note 22, p. 31.
[47]   T. W. Waelde, *supra* note 44, p. 41; UNCTAD, *supra* note 2, p. 55; World Bank, *supra* note 41, p. 154; K. J. Vandevelde, *supra* note 34, p. 77.
[48]   T. W. Waelde, *supra* note 44, p 41; Xu Chongli, *supra* note 20, p. 122.

between developing countries, it is stipulated that full protection and security should be subject to the laws of the other contracting party.[49]

The MAI's principle of full and constant proteciton and security is subject to the above comments. It is also regarded as an onerous burden.[50]

7.2.4   Minimum Standard of International Law

The MAI incorporates international law by reference of it into its general treatment clause. International law standard is adopted by some BITs of developed countries and few international treaties such as the ECT and NAFTA to which developed countries are key proponents. But it is rarely found in the BITs between developing countries.[51] On the contrary, most developing countries are opposed to this standard in their BITs. For example, during the negotiations on the BIT between China and the United States, China rejected the wording in the BIT of "fair and equitable treatment shall in no case be less favourable than that required by international law".[52] Also during the negotiations on the United Nations Code of Conduct on Transnational Corporations, this standard was insisted upon by industrialized countries, but opposed by developing countries.[53]

There are also differences as to the content of international minimum standard. As mentioned above, international law standard is regarded by some scholars as an equivalent to the fair and equitable treatment. NAFTA considers international law standard as consisting of fair and equitable treatment and full protection and security.[54] ECT and the MAI consider it as an independent and separate standard. Such differences add to the difficulties in the interpretation of this standard.

Reasons for the developing countries to oppose this standard is that developing countries consider that this standard has often been misused in the past to secure privileged treatment for foreigners in economic matters, to exploit their natural resources, and even to justify military intervention by foreigners' home countries on their behalf.[55]

In the perspective of developing countries, the possible unfavourable results of incorporating international law by reference are as follows: (1) the treatment to foreign investment by a host country that falls below the international law standard would violate the clause.[56] (2) The principles of international law could be invoked or enforced in investor-state or state-state dispute resolution mechanisms.[57] (3) The clause might serve as a choice of

---

[49]   For example, the Agreement between China and Thailand for the Promotion and Protection of Investment, Art. 3 (2). See also Xu Chongli, *supra* note 20, p. 122.
[50]   R. H. Thomas, "The Need for a Southern African Development Community Response to Proposals for a Multilateral Agreement on Investment," 21 *World Competition* (1998), no. 4, p. 97.
[51]   G. Sacerdoti, *supra* note 30, p. 347.
[52]   Xu Chongli, *supra* note 20, p. 128.
[53]   G. Sacerdoti, *supra* note 30, p. 347; UNCTAD, *supra* note 2, p. 57, footnote 69.
[54]   NAFTA, Art. 1105 (1).
[55]   UNCTAD, *supra* note 2, p. 57; UNCTC, *supra* note 22, p. 31.
[56]   UNCTAD, *supra* note 2, p. 57.
[57]   K. J. Vandevelde, *supra* note 34, p. 78; UNCTAD, *supra* note 2, p. 57.

law provision for all dispute settlement mechanisms, the reason being that the investment treaty provides that the treatment accorded to foreign investors shall be not less favourable than that is required by international law, so both treaty clauses and principles of international law can be used as governing law in the case of treatment dispute.[58]

For the MAI, it is unscientific and unobjective to adopt international law standard whose content is vague, disputed and lack of precision, and to deem it as an absolute obligation of host state to foreign investors. Even the MAI negotiators admitted that what components an international minimum standard should have is a question.[59] Under the current circumstances that developing countries have strong fear and objection to international minimum standard, the incorporation of this standard into the MAI would surely prevent developing countries from access to the MAI, even if the MAI was intended to be open to them.

7.2.5 Prohibition of Unreasonable and/or Discriminatory Measures

Another clause of the MAI's general treatment of investment protection is the prohibition of unreasonable and/or discriminatory measures by host government to foreign investment. Such a clause is not a common practice in BITs or international investment instruments. Two approaches are adopted by those few BITs and multilateral treaties in this regard: "unreasonable *or* discriminatory measures" and "unreasonable/arbitrary *and* discriminatory measures" (emphasis added).[60] For the first approach, the host country would have less latitude for action since any regulatory measure which is either unreasonable or discriminatory would be prohibited. For the second approach, the host state could have greater latitude for action. It would be free to impose discriminatory measure on foreign investment as long as the discriminatory measure was not unreasonable, and *vice versa*.[61] For instance, a developing country may grant special incentives to its national investors but deny them to foreign investors based on the argument that such differentiation is reasonable in view of its status as a developing country.[62]

In drafting Article 1.2, three formulations were suggested. One formulation calls for no additional standards with respect to which a government's action would be measured.[63] The other two concerns a choice between the above two approaches. Those who supported the first approach argued that

---

[58]   Id.
[59]   OECD, *supra* note 13, p. 150.
[60]   For the first approach, examples are: the BIT between Denmark and Lithuania (1992), Art. 3 (1), the BIT between Ghana and Switzerland (1991), Art. 3, and the BIT between Lithuania and the Netherlands (1994), Art. 3 (i). The ECT, Art. 10 (1) also adopts this approach. For the second approach, the United States Model BIT (1984) uses "arbitrary and discriminatory measures" and the United States Model BIT (1994) uses "unreasonable and discriminatory measures".
[61]   UNCTAD, *supra* note 2, p. 55.
[62]   Id.
[63]   Commentary to the MAI, IV. Investment Protection, 1. General Treatment, para. 7.

it would be too narrow to cover only measures which are both "discriminatory" and "unreasonable" because there may be severe interference with the investor's activities without discrimination or unreasonableness.[64] Those who supported the second approach argued that, the term "unreasonable" is too vague and it would go too far to prohibit measures that are only "unreasonable".[65] Since no consensus could be reached, the MAI had to put the two approaches into the MAI text.

Such a clause may provide additional protection for foreign investors when they are subject to certain regulatory measures of host state which are unfavourable to them but do not fall within the scope of expropriation. In such a case, for their private benefit, foreign investors may take advantage of the above treatment to challenge host state's measure as being unreasonable or discriminatory.[66] Examples of such measure could include some investment conditions which are for the public interest of one state and are not on the list of performance requirements prohibited by the MAI, such as the requirement of minimum salary for living, policies to create high quality job for local residents, etc.[67]

It is inappropriate for the MAI to employ the standard of reasonableness and non-discrimination to measure or judge the regulatory measures of host states. Firstly, the term "unreasonableness" is quite vague and lack of measurable, objective and precise criteria. The term "discrimination" in the context of the MAI would include both *de jure* and *de facto* discrimination.[68] Thus, the measures, administrative or judicial decisions, laws and regulations of host state which would put strict conditions on foreign investments or be unfavourable to foreign investors but would benefit nationals would be easily challenged by foreign investors on the ground of unreasonable or discriminatory measures. Secondly, to tailor the measures of host state on foreign investment with the criteria of reasonableness and non-discrimination is an intervention and restriction on the economic sovereignty of host state to regulate foreign investment. Host states should have had great discretion to decide whether measure and what measures are to be imposed on foreign investments based on domestic policy necessities. Thirdly, since the MAI does not give further clarification of how to apply the criteria of reasonableness and non-discrimination to the disputes arising out of this treatment standard, judges or arbitrators hearing the relevant cases could have more discretion.[69] Finally, the treatment standard of reasonableness and non-discrimination could overlap with other treatment standards, such as NT/MFN treatment, fair and equitable treatment, international minimum standard and the full and constant protection and security. In other words, the other standards have implicitly excluded unreasonable or discriminatory

---

[64]   J. Karl, *supra* note 12, p. 15.
[65]   Id., pp. 14–15.
[66]   M. Sforza, "MAI Provisions and Proposals: An Analysis of the April 1998 Text," *Public Citizen's Global Trade Watch*, July 1998, p. 20.
[67]   Id.
[68]   For an analysis of the discriminatory measure in the context of the MAI, see Chapter Five of this book; see also K. J. Vandevelde, *supra* note 34, p. 78; UNCTAD, *supra* note 2, p. 77.
[69]   M. Sforza, *supra* note 66.

treatment.[70] It could be said that it is hard to separate reasonable or discriminatory treatment completely from other treatment standards.[71]

7.2.6 Conclusion

To sum up, the MAI adopts both NT/MFN treatment and all the four models of the general treatment standards which are interrelated, overlapped and mainly supported by developed countries for investment protection, for the purpose to provide full and adequate protection for foreign investments. This is not acceptable from the viewpoints of developing countries.

Moreover, the terms of the above standards are generally too vague with differentiated implications by different scholars. These treatment standards being absolute requirement by the MAI, in their future practical application, would easily lead to disputes between contracting states and between host states and foreign investors. Regulatory measures for foreign investment of developing countries would be easily subject to challenges by foreign investors and thus puts developing countries in a relatively disadvantageous position. Furthermore, for developing countries, the treatment guaranteed by the MAI to foreign investors by the MAI could be higher than whatever domestic investors could have based on their domestic laws and regulations. As a subsequence, domestic investors who have been in a financially and technically weak position would not be equally treated with their foreign competitors in their own countries and thus makes it harder for them to compete with foreigners from the same point of running. The above possible adverse impact of the MAI principles is one of the grounds for many developing countries and NGOs to object the MAI.

The MAI itself was dead so there was not any case in this regard. But the potential adverse consequences of its general treatment principles for investment protection can still be predicted from the existing cases arising from NAFTA which is the "prototype" of the MAI. In the Loewen Group, Inc. v. the United States case under NAFTA Chapter 11,[72] the Canadian-based Loewen Group was not satisfied with the verdict of jury in the state of Mississippi and thus registered its case at the Additional Facility of ICSID. The complainant claimed that it was victimized by racial and national discrimination on the part of a Mississippi judge, jury and plaintiff's counsel—all of whom were black. It also claimed that the conduct of the trial judge, the size of the jury award, the courtroom strategy of the plaintiff's attorneys and the ruling of the Mississippi Supreme Court, and thus the civil justice system in Mississippi—allowing jury trials—violated its NAFTA-guaranteed rights to fair and equal treatment and non-discrimination. Based on Article 1105 of the NAFTA—international minimum standard of treatment,

---

[70] UNCTAD, *supra* note 2, p. 55.
[71] T. W. Waelde, *supra* note 44, p. 42.
[72] For an introduction to the case, see "The Loewen Group, Inc. v. The United States", available at http://www.citizen.org/pctrade/nafta/cases/loewen.htm, see also "NAFTA Can Overturn Supreme Court", available at http://www.spotlight.org/03_18_01/NAFTA_Can Overturn_Supreme_Cou/nafta_can_overturn_supreme_cou.html

fair and equitable treatment and full protection and secury, the NAFTA panel ruled that NAFTA had jurisdiction over complaints from foreign countries about court decisions in the United States. It also claimed jurisdiction over complaints about state and federal administrative agency actions.[73] Some warning can be taken from the case.

7.3   SPECIFIC TREATMENT STANDARDS

Expropriation and compensation, protection from strife and transfer of payment are the most essential issues in the field of investment protection. To afford full and adequate protection to foreign investment, the MAI, in addition to the general treatment standards for investment protection, formulates specific treatment standards with respect to the above issues. These specific treatment standards represent the highest standards so far in comparison with corresponding standards in BITs or regional investment treaties, which will be discussed in details as follows. The MAI also makes rules on subrogation and existing investments, but these rules will not be discussed here because they are almost the same as those in most BITs and other international investment treaties.

7.3.1   Expropriation and Compensation

The issues of expropriation and compensation have been always the contentious issues between developed and developing countries, among which the legality of expropriation, indirect expropriation and compensation standard account the most weight.[74] These controversies, among others, are the main reasons for the failure of conclusion of multilateral investment treaties. However, the MAI takes the position of developed countries in this regard and thus criticized by developing countries and many NGOs.

7.3.1.1   *Controversies with Regard to Expropriation and Compensation between Developed and Developing Countries*

Developing countries are of the opinion that according to state's economic sovereignty, any country has the right to nationalize or expropriate properties of foreign investors. But most developed countries had denied this right and alleged that expropriation or nationalization of host state constituted international wrongful act until 1950s. Then they switched to the view that it is lawful for host state to expropriate foreign property if the expropriation

---

[73] "NAFTA Can Overturn Supreme Court", available at http://www.spotlight.org/03_18_01/ NAFTA_Can Overturn_Supreme_Cou/nafta_can_overturn_supreme_cou.html
[74] Xu Chongli, "Controversial Issues in International Investment Law and China's Countermeasures" (Chinese edition), 1 *Chinese Social Science* (1994), pp. 27–28.

is accompanied by prompt, adequate and effective compensation. But the condition of prompt, adequate and effective compensation in effect weakens, limits and even eliminates the right of host state to expropriate, because such compensation is a big sum for host state. Now it is acknowledged that states have the right to nationalise or expropriate the assets of foreign investors.[75]

There is not a uniform definition of expropriation or nationalization. The two concepts of expropriation and nationalization are regarded as interchangeable. Since 1970's, the concept of creeping expropriation (indirect expropriation) emerged. There is also disagreement between developed and developing countries as to the scope of indirect expropriation. Developed countries, the United States in particular, tried their best to give broad definition to indirect expropriation. Examples of indirect expropriation could cover confiscatory taxation, total or partial compulsory sale, impairment or deprivation of management, control or economic value, forced divestment of shares of a company, refusal of access to labour or raw materials, foreign exchange control, forced export, change of foreign policy, etc.[76] Developing countries strongly opposed to the broad definition, the reasons being that, according to the above opinion, many regulatory measures of host state which are derived from state sovereignty and are necessary for the administration of foreign investment could risk of being deemed as expropriation.

The issue of standard of compensation is also controversial. There exist three formulas of standard of compensation. The first is no compensation. This formula was the practice of France in 1789, former Soviet Union after 1919 and some eastern countries soon after the Second World War.[77] Now there is no support of this practice.[78] The second formula is appropriate compensation. Appropriate compensation is established by the UN Resolution on Permanent Sovereignty over Natural Resources[79] and the Charter of Economic Rights and Duties of States.[80] This formula is universally accepted by developing countries in their national laws and BITs. The third is the so-called "Hull Formula" — prompt, adequate and effective compensation. This formula was first forwarded and then insisted by the United States as "minimum standard of international law" and now accepted by many developed countries.[81] But scholars among developed countries have disagreement in this regard. There are also departures from the Hull formula in the treaty practice of developed states.[82] Even those countries who insist on Hull

---

[75]   L. Brazell, "Catalysing Growth: the Main Treaty Provisions, their Interaction and Effect", *Energy Charter Treaty: Selected Topics*, T. W. Waelde & K. M. Christie (ed.), 1995, p. 3.31; M. Sornarajah, *The International Law on Foreign Investment*, Cambridge University, 1994, p. 209.

[76]   M. Sornarajah, *supra* note 75, p. 254; UNCTAD, *Taking of Property*, United Nations, 2000, p. 12; Chen An, Zeng Huaqun (ed.), International Investment Law (Chinese edition), Peking University Press, 1999, p. 448.

[77]   Yu Jingshong, "Basis of the Compensation of Nationalization in International Investment Law" (Chinese edition), 2 *Chinese Social Science* (1986), pp. 59–61.

[78]   M. Sornarajah, *supra* note 75, p. 209.

[79]   See 1.4 of the Resolution.

[80]   Article 2, para. 2.3 of the Charter.

[81]   P. Peters, "Recent Developments in Expropriation Clauses of Asian Investment Treaties", 5 *Asian Yearbook of International Law* (1997), p. 57.

[82]   M. Sornarajah, "Nationalization of Foreign Investment", *International Transactions, Trade and Investment, law and Finance*, K. C. D. M. Wilde (ed.), The Law Book Company Limited, 1993, p. 256.

Formula sometimes accept arrangement of "partial compensation".[83] At the multilateral level, heated debate on standard of compensation between developed and developing countries was reflected both in the UNCTC Draft Code of Conduct on Transnational Corporations and the World Bank Guidelines on the Treatment of Foreign Investment. For the former draft code, it was not decided whether appropriate compensation or Hull Formula should be adopted.[84] For the latter Guideline, the phrase of "appropriate compensation" is adopted but it is interpreted as "adequate, effective and prompt".[85] It is worth of noting that ever since 1990, the investment treaties concluded among developed countries, such as ECT, NAFTA and the MAI, adopt the Hull Formula.[86]

7.3.1.2   MAI's Rules on Expropriation and Compensation

With respect to the scope of expropriation and the standard of compensation, the MAI takes the position of developed countries. The MAI has also a lot of "inventions".

The MAI provides that "A Contracting Party shall not expropriate or nationalise directly or indirectly an investment in its territory of an investor of another Contracting Party or take any measure or measures having equivalent effect except ...".[87] This provision does not give a definition of expropriation or nationlization, so that it can be flexibly and willfully interpreted to render as broad as possible the protection to foreign investment. However, the expropriation in the MAI covers both direct and indirect expropriation (creeping expropriation), which is the result of the negotiators' intention to make the scope of expropriation as broad as possible, with the belief that a broad definition would be a safeguard against new forms of expropriation.[88] Therefore, all measures adopted by a state — whether direct or indirect—that have the effect of depriving the investor of its investment should be regarded as expropriation.[89] According to the MAI's definition of investment, investment should include both property and contractual rights. Therefore, any "breach" of an agreement could be regarded as expropriation. Although the MAI itself does not list any such measures, the negotiators mentioned that such measures should include, *inter alia*, confiscations, seizure, interventions, temporary takings, modalities on the use and disposal of the investment, interference, government administration, even if it does not affect the title or ownership of the investment, and forced sales and

---

[83]   Id., p. 339.
[84]   See para. 54 of the Draft Code.
[85]   See Chapter IV, Art. 2 of the Guideline.
[86]   See ECT, Art. 13 (1) (d). Although NAFTA Article 1110 does not use the terms "prompt, adequate and effective", it essentially adopts the Hull Formula. See T. Levy, "NAFTA's Provision for Compensation in the Event of Expropriation: A Reassessment of the "Prompt, Adequate and Effective" Standard", 31 *Stanford Journal of International Law*, no. 2, p. 441.
[87]   The MAI, IV. Investment Protection, 2. Expropriation and Compensation, para. 2.1.
[88]   OECD, *supra* note 13, p. 138.
[89]   Id.

partial takings.[90] As long as the measures of host state have negative effect on the profitability of an investor, such measures should constitute expropriation, and foreign investor may ask for compensation. The broad scope of expropriation is thus self-evident. The scope of indirect expropriation in the MAI is much broader than that of most BITs so far.[91]

Large-scale expropriation will not take place in any country in the current situations and in the predicted future. The direct expropriation of individual case will rarely happen. Then what foreign investors can challenge is indirect expropriation. But the broad scope of indirect expropriation makes host governments difficult to prevent effectively the happening of indirect expropriation, because even government administration could be deemed as expropriation. Although the negotiators have stated that regulatory acts of general application should not normally be considered an expropriation,[92] and the OECD Ministerial Declaration explicitly stated that "the MAI... would not inhibit the normal non-discriminatory exercise of regulatory powers by governments and such exercise of regulatory powers would not amount to expropriation",[93] the experience of NAFTA cases show that new laws of host government on non-discriminatory basis for the purpose of environmental protection are regarded as "regulatory taking" and thus is expropriation.[94] We are not sure whether the Ministerial Declaration would prevail if foreign investor, based on the MAI provision of expropriation, would challenge such laws of host state, if we presume that the MAI came into effect. Moreover, any judicial decision or even judicial system of host state which is unfavourable to foreign investor could be challenged as expropriation.[95] In such a case, "regulatory freeze" or even "judicial freeze" of host state would be a possible consequence — host state would be prevented from making any new laws or changing any existing laws, and courts at all levels would be prevented from making any judgements or decisions that are not favourable to foreign investors. Therefore, it was felt necessary to issue a political declaration on the relation between regulation and expropriation.[96]

In general, there are four models of conditions for expropriation: for public purpose, non-discrimination, due process of law and compensation. According to a review of 335 BITs concluded before 1995, many BITs adopt

---

[90]   Id.
[91]   UNCTAD, *supra* note 76, p. 23.
[92]   R. Geiger, "Towards a Multilateral Agreement on Investment", 31 *Cornell International Law Journal* (1998), no. 3, p. 471.
[93]   OECD, "Ministerial Statement on the Multilateral Agreement on Investment (MAI)" (April 28, 1998), available at http://www.oecd.org/media/release/nw98-50a.htm.
[94]   Examples of such cases are: Ethyl Corporation vs. Government of Canada, available at http://www.citizen.org/pctrade/nafta/cases/Ethylbri.htm, Metalclad Corp. v. Mexica, available at http://www.citizen.org/pctrade/nafta/cases/metalcla.htm, S. D. Myers Inc. v. Canada, available at http://www.citizen.org/pctrade/nafta/cases/canada.htm. Regulatory taking is the taking of property that falls within the policy powers of a state, or otherwise arises from state measures like those pertaining to the regulation of the environment, health, morals, culture or economy of a host country. Whether regulatory taking is expropriation is a new and difficult issue. See UNCTAD, *supra* note 76, p. 12.
[95]   The Loewen Group, Inc. v. The United States of NAFTA is an example. This case is available at http://www.citizen.org/pctrade/nafta/cases/Loewen.htm,
[96]   UNCTAD, *supra* note 76, p. 24.

one or two or three of the above conditions.[97] The MAI uses all the four conditions and makes them stricter. Under the MAI, non-discrimination means national treatment and MFN treatment. Due process of law includes, in particular, the right of an investor of a contracting party which claims to be affected by expropriation by another contracting party to prompt review of its case, including valuation of its investment and the payment of compensation, by a judicial authority or another competent and independent authority of the latter contracting party.[98] Compensation means prompt, adequate and effective compensation, the so-called Hull Formula.[99]

The MAI adopts the Hull Formula for the compensation of expropriation despite of the objection of developing countries. Pursuant to the MAI, "prompt" means the compensation shall be paid without delay;[100] "adequate" means compensation shall be equivalent to the fair market value of the expropriated investment immediately before the expropriation occurred. At the same time the fair market value shall not reflect any change in value occurring because the expropriation had become publicly known earlier.[101] But the MAI does not say how to determine the "fair market value". One delegation suggested that the valuation criteria include going concern value, asset value and other appropriate criteria.[102] These criteria are always opposed by developing countries. "Effective" means compensation shall be fully realisable and freely transferable.[103] The MAI further provides that compensation shall include interest at a commercial rate established on a market basis for the currency of payment from the date of expropriation until the date of actual payment.[104]

In addition, the MAI has a lot of "invention" with respect to expropriation in order to guarantee full protection for foreign investors.

First, the MAI's rules of expropriation apply not only to property but also to contractual rights and to any "breach" of an agreement. Therefore, the MAI's investment protection provisions exceed not only the standard established by generally accepted customary international law, but also that of the Hull standard put forward by the United States and other capital-exporting countries.[105]

Second, the MAI's articles of general exceptions do not apply to expropriation and compensation,[106] the reason being that no exception would be allowed to absolute treatment standards, e.g., specific treatment for expropriation and compensation. Further, the MAI provides that, when one state does not comply with its obligations to another state as determined in an arbitral award rendered in accordance with the MAI's state-state mechanism,

---

[97] Chen An, Zeng Huaqun (ed.), *supra* note 76, p. 449.
[98] The MAI, IV. Investment Protection, 2. Expropriation and Compensation, para. 2.6.
[99] Id., para. 2.1.
[100] Id., para. 2.2.
[101] Id., para. 2.3.
[102] Commentary on the MAI, Chapter 2.15.
[103] The MAI, IV. Investment Protection, 2. Expropriation and Compensation, para. 2.4.
[104] Id., para. 2.5.
[105] S. Picciotto, "Linkages in International Investment Regulation: the Antinomies of the Draft Multilateral Agreement on Investment", 19 *University of Pennsylvania Journal of international Economic Law* (1998), no. 3, pp. 757–758.
[106] MAI, Chapter VI, General Exceptions. For a detailed discussion of general exceptions, see Chapter Five of this book.

the latter state may take responsive measures to suspend the application to the former state of obligations under the MAI.[107] However, such measures may not include suspension of the application of the article on expropriation.[108] This exception shows again the status of treatment of expropriation as an absolute treatment standard.

Third, due to the disagreement of negotiators on the inclusion of taxation, the MAI provides that as a general rule, the MAI does not apply to taxation measures.[109] But the MAI's article on expropriation shall apply to taxation measures.[110] This is the reflection of the fear that taxation measures may be used by some states for the purpose of creeping expropriation. In other words, the MAI tries its best to protect foreign investors from any possible negative measures from host states.

Fourth, according to the MAI, federal government or central government shall be responsible for any expropriating measures by sub-federal, provincial, or local authority, the reason being that measures in the MAI include measures by governments at all levels.[111] The NAFTA cases of the Loewen Group, Inc. v. the United States and Metalclad Corp. v. Mexica have proved the proposition.

Fifth, the MAI's investor-state dispute settlement mechanism is used as an effective way to enforce foreign investors' right guaranteed by the specific treatment for expropriation and compensation. The above-mentioned NAFTA cases are examples and evidence.

All in all, the MAI's clauses of the specific treatment for expropriation and compensation are the highest standard so far. They are regarded as the most dangerous clauses even by western scholars.[112] This treatment rule grants foreign investors the right to challenge any laws, policies, or judicial decisions of host states, because any of these laws, policies or judicial decisions could impose potential threat on the interest of foreign investors. In other words, host governments have to pay for foreign investors for expropriation because of regulations they have imposed on them in order to conduct domestic policies.[113] Moreover, the broad definition of expropriation is equivalent to a fetter and infringement of the controlling power of host government on foreign investment. Third, the rule of prompt, adequate and effective compensation is unaccetable by developing countries. Last, we should be alert that the MAI's above rules have been imitated by some BITs.

7.3.2   Protection from Strife

Strife refers to war, armed conflict, state of national emergency, insurrection, riot, and rebellion or other civil disturbance, etc. Under customary international law, host state is not liable for any losses caused by military

---

[107]   MAI, Chapter V, C. 9. a.
[108]   MAI, Chapter V, C. 9. b.
[109]   MAI, Chapter VIII, Art. 1.
[110]   MAI, Chapter VIII, Art. 2.
[111]   For this point, see Chapter Five of this book.
[112]   "Everything You Wanted to Know About the Multilateral Agreement on Investment (MAI)", available at http://www.citizen.org/pctrade/otherissues/MAI/what%20is/maievery.htm.
[113]   A. Böhmer, *supra* note 32, p. 288.

necessity.[114] Normally, only when the host state does not exercise its "due deligence" on alien property in the situation of strife can the host state be held liable for the losses arising therefrom. From 1980s, some BITs began to adopt a clause of protection from strife. The purpose is to bypass customatory international law in this regard and therefore provide additional protection to foreign investors. But most of those BITs with such a clause do not impose strict liability on host state for compensation; instead, they only require for non-discrimination with respect to compensation.[115] Among those BITs with a clause of protection from strife, the British BITs and the United States BITs adopt the highest standard. The ECT takes almost the same position as the American BITs.[116] In contrast with the British and American BITs and the ECT, the MAI takes even higher standard in this regard.

As to the types of damages protected under this clause, the British BITs enumerate seven specific types: war, other armed conflict, revolution, state of national emergency, revolt, insurrection and riot.[117] The American BITs, except for a specific enumeration of war, other armed conflict, revolution, state of national emergency, insurrection and civil disturbance, add the phrase of "similar events".[118] "Similar events" are vague and subject to broad interpretation and therefore is easy to be abused by foreign investors. The MAI has a broader scope of strife to cover war, other armed conflict, and state of emergency, revolution, insurrection, civil disturbance and any other similar events.[119]

The British BITs, the American BITs, ECT and the MAI make a distinction between damages caused by strife without direct action by the host states and damages caused by action by the state itself in situations of strife. In the former situation, foreign investors shall be accorded non-discriminatory treatment as regards restitution, indemnification, compensation or other settlement. The latter situation covers damages resulting from the requisition of foreign investment or part of it by host state's forces or authorities, and from destruction of foreign investment or part of it by host state's forces or authorities. In the latter situation, not only non-discriminatory treatment applies, foreign investors shall also be accorded restitution or compensation.[120] For the latter situation, the British BITs provide two exceptions to the destruction by host forces or authorities: combat action and necessity of the situation. The American BITs, ECT and the MAI provide only one exception: necessity of the situation. As for compensation in the latter situation, British BITs require for adequate compensation. The American BITs, ECT and the MAI require for prompt, adequate and effective compensation which is the same standard of compensation in case of expropriation.

---

[114]   UNCTAD, *supra* note 2, p. 73.

[115]   Chen An & Zeng Huaqun (ed.), *supra* note 76, p. 479.

[116]   ECT, Art. 12.

[117]   For example, Article 5 of the BIT between the United Kingdom and Ukraine (1993).

[118]   Article IV of the Model BIT (1994) of the United States.

[119]   MAI, IV., 3.1.

[120]   For example, Article 5 of the BIT between the United Kingdom and Ukraine (1993); Article IV of the United States Model BIT (1994)of the United States; ECT, Art. 12; MAI, IV., 3.2.

Like the MAI's rules of expropriation, the MAI's articles of general exceptions do not apply to protection from strife.

The essence of this clause is to shift the risk of losses which arise from strife in host state and should be borne by foreign investors to host state. This is unfair because host state itself also suffers from such strife. Such a clause is equivalent to requiring host state to guarantee to foreign investors that no strife which would damage their profitability would happen. But in fact, no host state wishes to have such strife taken place and no host state is able to stop the happening of such strife. In other words, in order to avoid such strife, host state has to put strict limit on or even eliminate those strifes which can be controlled by it, such as protest, strike. But in most cases, protest and strike is tool of social justice and any limit or elimination of them is a deprivation of civil rights. On the other hand, this clause will give foreign investors more opportunities to seek compensation from host state. This is another important reason for the objection of the MAI by many developing countries and NGOs. Moreover, only foreign investors can enjoy the benefit of this clause, while domestic investors can not. So domestic investors are treated unfavourably in this regard.

7.3.3   Transfer of Payments

Transfer of payments is an essential issue in the field of international investment. For host states, the sudden repatriation of large profits or the proceeds from sale or liquidation can have an adverse effect on their balance of payments, thereby hindering economic development.[121] For foreign investors, their benefit from investment projects can not be finally effectuated if their profit, capital and other payments can not be freely transferred. But under customary international law, host countries do not have the obligation of allowing free transfer of payments of foreign investors.[122] Therefore, in concluding BITs or other international investment agreements, there are great controversies between developing countries and developed countries with respect to the clause of free transfer. Developing countries always seek broad guarantee of free and unrestricted transfer, while developing countries which have more or less difficulties in foreign exchange, have to impose control on foreign exchange and thus have certain degree of restriction on the transfer of payments of foreign investors. Disregarding the above differences and controversies between developing and developed countries, the MAI takes the highest standard as to the transfer of payments. The high standard of the MAI is embodied in the following aspects.

Type of payments.   There are two approaches as to the type of payments in BITs and other international agreements. The first approach is to have an exhaustive list of payments covered by the clause, examples being most BITs concluded by Denmark, France and Sweden.[123] The second approach is to

---

[121]   UNCTAD, *supra* note 2, p. 75.
[122]   Chen An & Zeng Huaqun (ed.), *supra* note 76, p. 460.
[123]   UNCTAD, *supra* note 2, p. 76.

have a non-exhaustive (illustrative) list of payments, examples being most BITs concluded by Germany and the United States, NAFTA and ECT. In contrast, the non-exhaustive list is generally broader than the exhaustive list. The MAI adopts the second approach and gives the broadest illustration of payments to include the initial capital and additional amounts to maintain or increase an investment, returns, payments made under a contract including a loan agreement, proceeds from the sale or liquidation of all or any part of an investment, payments of compensation resulting from expropriation and strife, payments arising out of the settlement of a dispute, and earnings and other remuneration of personnel engaged from abroad in connection with an investment.

Type of currency.   Many BITs require that transfer should be permitted in the convertible currency in which the investment was made or in any convertible currency to which the parties agree.[124] The MAI, NAFTA, ECT and the BITs concluded by the United States require that transfer should be permitted in any freely convertible currency. This approach gives foreign investors the greatest protection.[125]

Timing of transfer.   Some BITs provide that transfer should be permitted "without undue delay" and some other BITs permit a reasonable period of delay.[126] The MAI, NAFTA, ECT and some BITs provide that transfer should be permitted "without delay". The latter approach is much stricter than the former one.

Exchange rate.   Some BITs provide that transfer should be made at the official exchange rate which is subject to the control of the host state.[127] Some BITs and other investment agreements specify the market rate of exchange. Some other BITs specify the exchange rate for conversion of currencies into Special Drawing Rights.[128] The MAI precludes the official exchange rate but adopts the market rate of exchange and the exchange rate for conversion of currencies into Special Drawing Rights in the absence of a market rate.[129] It also specifies that the market rate of exchange should be that prevailing on the date of transfer.

Exceptions.   Many BITs allow both ordinary exceptions and specific exceptions (emphasized by developing countries in particular) to the free transfer of payments. Specific exceptions include the restrictions on transfer in case of serious shortage of foreign currency and the transfer subject to host state's applicable laws and regulations. The MAI only takes into consideration the ordinary exceptions so as to delay or prevent a transfer: to protect the rights of creditors; to ensure the compliance with laws and regulations on the issuing, trading and dealing in securities, futures and derivatives, or concerning reports or records of transfers; and in connection with criminal offences and orders or judgments in administrative and adjudicatory proceedings.[130] In addition, the above exceptions should be based on the

---

[124]   Id., p. 78. Examples are the BITs concluded by Denmark and the United Kingdom.
[125]   UNCTAD, *supra* note 2, p. 78.
[126]   Id.
[127]   Id.
[128]   Id., pp. 78–79.
[129]   The MAI, IV., 4.3 & 4.4.
[130]   The MAI, IV., 4.6.

conditions of equitable, non-discriminatory and good faith application of measures, and that the measures and their application shall not be used as a means of avoiding the contracting party's commitments or obligations under the MAI. However, the MAI pays almost no attention to the specific exceptions favoured by developing countries, except that according to the MAI's general exception provisions, temporary safeguard measures may be adopted in the event of serious balance-of-payments and external financial difficulties or threat thereof.[131]

7.4   CONCLUSION

The above detailed comparison and analysis makes the conclusion clear and obvious: the MAI's general treatment standard and specific treatment standard with respect to investment protection are the highest so far among all the BITs and other international investment agreements.

---

[131]   The MAI, VI., Temporary Safeguard, 1.

8. The MAI's Dispute Settlement Mechanism

8.1 INTRODUCTION

In general, there are two approaches for the rights and obligations imposed on contracting parties by investment treaties to be enforced: peer pressure from member states and the dispute settlement mechanism designed by the treaties. The OECD's two Liberalization Codes adopt the former approach which has the weakness of lack of enforceability in the event of the failure of contracting members to comply with their obligations. The recent BITs, Energy Charter Treaty (ECT) and NAFTA take the latter approach. The two advantages of the dispute settlement mechanism are: first, the mechanism will provide a formal channel for the settlement of disputes arising from the treaty and thus give greater confidence to investors; second, the mechanism can play a role in encouraging the avoidance of disputes or the avoidance of the settlement of dispute by formal channel, the reasons being that on one hand, with the dispute settlement mechanism any party has no way to escape its duty in breaching the treaty, and on the other hand, it is time, money and effort-consuming to recourse to court or arbitration in contrast with other informal channels.

In order to properly implement the high standards of the MAI for the treatment and protection of investments, the drafters of the MAI thought it necessary to have an effective dispute settlement system contained in the MAI.[1] Therefore, the OECD changed its former practice of relying on peer pressure to preferring the formal and strong dispute settlement procedures.[2] In the process of the draft of dispute settlement provisions of the MAI, the relevant provisions of dispute settlement in many BITs, WTO, ECT and the NAFTA were reviewed and referred as important references. Therefore, the dispute settlement mechanism of the MAI is so far the most comprehensive, advanced and detailed one in comparison with other investment treaties in the following two facets. First, the MAI consists of two sets of dispute settlement procedures: state-state mechanism and the investor-state mechanism.

---

[1] M. Baldi, "Dispute Settlement," *Proceedings of the Special Session on the Multilateral Agreement on Investment Held in Paris on 17 September 1997*, p. 28. The author is Chairman of the Expert Group on Dispute Settlement and Geographical Scope.
[2] OECD, "Dispute Settlement: Report by Working Group D," *Towards Multilateral Investment Rules, 1996*, p. 151.

Second, the MAI contains a large number of clauses with detailed contents with respect to the two sets of dispute settlement procedures, including the scope of disputes, the modalities of dispute settlement, applicable law, constitution of arbitral tribunal, the forms of remedies in the arbitral awards, the consequences of non-complying and many other procedural aspects.

The drafters of the MAI use 14 pages to address the issue of dispute settlement in the MAI,[3] which shows that the issue of dispute settlement takes an important position in the whole MAI. Based on the procedural and technical characteristics of dispute settlement, this chapter introduces and makes comments on the MAI's state-state dispute settlement mechanism and the investor-state dispute settlement mechanism.[4]

8.2   STATE–STATE DISPUTE SETTLEMENT MECHANISM

The state-state dispute settlement is a main subject for most BITs, WTO, ECT, NAFTA, etc. But the MAI's relevant mechanism has its own attributes in addition to the common features with other treaties.

8.2.1   Applicable Scope

The MAI's state-state dispute settlement mechanism applies to the disputes between two or more contracting parties regarding the interpretation or application of the MAI.[5] A dispute over whether a party has acted in contravention of the MAI thus falls under the scope. It should be noted that "action" in this context also includes failure to act.[6] Therefore, the implication of the scope is quite broad.

However, this mechanism is not the only way to resolve these disputes. The parties may agree to select other rules or procedures for the resolution of their disputes in this regard.[7] Though neither the MAI text nor the MAI's Commentary gives specific mentions as to these other rules or procedures, the author is of the opinion that the WTO dispute settlement rules and procedures are among them, since: first, it is possible for the parties' violative actions of the MAI to be overlapped with the violation of obligations of the TRIMs or TRIPs where the WTO's dispute settlement procedures apply; second, this approach is likely borrowed from the provisions of the NAFTA

---

[3]   There are totally 106 pages for the mere text of the MAI and 145 pages for the whole text of the MAI including the two annexes to the MAI. The issue of dispute settlement accounts for more than 10 percent of the text of the MAI.
[4]   The MAI's text of dispute settlement was prepared by the Chairman of the Expert Group on Dispute Settlement on the basis of the discussion in the Group, and was intended to be subject to further discussion and revision. Some of the provisions were challenged by delegations during the MAI's negotiations.
[5]   The MAI, V. Dispute settlement, Article A. 1.
[6]   The MAI, V. Dispute Settlement, Article C.1.a; Commentary on the MAI, V. Dispute Settlement, Article C.1.a, para. 1.
[7]   The MAI, V. Dispute Settlement, Article A. 1.

which provides that disputes regarding any matter arising under both the NAFTA and the *General Agreement on Tariffs and Trade*, any agreement negotiated thereunder, or any successor agreement (GATT), may be settled in either forum at the discretion of the complaining Party.[8]

8.2.2   Steps to be taken in the Resolution of Disputes

If the disputing parties decide to follow the MAI's rules and procedures, they have two options: non-binding methods including consultation, conciliation and mediation, and legally binding method, i.e., arbitration.

The first step is consultations. Any contracting parties may request in writing any other contracting party to enter into consultations regarding any dispute between them about the interpretation or application of the MAI.[9] The Parties Group shall be provided with a copy of the request for consultation. The consultation procedure is a mandatory phase before any arbitration proceedings can be initiated,[10] with the intention to encourage amicable resolution of the dispute. For most BITs, negotiation is only suggested as a possible way rather than a mandatory way to settle disputes.[11] The MAI's consultation rules are similar to that of the WTO, while the MAI's Parties Group functions as the WTO's Dispute Settlement Body.[12]

BITs only have the procedure of negotiation, while the MAI have other approaches. The MAI provides that if the disputing parties can not resolve the dispute within 60 days, they may agree to request the Parties Group to consider the matter.[13] The latter may make recommendations. This is called multilateral consultation by the MAI. This procedure is not mandatory but may be used upon the agreement of the relevant parties. Some delegations supported that any parties should have a unilateral right to request multilateral consultations.[14]

If consultations fail, the parties may have recourse to good offices or to mediation or conciliation.[15] Likewise, these methods are not mandatory phases, either.

The above proceedings involving consultations, mediation or conciliation shall be confidential and any mutually agreed solution there from shall be informed to the Parties Group.[16]

---

[8]   NAFTA, Article 2005.
[9]   The MAI, V. Dispute Settlement, Article B. 1. a.
[10]   The MAI, V. Dispute Settlement, Article B. 1. b. and Article C. 1. a; see also P. Malanczuk, "State-State and Investor-State Dispute Settlement in the OECD Draft Multilateral Investment Agreement," *Multilateral Regulation of Investment*, E.C. Nieuwenhuys and M.M.T.A. Brus (ed.), Kluwer Law International, 2001, p. 142.
[11]   UNCTAD, *Bilateral Investment Treaties in the Mid-1990s*, p. 100.
[12]   For the WTO's consultation rules, see Understanding on Rules and Procedures Governing the Settlement of Disputes (generally referred to as "Dispute Settlement Understanding" or "DSU"), Article 4.
[13]   The MAI, V. Dispute Settlement, Article B. 2. a.
[14]   M. Baldi, *supra* note 1, p. 30.
[15]   The MAI, V. Dispute Settlement, Article B. 3.
[16]   Id., ArticleB. 4.

The second step is arbitration. The dispute between contracting parties can be submitted before an arbitral tribunal for decision after the failure of the proceeding of consultation. A request for arbitration and a copy of it shall be delivered to the other party and the Parties Group respectively.[17]

Two points need to be noted as to the submission of dispute for arbitration. One is concerning the traditional principle of exhaustion of local remedies. The other is concerning the principle of one lawsuit for one subject matter.

In tradition, many countries such as Latin American countries require that local remedies should be exhausted before a case could be submitted for decision to an international court or tribunal. The MAI text itself keeps silent on the requirement of exhaustion of local remedies but the Commentary to the MAI clearly states that there is no requirement of exhaustion of local remedies before MAI dispute settlement could be invoked.[18]

Two situations arising from the MAI could be related to the principles of one lawsuit for one subject matter. One situation is that a dispute arising from the MAI Agreement is both a dispute between contracting parties concerning the interpretation or application of the MAI and a dispute between a foreign investor and the contracting host state concerning a breach of an obligation of the latter under the MAI. In this case, the dispute could be submitted for arbitration according to both state-state dispute settlement procedure and the investor-state dispute settlement procedure which will lead to the result that a same subject matter is tried by two different tribunals. Such a result will have two disadvantages: in-economic and there could be two different or inconsistent judgements of awards. To avoid such a result, the MAI provides that if the dispute has been submitted or has been consented to be submitted by a foreign investor for arbitration, the same dispute can not be submitted by the contracting party for arbitration. But if the defendant state fails to comply with the arbitral award rendered by the investor-state proceeding, or the proceeding terminates without resolution, the other contracting party may initiate the state-state proceeding.[19] The wording of this provision of the MAI is based on Article 27 of the Convention on the Settlement of Investment Disputes between States and Nationals of Other States.

The other situation is that a dispute between contracting parties concerns the violation by one party of an obligation under both the MAI and another agreement to which both are parties. For example, certain measures concerning performance requirements taken by one contracting party could be a violation of both the MAI and the TRIMs of the WTO. Likewise, the dispute could be submitted for resolution under both agreements, and to avoid thus a result, the MAI provides that the complaining party has the right to submit the dispute for resolution under either agreement and its right to resort to the other agreement not chosen is deemed to be waived.[20]

---

[17]   Id., ArticleC. 1. a.
[18]   Commentary to the MAI, V. Dispute Settlement, Article C. 1. a, para. 2.
[19]   The MAI, V. Dispute Settlement, Article C. 1. b.
[20]   Id., Article C. 1. c.

8.2.3 The MAI's Rules Concerning Arbitration

The MAI provides specific rules as to the procedure of arbitration.

8.2.3.1 *Formation of the Arbitral Tribunal*

The Parties Group maintains a roster of highly qualified individuals serving on arbitral tribunals under the MAI. Each contracting party may nominate up to four persons for this roster.[21] Generally, arbitrators of the tribunal shall be appointed from the roster. Normally, the tribunal consists of three members.

8.2.3.2 *Arbitration Rules*

The MAI has its own rules as to the rules and procedures of arbitration which will be discussed later. In addition, the MAI refers to the Permanent Court of Arbitration's (PCA) Optional Rules for Arbitrating Dispute between Two States as default rules to supplement provisions of the MAI.[22]

The maintained roster of arbitrators and the arbitration rules provided by the MAI show that the arbitration in the context of the MAI's state-state dispute settlement procedure is not ad hoc arbitration like the one in most BITs, and if it is not qualified as arbitration before an existing institution, it can at least be regarded as quasi-institutional arbitration.

8.2.3.3 *Applicable Law*

The applicable law for the resolution of dispute is the MAI alone.[23] But the MAI may be interpreted and applied in accordance with the applicable rules of international law.[24] The applicable rules are those concerning the interpretation and application of treaties,[25] including mainly the Vienna Convention on Treaty Law. The MAI's above provision would not provide a basis for a panel to rule on a dispute about a contracting party's compliance with other international legal obligations.[26]

8.2.3.4 *Provisional Measures*

Like other tribunals, the tribunal under the MAI may, at the request of a party, recommend provisional measures which either party should take to avoid serious prejudice to the other pending its final award.[27]

---

[21] Id., Article C. 2. a.
[22] Id., Article C. 8.
[23] Id., Article C. 6. a.
[24] Id.
[25] Commentary to the MAI, V. Dispute Settlement, Article C. 6, para. 1.
[26] Id.
[27] The MAI, V. Dispute Settlement, Article C. 6. b.

8.2.3.5   *Arbitral Awards*

The MAI has distinctive provisions as to the arbitral awards. It provides that before the issuance of a final award, the award shall be issued in provisional form to the parties for their written comments upon any portion of it. The tribunal shall consider those comments and may solicit additional written comments of the parties and then issue its final awards.[28] The provisional award system is borrowed from the interim report system of the WTO's dispute settlement procedure.[29] The final award shall be issued within 15 days after the closure of the comment period.[30] A copy of the final award shall be transmitted to the Parties Group.[31] The MAI provides that the final award shall set forth its findings of law and fact, together with the reasons therefore.[32] Generally speaking, the final award is final and binding.

The MAI provides various forms of remedies which may be awarded by the tribunal as follows:

i.   a declaration that an action of a party is in contravention of its obligations under the MAI;

ii. a recommendation that a party bring its actions into conformity with its obligations under the MAI;

iii. pecuniary compensation for any loss or damage to the requesting party's investor or its investment; and

iv. any other form of relief to which the party against whom the award is made consents, including restitution in kind to an investor.

Among the above forms of remedies, the second one is unique in contrast with those forms of remedies allowed by the investor-state dispute settlement procedure.[33] This form of remedy is of significance because it may require the party to correct its action to conform with the MAI. This will be a motivation for the home state to choose the state-state procedure rather than the investor-state procedure since the latter procedure does not have the power to order the violating contracting party to correct its action.

8.2.3.6   *Nullification of the Awards*

There is not any innovation of the MAI's rules on the nullification of the awards which are almost the same as those of the ICSID.[34] The grounds for

---

[28] Id., Article C. 6. d.
[29] DSU of the WTO, Article 15.
[30] The MAI, V. Dispute Settlement, Article C. 6. d.
[31] Id., Article C. 6. e.
[32] Id., Article C. 6. c.
[33] As to the forms of remedies allowed by the investor-state dispute settlement procedure, see the MAI, V. Dispute Settlement, Article D. 16. a.
[34] For the ICSID's rules on the nullification of awards, see Article 52 of the ICSID Convention.

any party to the dispute to request the annulment of an award in whole or in part are as follows:[35]

  i. the Tribunal was not properly constituted;
 ii. the Tribunal has manifestly exceeded its powers;
iii. there was corruption on the part of a member of the Tribunal or on the part of a person providing decisive expertise or evidence;
 iv. there has been a serious departure from a fundamental rule of procedure; and
  v. the award has failed to state the reasons on which it is based.

A new tribunal will be constituted to decide the request of the annulment.[36] The tribunal may nullify the award in whole or in part. In such a case, the dispute may be submitted for decision to another new tribunal constituted under the MAI or to any other available forum.[37]

8.2.3.7 Non-execution of the Award

The MAI does not provide that how the award shall be executed by the losing party. On the other hand, it provides what responsive measures can be taken if the losing party fails to comply with its obligations as determined in the award.

First, the two parties to the award shall enter into consultation to find a mutually acceptable solution.[38]

Second, if no satisfactory solution is reached within thirty days, the winning party may take measures in response (retaliate) or suspend the application to the non-complying party of its obligations under the MAI.[39] As to what specific measures may be taken to retaliate, there were differing views among delegations during the negotiations. Some delegations favoured broad responsive measures permitted under customary international law, including measures in the field of trade. Some favoured limiting the responsive measures to suspension of benefits under the MAI itself.[40] However, the effect of any responsive measures or suspension must be proportionate to the effect of the other party's non-compliance. Nevertheless, the winning party can not suspend the application of the MAI's articles concerning general treatment and expropriation and can not deny other protections to established investment.[41] The reason for the above restrictions is that the parties' obligation under the MAI's rules on general treatment and expropriation is absolute obligation which can not be shaken in any situation and

---

[35] The MAI, V. Dispute Settlement, Article C. 7. a.
[36] Id., Article C. 7. b.
[37] Id., Article C. 7. d.
[38] Id., Article C. 9. a.
[39] Id., Article C. 9. a.
[40] Commentary to the MAI, V. Dispute Settlement, Article C. 9, para. 2.
[41] The MAI, V. Dispute Settlement, Article C. 9. b.

the retaliatory measures aiming at the non-complying party may not prejudice any protection to established investment.

Third, any party to the award may request the Parties Group to consider such matters as the non-compliance of the losing party and the responsive measures taken by the winning party.[42] The Parties Group may take the following measures:[43]

i.   make recommendations, by consensus minus the disputing contracting parties;
ii. suspend the non-complying party's right to participate in decisions of the Parties Group, by consensus minus the non-complying contracting party; and
iii. by consensus minus the contracting party which has intended to take responsive measures, decide that some or all of the responsive measures shall not be taken. The contracting party shall comply with that decision.

According to the MAI, the Parties Group has the right to supervise or even interfere with the execution of the awards. The MAI also creates a new system of consensus through which the decision of the Parties Group shall be agreed by all the contracting parties minus the interesting parties—the non-complying party, the party to take response, or both of them.

Fourth, if there is a dispute as to the alleged failure of the losing party to comply with the award or the lawfulness of any responsive measures, the dispute shall be submitted at the request of any party to the dispute for decision to the original tribunal which rendered the award.[44] If the original tribunal is unavailable, a new tribunal whose single member or three members are designated by the Secretary-General of the ICSID shall be constituted. The tribunal will follow the same rules in the proceedings with some appropriate modifications.[45] From the time of submission of the dispute, no responsive measures may be taken.[46]

The author is of the view that such arbitration can be called "second arbitration" compared with the arbitration of the original dispute. Although the second arbitration could be a method to settle dispute concerning the non-compliance of the award and the lawfulness of responsive measures, it is not a practical way for many developing countries not only because arbitration is a time and money-consuming matter but also because developing countries are lack of necessary expertise in this regard. Furthermore, this second arbitration can not guarantee the complete resolution of the dispute. In case the losing party does not comply with the obligations under the second arbitral award, shall the above procedures of non-compliance be followed again? If another dispute arises as to the non-compliance of the second award, can such a dispute be submitted for a third arbitration? Since the MAI does not

---

[42]   Id., Article C. 9. c.
[43]   Id., Article C. 9. c.
[44]   Id., Article C. 9. d.
[45]   Id.
[46]   Id.

limit the times of arbitration, in theory, a third or fourth arbitration is possible. Therefore, the second arbitration approach could be taken advantage by the rich losing party as a vehicle to deny or delay the execution of the obligations under the first award.

8.2.3.8   Other Rules Concerning Arbitration

The MAI also provides rules for the consolidation of arbitration over the disputes between some contracting parties and one same contracting party over the same matter, the consultation rights of third parties, and the advice of scientific and technical expertise,[47] which are not discussed in detail in this chapter.

8.3   INVESTOR–STATE DISPUTE SETTLEMENT MECHANISM

Under international law, any individual including natural person and legal person can not be the subject of international law, and thus an individual can not be a contracting party to an international treaty. This is also true for international investment treaties and no obligations can be imposed on foreign investors thereunder. For the settlement of the dispute between foreign investor and host state concerning investment matter, the traditional two ways are: the claim brought by investor against host state in a domestic court, and the exercise of diplomatic protection by home state.[48] Lately, many BITs, the NAFTA and the ECT provide investor-state dispute settlement mechanism to give more options to foreign investors for the resolution of disputes between foreign investor and host state. It should be noted that WTO does not contain such a mechanism. The ICSID is specifically designed to settle investment disputes between foreign investors and host state by arbitration or conciliation.[49]

In view that investors generally wish to have at their disposal a dispute settlement mechanism that they can activate,[50] investors' direct recourse to arbitration will increase legal certainty and add credibility to the MAI, investors will avoid potential political conflicts, they no longer have to depend on their home governments to espouse their claims,[51] and that governments also see advantages in investor-state dispute settlement mechanism to which they do not need to become a party,[52] the MAI drafters decided to imitate relevant

---

[47]   The MAI, V. Dispute Settlement, Article C. 3, 4 and 5.
[48]   UNCTAD, *supra* note 11, p. 89.
[49]   ICSID is the abbreviation of International Center for the Settlement of Investment Disputes. The full name of the ICSID Convention is Convention for the Settlement of Investment Disputes between States and Nationals of Another State which was signed in Washington on March 18, 1965.
[50]   M. Baldi, *supra* note 1, p. 29.
[51]   R. Geiger, "Towards a Multilateral Agreement on Investment", 31 *Cornell International Law Journal* (1998), no. 3, p. 471.

provisions of the NAFTA and the ECT to create its own investor-state dispute settlement procedures. The investor-state procedures of the MAI have a number of its own features which will be discussed in the following subsections.

8.3.1 Applicable Scope

The investor-state mechanism applies to two categories of disputes between a contracting party and an investor of another contracting party: (1) the disputes concerning an alleged breach of an obligation of the state under the MAI which causes loss or damage to the investor or its investment;[53] and (2) the disputes concerning any obligation under some agreements concluded between the contracting parties and the investors.

The scope of the first category of disputes is very broad for two reasons: the heavy obligations of contracting states under the MAI, and the broad implications of loss or damage in the MAI. The obligations of contracting states under the MAI cover those obligations relating to both pre-establishment phase and post-establishment phase of an investment. At the beginning of the negotiations, there was great debate on whether the investor-state procedures shall apply to all MAI obligations or shall only apply to post-establishment obligations, because the investor-state procedures of the NAFTA treat obligations under pre-establishment phase and post-establishment phase differently.[54] The application of investor-state dispute settlements to the pre-establishment obligations will cause such a result that an investor who wishes to make an investment but is precluded from doing so by a potential host government may be able to start proceedings against that government. Because the establishment questions are too closely linked to a country's sovereignty to allow an investor to start proceedings, some countries suggested that it would be more properly dealt with under state-state procedures.[55] But the negotiating group eventually decided not to treat the obligations under the two phases differently alledging that it was not practicable to distinguish them, and hence all MAI obligations are subjected to the dispute settlement mechanism.[56] Therefore, this Article of the MAI applies to all the investor's rights including those relating to establishment.[57]

The MAI also confers broad implications to loss or damage to the investor or its investment. The Commentary especially points out that a lost opportunity to profit from a planned investment would be a type of loss sufficient to give an investor standing to bring an establishment dispute.[58] Although the Commentary stresses that the alleged breach of the MAI must be causally linked to loss or damage for the investor to have standing to bring

---

[52] M. Baldi, *supra* note 1, p. 29.
[53] The MAI, V. Dispute Settlement, Article D. 1. a.
[54] M. Baldi, *supra* note 1, p. 31; see also OECD, *supra* note 2, p. 153.
[55] F. Engering, "The Multilateral Investment Agreement," 5 *Transnational Corporations*, no. 3 (December 1996), pp. 157–158.
[56] M. Baldi, *supra* note 1, p. 31.
[57] Commentary to the MAI, V. Dispute Settlement, Article D. 1. a. 2.
[58] Id., Article D. 1. a. 1.

a claim against the host state, the damage or loss would not need to have been incurred before the dispute is ripe for arbitration.[59]

On the other hand, according to the broad definition of expropriation under the MAI, the governmental regulations on environment, health, workers' rights which would have negative effect on investors' profitability would amount to expropriation. Investors may thus initiate proceedings against the host state. Several cases under the NAFTA are good examples in this regard.[60] To avoid such a result, some scholars suggested appropriate drafting of the expropriation provision together with an interpretative statement that the exercise of general regulatory powers did not normally amount to expropriation.[61] Unfortunately, neither the expropriation provision is appropriately drafted in the MAI, nor such an interpretative statement appears either in the text of MAI or in the Commentary.

The second category of disputes is concerning any obligation which the contracting state has entered into with regard to a specific investment of the investor through: (i) an investment authorization granted by its competent authorities specifically to the investor or investment; and (ii) a written agreement granting rights with respect to some subject matters, on which the investor has relied in establishing, acquiring, or significantly expanding an investment.[62] This means that if host state violates its obligations under the contracts with foreign investor, it would be subject to the investor-state procedures. In fact, this category of disputes has nothing to do with the MAI itself, but the MAI still confers investors the standing to bring a claim against host state. For many countries, *inter alia* developing countries, such contracts are categorized as domestic contracts rather than international contracts and thus are subject to the jurisdiction of domestic courts. Therefore, this article is challenged by some countries. Six delegations expressed their wish to reserve their position.[63] But the MAI keeps silent on whether this article may be reserved. In contrast, the ECT has a similar clause which allows exceptions by contracting states,[64] and four countries make reservations on their consent to the submission of such disputes to arbitration.[65]

A careful analysis of the aforementioned articles shows that only the investors can be the potential claimants of the arbitration for the resolution

---

[59]   Id.

[60]   Examples of the cases are The Loewen Group, Inc. v. The United States, Ethyl Corporation vs. Government of Canada, Metalclad Corp. v. Mexica, S. D. Myers Inc. v. Canada. For sources of these cases, see Footnote 94 of Chapter Seven of this book.

[61]   R. Geiger, *supra* note 51, pp. 471–472.

[62]   The MAI, V. Dispute Settlement, Article D. 1. b.

[63]   Commentary to the MAI, V. Dispute Settlement, Article D. 1. b. 1.

[64]   Article 10 (1) of the ECT stipulates that "… Each Contracting Party shall observe any obligations it has entered into with an Investor or an Investment of an Investor of any other Contracting Party". Article 26 (3) (c) allows countries not to give unconditional consent to the investor-state procedures with respect to the submission of any dispute arising under the above quoted provision. Article 27 (2) provides that any such dispute is not subject to state-state procedures for those countries which do not give unconditional consent under Article 26 (3) (c). In other words, for those dissenting countries under Article 26 (3) (c), the disputes arising under the contracts between host states and foreign investors are subject to neither state-state dispute settlement proceedings nor investor-state dispute settlement proceedings.

[65]   The four countries are: Australia, Canda, Hungary and Norway. See Annex IA to the Energy Charter Treaty.

of the above two categories of disputes. The reasons are as follows: firstly, the MAI is an agreement among countries which only imposes obligations on these countries. Foreign investors do not bear any obligations under the MAI, so for foreign investors, there is no violation of the obligation at all. Since the first category of dispute is concerning the breach of an obligation of contracting states under the MAI, it can be easily inferred that if the dispute is to be submitted to arbitration for resolution, only investor can be the claimant and the contracting state will always be the respondent. Secondly, the second category of disputes is concerning the obligation under some contracts between a contracting state and a foreign investor, but the MAI's wording that "An investor ... may also submit to arbitration ..."[66] implies that only the investor can be the claimant of the arbitration and the contracting state will be respondent. Therefore, in the context of the investor-state mechanism of the MAI, investor will be always in the position of claimant who has the initiative to attack the state, while the state will land itself in a passive position as respondent. This result is unfair for contracting states. In contrast, the ICSID mechanism allows both foreign investors and host states to be claimants or respondents. So far, there is at least one case where host state brought the dispute as claimant to the ICSID.[67]

In addition, the investor-state mechanism is only available for foreign investors. No domestic investors of the contracting states may resort to this mechanism. In this sense, foreign investors are in a more advantageous position than that of domestic investors. Thus inequality between foreign investors and domestic investors is artificially created, which is contrary to the MAI's principle of national treatment.

8.3.2   Means of Settlement

The MAI provides various means for the settlement of the disputes between investors and states except for negotiation or consultation, which include: (1) resolution by courts or administrative tribunals in host state; (2) resolution in accordance with any dispute settlement procedure agreed upon prior to the dispute; (3) resolution by arbitration.[68] With respect to the arbitration rules to be followed, the MAI refers to the ICSID Convention if it is available, the ICSID Additional Facility if it is available, the Arbitration Rules of the United Nations Commission on International Trade Law ("UNCITRAL"), and the Rules of Arbitration of the International Chamber of Commerce ("ICC").[69] Investors may choose from the above three means and choose from the four available arbitration rules if the means of arbitration is chosen. It is clear that the MAI tries to provide sufficient options for investors so as to enable them to have a satisfactory resolution of their cases.

As far as the investor's choosing of the means of settlement is concerned, investor may choose but is not limited to choose the local remedy, i.e.,

---

[66]   See the MAI, V. Dispute Settlement, Article D. 1. b.
[67]   The case is Gabon v. Société Serete S.A. (Case No. ARB/76/1).
[68]   The MAI, V. Dispute Settlement, Article D. 2.
[69]   Id., Article D. 2. c.

resolution by courts or administrative tribunals in the host state. Here, the MAI again throws away the traditional requirement of the exhaustion of local remedy. Further, the MAI permits investor to choose other means of settlement even if there is a dispute settlement procedure agreed upon between the investor and the host state prior to the dispute arising. This permission is to allow investors not to comply with the original agreement on dispute settlement procedure between host state and investor.

There is a further question as to "forum shopping" between domestic remedies and international arbitration. In other words, this is a question concerning whether investor may resort to international arbitration even though it has initiated a case in local court. There are different practices in this regard. The BIT Model of the United States provides that if investor has not submitted the dispute to domestic remedies, it may submit the dispute for settlement by binding arbitration,[70] from which we may conclude that foreign investor should choose from the outset domestic remedies or international arbitration. European BITs generally permit the investor to initiate local remedies and then resort to arbitration after a delay of three to six months. But it is not clear whether the local remedies shall be abandoned when international arbitration is initiated.[71] NAFTA, on the contrary, prohibits investor to initiate or continue local remedies once arbitration is initiated.[72] The ECT is more flexible which provides alternatives to contracting parties: the general rule is that investor is allowed to seek arbitration despite domestic remedies have been initiated; exception to the general rule is that contracting parties may withhold their consent to arbitration once domestic remedies have been initiated.[73] During negotiations, the MAI delegations expressed different approaches as to "the fork in the road" when a foreign investor must irrevocably choose between domestic remedies and international arbitration.[74] One delegation pointed out in particular that tying the investor to only one procedure might entail risks,[75] which is against the MAI's target to provide high standard of protection for investors. The Chairman of the Expert Group on Dispute Settlement was of the opinion that contracting parties would be entitled to impose a "fork in the road".[76] In other words, he held that as a general rule, investor was allowed to resort to arbitration despite of the initiation of local remedies, and as an exception, contracting parties might withhold their consent to arbitration in cases of the initiation of local remedies. Finally, the MAI follows the approach adopted by the ECT, i.e., it generally stipulates that investors have the options of local remedies and international arbitration without saying "the fork in the road",[77] then it provides that contracting parties may give their consent to the submission of disputes to arbitration on the condition that the investor and the investment waive in writing the right to initiate any other dispute

---

[70] The BIT Model (1994) of the United States, Article IX (3).
[71] OECD, *supra* note 2, p. 152.
[72] NAFTA, Article 1121 (1) (b).
[73] ECT, Article 26 (2), (3) (b) (i); OECD, *supra* note 2, p. 152.
[74] OECD, *supra* note 2, p. 152.
[75] Id.
[76] M. Baldi, *supra* note 1, p. 31.
[77] The MAI, V. Dispute Settlement, Article D. 2.

settlement procedure with respect to the same dispute and withdraw from any such procedure in progress before its conclusion.[78]

As far as arbitration rules are concerned, the ICSID Convention is available only when both the host states and the home states of investors are contracting states. At present, there are 149 contracting states where Canada, Mexico and Poland who are OECD members are not contracting states.[79] This means that disputes between these three countries and foreign investors, and disputes between investors from these three countries and any other contracting countries, will be excluded from the ICSID facility. The ICSID Additional Facility is available when either the state party to the dispute or the state whose national is a party to the dispute is not a contracting state to the ICSID Convention. This facility can resolve part of the above mentioned disputes. However, the disputes between these three countries and investors from these three countries do not fall within the scope of either the ICSID facility or the ICSID Additional Facility. Taking this situation into consideration, the MAI refers to the Arbitration Rules of the UNCITRAL and that of the ICC as possible options.

8.3.3   Issues Related to the MAI's Arbitration Rules

By incorporating the above possible arbitration rules into the MAI, the MAI has no need to make a set of detailed arbitration rules of its own which would be similar to those existing rules. It only needs to make those special rules fitting the MAI's expectations and features. Such an elaborate arrangement can avoid troubles of making detailed rules, and save space for the text and integrate the MAI rules with main international arbitration rules.

The MAI's special rules of arbitration mainly concern the contracting parties' consent to arbitration, time periods for submission to arbitration, standing of the investment, consolidation of multiple proceedings, applicable law, and final arbitral awards. The MAI also mentions rules on the appointments to arbitral tribunals, preliminary objections, indemnification, third party rights, scientific and technical expertise, interim measures of relief, confidential and proprietary information, place of arbitration and enforceability, and tribunal member fees. Since these rules contain few new contents,[80] the following will focus on the MAI's some main or special rules of arbitration and the issues arising therefrom.

8.3.3.1   The Contracting Parties' Consent to Arbitration

For all international arbitration rules, the precondition to submit a dispute to arbitration for decision is the consent to arbitration in writing by parties to the dispute. Arbitral tribunal can only accept and hear those cases submitted with consent by both parties to the dispute. Likewise, the ICSID

---

[78]   Id., Article D. 3. b.
[79]   The data is available at http://www.worldbank.org/icsid/constate/c-states-en.htm.
[80]   For the specific contents of these rules, see the MAI, V. Dispute Settlement, Article D. 3, 7, 10, 11, 12, 13, 15, 17, 18 and 19.

Convention, the UNCITRAL Arbitration etc., also have the requirement of consent in writing.[81] The ICSID Convention does not limit the form of consent to "arbitration agreement" or "arbitration clause" in a contract, and thus host government may express its consent in the BITs it concludes with other countries. Such an expression is like an "offer" and the submission to the ICSID by foreign investor in case that a specific dispute arises is an "acceptance".[82]

To satisfy the requirement of written consent in the arbitration rules referred to by the MAI, the MAI stipulates that each contracting party gives its unconditional consent to the submission of a dispute to international arbitration when it adopts the MAI.[83] The MAI does not mention any possibility for country specific reservations, but mentions that contracting party may be allowed to withhold its consent in cases where the investor has previously submitted to local remedies. The latter issue has been discussed earlier. However, this withholding is not equal to an exception or reservation to the rule of prior consent in that if investor waives its right to resort to local remedies and seeks arbitration to settle the dispute, host state has no way to withhold its consent. The unconditional consent expressed in the MAI constitutes the written consent of the host state. The MAI further stipulates that the written submission of the dispute to resolution by the investor or the investor's advance written consent to such submission constitutes the written consent of the investor and further constitutes the written agreement of the parties to the dispute required by the arbitration rules.[84]

Prior consent by the contracting parties practically means that in a given case it is exclusively up to the investor to decide whether or not to refer the dispute to arbitration.[85] The investors' right to exclusive decision, together with their various opinions to both the means of settlement and international arbitration rules, makes investors always in an advantageous position to attack while host states in a passive position to defend. The MAI's tendency to give investors adequate protection is thus clearly revealed.

In view of the fact that adoption of the MAI constitutes contracting parties' unconditional prior consent to arbitration makes host states in a disadvantageous position, delegations had great controversies with this issue among themselves. One delegation had serious concern with prior concern and two delegations had problems of constitutional nature with it.[86] A few delegations do not accept the idea of prior consent at all.[87] The rule of prior consent will also be an obstacle to non-OECD members' accession to the MAI. To settle these controversies and to make the MAI acceptable by many countries, the MAI should learn some good solutions from the successful experience of the ICSID Convention. The ICSID Convention was created

---

[81] For example, Article 25 (1) of the ICSID Convention; Article 4 (2) of the ICSID Additional Facility Rules; Article 1 of the UNCITRAL Arbitration Rules.
[82] "Report of the Executive Directors on the Convention on the Settlement of Investment Disputes between States and Nationals of Other States," *ICSID Doc. 2*, March 18, 1965, para. 24.
[83] The MAI, V. Dispute Settlement, Article D. 3. a.
[84] Id.
[85] M. Baldi, *supra* note 1, p. 29.
[86] Commentary to the MAI, V. Dispute Settlement, Article D. 3.
[87] M. Baldi, *supra* note 1, p. 31.

especially to settle through arbitration or conciliation any legal disputes arising directly from investment. But the mere adoption of the Convention by contracting states does not constitute prior consent to arbitration. Furthermore, the notifying of the ICSID of the class or classes of disputes which host state would or would not consider submitting to the jurisdiction of the Centre does not constitute prior consent to arbitration.[88] In addition, even the consent by a constituent subdivision or agency of a Contracting State shall generally require the approval of that State.[89] The strict requirement of consent of the ICSID Convention does not decrease the number of cases submitted to the Centre; instead, it attracts more countries to accede to the Convention.[90]

8.3.3.2   Time Periods for the Submission to Arbitration

The time periods of both the permitted earliest and latest time for an investor to submit a dispute to arbitration are new ideas created by the MAI. According to the MAI, an investor can not refer a dispute to arbitration immediately after the arising of the dispute. Before submitting to arbitration, the investor shall send a notice of intent and a copy of it to the host state in the dispute and the Parties Group respectively. The notice of intent shall specify the name and address of the disputing investor, the name and address of the investment, the provisions of the MAI alleged to have been breached and any other relevant provisions, the issues and the factual basis for the claim, and the relief sought, including the approximate amount of any damages claimed.[91] Only after sixty days following the date on which the host state received the notice of intent may the investor submit the dispute for resolution. The notice of intent enables the host state to gain knowledge in advance of the means of settlement being adopted, the arbitration rules to be followed, and the relief to be sought. The time period of sixty days gives time to the host state who is in the passive position of defending to assess and judge the dispute seriously. It also provides opportunities for both parties to reach reconciliation in the dispute. Therefore, this time period is also called "cooling period". However, it is not good to postpone the submission to arbitration for a too long time period. The MAI stipulates that the submission of a dispute to arbitration can not be later than five years from the date the investor first acquired or should have acquired knowledge of the events which gave rise to the dispute.[92] This time period of five years is quite long.

---

[88]   ICSID Convention, Article 25 (4).
[89]   ICSID Convention, Article 25 (3).
[90]   Until now there are 95 cases submitted before the ICSID, 58 of which have been concluded and the rest 37 are still pending. The number of cases submitted to the Centre has increased significantly in recent years. At present 149 states have signed the Convention. See the website of the ICSID at http://www.worldbank.org/icsid.
[91]   The MAI, V. Dispute Settlement, Article D. 4.
[92]   Id.

8.3.3.3 Standing of the Investment

According to the law of almost all countries, a company invested by a foreign investor but constituted or organized under the law of a host state has the nationality of this host state. In such a case, this company is not a foreign investor but merely an investment of foreign investor who owns or controls it. In a strict sense, such a company does not have the standing to bring a claim to arbitration against the host state. If any dispute arises between this company and the host government, only the foreign investor who owns or controls this company has the standing to bring the case to arbitration. But for the purpose of giving full protection to foreign investor and its investment, such a company is treated as a company of another state by the ICSID, the ECT and some BITs. Article 25(2)(b) of the ICSID Convention provides that "National of another Contracting State means… (b) any juridical person which had the nationality of a Contracting State other than the State party to the dispute on the date on which the parties consented to submit such dispute to conciliation or arbitration and any juridical person which had the nationality of the Contracting State party to the dispute on that date and which, because of foreign control, the parties have agreed should be treated as a national of another Contracting State for the purposes of this Convention". Article 1(6) of the ICSID Additional Facility Rules provides that "National of another State means a person who is not, or whom the parties to the proceeding in question have agreed not to treat as, a national of the State party to that proceeding". The ECT stipulates that for the purpose of the relevant articles of the ICSID Convention and the Additional Facility Rules, an investor which has the nationality of a contracting state and is controlled by an investor of another contracting state shall be treated as a national of another state.[93] The BIT Model (1994) of the United States stipulates that for the purpose of Article 25 (2)(b) of the ICSID and the BIT's article of investor-state procedure, a company of a party that, immediately before the occurrence of the event or events giving rise to an investment dispute, was a covered investment, shall be treated as a company of the other party.[94]

During the MAI's negotiations, whether such a company would have standing to act as the foreign investor in bringing a claim to arbitration against the host state was much debated.[95] The MAI finally gives the standing to the investment by providing that an enterprise constituted or organized under the law of a contracting party shall, for the purpose of disputes concerning that investment, be considered an investor of another contracting party under the MAI's article on investor-state mechanism and the relevant article of the ICSID Convention.[96] This clause is a variant of aforementioned articles of the ICSID Convention, ECT and the BITs. To make a compromise, the Commentary points out that countries are allowed to make specific reservations with respect to this clause.[97]

---

93 The ECT, Article 26 (7).
94 The BIT Model (1994) of the United States, Article IV. 8.
95 M. Baldi, *supra* note 1, p. 31.
96 The MAI, V. Dispute Settlement, Article D. 8.
97 Commentary to the MAI, V. Dispute Settlement, Article D. 8. See also M. Baldi, *supra* note 1, p. 31.

8.3.3.4   Consolidation of Multiple Proceedings

As a party to a multilateral agreement, a host state's violation of its obligations under the agreement would exert influence on investors from a same contracting state or from different contracting states and two or more disputes would thus arise between the host state and the investors. In this event, different investors may, under the investor-state procedure, bring the disputes arising from the same fact or law before different tribunals. Therefore, the host state would be involved in multiple proceedings as a defendant. It would be inefficient, time, money and energy consuming for the host state to deal with these proceedings. Awards made by different proceedings would be inconsistent with each other and thus create unfairness among different investors. To solve these problems, the MAI confers the contracting party the right to request the consolidated consideration of all or part of these disputes. A separate arbitral tribunal would be constituted to decide on the disputes. The investor parties shall act as one side for the purpose of the formation of the tribunal. This arbitral tribunal may stay or adjourn the other arbitral proceedings having been initiated by different investors.[98] The detailed rules as to relevant issues including the formation of tribunal will not be addressed here.

8.3.3.5   Applicable Law

The MAI applies different applicable laws to different categories of disputes. For the first category of disputes between a contracting party and an investor of another contracting party concerning an alleged breach of obligation of the former under the MAI, those laws applicable to the disputes between contracting parties are applicable. To be specific, the applicable law is the MAI itself, but the MAI should be interpreted and applied in accordance with applicable rules of international law.[99]

For the second category of disputes between a contracting party and an investor of another contracting party where the former is alleged breaching the contracts with the latter, the applicable law is the rules of law which may be agreed by the parties. This provision reflects the traditional rule of "autonomy of parties". But since the MAI or the Commentary does not give further explanation as to what the rules of law are, such rules of law could be any rule of law including domestic law or international law. In the absence of such agreement, the applicable law is the law of the contracting party to the dispute (including its rules on the conflict of laws), the law governing the authorization or agreement and such rules of international law as may be applicable.[100] This provision is very similar to that of the ICSID Convention.[101] Referring to the drafting history of the ICSID Convention, this provision is a compromise between developing countries and developed

---

[98]   The MAI, V. Dispute Settlement, Article D. 9.
[99]   Id., Article D. 14. a.
[100] Id., Article D. 14. b.
[101] For the provision of the ICSID Convention, see Article 42 (1).

countries because the former contended the application of domestic law of host state while the latter insisted on the application of rules of international law.[102] Since the MAI does not say the relations among the three applicable laws, problems still will arise as to whether the three applicable laws should be applied simultaneously or whether the tribunal can choose one or two of them to be followed.

8.3.3.6 Final Awards

The final award should contain such contents as findings of law and fact, and the reasons for such findings of law and fact, as well as the relief. The available forms of relief are as follows: (1) a declaration that the contracting party has failed to comply with its obligations under the MAI; (2) pecuniary compensation, which shall include interest from the time the loss or damage was incurred until time of payment; (3) restitution in kind in appropriate case, provided that the contracting party may pay pecuniary compensation in lieu thereof where restitution is not practicable; and (4) with the agreement of the parties to the dispute, any other form of relief.[103] A comparison of these forms of relief with those of the state-state procedure shows that the tribunal under the investor-state mechanism only has the power to declare that the contracting party has failed to comply with its obligations under the MAI; it does not have the power to order the contracting party to correct its action.

The arbitration awards shall be final and binding.[104]

8.3.3.7 Enforcement of Final Awards

The MAI provides that the arbitration award shall be carried out without delay by the party against whom the award is issued.[105] Each contracting party shall provide for the enforcement of the pecuniary obligations imposed by an arbitral award.[106] But the MAI does not mention how the final awards shall be enforced. Among the four available arbitral systems under the MAI, only the ICSID Convention creates rules concerning the recognition and enforcement of the awards made under the Convention.[107] In addition, the United Nations Convention on the Recognition and Enforcement of Foreign Arbitral Awards (the "New York Convention") provides facilities for contracting states for the recognition and enforcement of foreign arbitral awards made under any arbitral system. The MAI intends the arbitral

---

[102] For the debate on the issue of applicable law in the ICSID Convention, see Chen An (ed.), *Arbitration of International Investment Disputes—A Research on ICSID Mechanism* (Chinese edition), Fudan University Press, 2001, pp. 130–168.
[103] The MAI, V. Dispute Settlement, Article D. 16. a.
[104] Id., Article D. 16. c.
[105] Id.
[106] Id., Article D. 18.
[107] See Arts. 53, 54 and 55 of the Convention.

awards to be recognized and enforced in accordance with the New York Convention because it provides that: any arbitration shall be held in a state that is party to the New York Convention; claims submitted to arbitration under the MAI shall be considered to arise out of a commercial relationship or transaction for the purpose of Article I of that Convention;[108] and the contracting party's unconditional consent to arbitration and the investor's submission of the dispute to arbitration or his advanced written consent to such submission shall constitute the written consent and the written agreement of the parties to the dispute for the purpose of Article II of the New York Convention.[109]

8.4   COMMENTS ON THE INVESTOR-STATE MECHANISM

The MAI's investor-state mechanism is an instrument created for the full protection of foreign investors' interest. Except for the defects discussed in the above parts, this mechanism has the following potential negative effects on host government which have been proved by the NAFTA cases.

Firstly, the combination of the procedural mechanism with the substantive contents of the MAI will produce far reaching impacts on host government's regulatory power and will pose a real threat to national sovereignty. For example, foreign investors can rely on the MAI's provisions on indirect expropriation and the MAI's investor-state procedure to challenge host state's environmental enactments as "regulatory taking". Such a challenge could result in the host government's revoking relevant enactments and paying compensation to the investor. In the NAFTA system which is the prototype of the MAI, there have been several such cases.[110]

Secondly, the submission of a dispute to arbitration by foreign investor will have political influence on host government. Host government would rather settle the dispute with foreign investor outside the tribunal than risk a politically embarrassing defeat in a tribunal. Foreign investor, on the contrary, will take advantage of host government's psychology i.e., not to "lost face" publicly, to ask for more compensation. The case of Ethyl Corp. v. Canada under the NAFTA system is the right example.[111] In April 1997, Canada enacted a public health law banning the import of its MMT gasoline additive. Five days later, the U.S.-based Ethyl Corp. slapped the Canadian Government with a $251 million lawsuit under NAFTA, charging the law was a "regulatory taking". In August 1998, the Canadian Government agreed to pay Ethyl Corp. $13 million in damages and to cover the company's legal

---

[108]   The MAI, V. Dispute Settlement, Article D. 18.
[109]   Id., Article D. 5.
[110]   Examples of the cases are: Metalclad Corp. v. Mexica, Ethyl Corporation vs. Government of Canada, The Loewen Group, Inc. v. The United States, and S.D. Myers Inc. v. Canada.
[111]   For details of the case, see "Ethyl Corporation vs. Government of Canada: Now Investor Can Use NAFTA to Challenge Environmental Safeguards," available at http://www.citizen. org/pctrade/nafta/cases/Ethylbri.htm; see also The Loewen Group, Inc. v. The United States, available at http://www.citizen.org/pctrade/nafta/cases/Loewen.htm.

costs rather than risk a politically embarrassing defeat in a NAFTA tribunal. Under the settlement, Canada was forced to publicly proclaim that MMT was "safe". Just one week after the Ethyl Corp. case, another U.S.-based company S.D. Myers Inc. initiated a C$ 10 million lawsuit against the Canadian Government charging Canada's PCB export ban.[112] At first the Canadian Government planned to settle the case through negotiations. Finally, the case was decided by a NAFTA tribunal in November 2000 with the decision that the Canadian Government paid US$ 20 million to S. D. Myers Inc. as compensation.[113]

Analysis and criticism on the investor-state procedure show that the MAI's present investor-state mechanism needs revision and restriction so as to balance the interests of both foreign investors and host governments. It was reported that in early 1999, Canada sought to introduce interpretative changes to NAFTA in order to limit the ability of private companies to seek compensation for government regulations that affect their business, after the initiations of so many cases against Canada under NAFTA.[114] Scholars also suggest that if the Bush Administration wishes to keep America united, it should first announce that the peculiar privileges for investors offered by Chapter 11 of NAFTA will not be proposed for any future trade agreements, and then suspend NAFTA's investor-state enforcement mechanism in agreement with Canada and Mexico.[115]

---

[112] For details of the case, see "NAFTA Case Shows Risks, Secrecy", available at http://www.canadians.org/release38.html; Canada Slapped with NAFTA Lawsuit against Another Environmental Law, available at http:www.citizen.org/pctrade/nafta/cases/canada.htm; U.S. Company Seeks Compensation from Canada under NAFTA, available at http://lawmoney.oyster.co.uk/public/news/hotnews/news9809/news980904.2.html.

[113] N. Judd, "Canada's PCB Export Ban Could Cost Taxpayer Dear," available at http://ens.lycos.com/ens/nov2000/2000L-11-14-11.html.

[114] P. Malanczuk, *supra* note 10, p. 156, footnote 143.

[115] W. Greider, "The Right and US Trade law: Invalidating the 20th century", Oct. 15, 2001. This article was circulated by E-mail by Prof. Sol picciotto, Head of UK Lancaster University Law School, E-mail: s.picciotto@lancaster.ac.uk.

9. Conclusion

Although the three-year MAI negotiations among OECD members failed, the MAI Negotiating Text is still worth studying because it represents the positions with ambitiously high standard of developed countries in every aspect of international investment treaty. But such a treaty text is not acceptable for developing countries. After analyses of the MAI negotiations and the MAI text, we conclude that:

- The MAI negotiation process behind closed door is unacceptable and inadvisable. For any future negotiation on investment rules, participants should be so wide to include developed countries, developing countries, NGOs, civil societies and interested groups. Only general participation can make the negotiation transparent and represent the most world-wide interests.
- The MAI is an agreement with high standards and thus is unreachable for developing countries. To make a universal investment agreement, the treatment standards should be acceptable for developing countries, and the balance of interests between developed countries and developing countries, the special circumstances of developing countries, and the balance of investors' rights and obligations should be taken into consideration.
- The MAI defines both investor and investment broadly so as to broaden its scope of application. Broad definitions and application scope make host governments' obligations much heavier.
- The MAI requires of host governments to accord national treatment and most-favoured-nation treatment to foreign investors and their investments. These treatment standards are too high and would have negative impacts on developing countries.
- The MAI develops high-standard disciplines on some special investment issues: key personnel, performance requirements, investment incentives, privatization, and monopolies, state enterprises and concession. There are few existing international rules for these special issues.
- The MAI provides that fair and equitable treatment, full and constant protection and security, minimum standard of international law and the prohibition of unreasonable and/or discriminatory measures are the general treatment standards of investment protection. These investment protection standards are vague and lack of certainty on one hand, they are

151

at the high level in contrast with the according standards of other investment instruments, on the other hand.

- The MAI also formulates specific treatment standards of investment protection for issues of expropriation and compensation, protection from strife, transfer of payments and etc. These standards are also at the high level for developing countries.
- The MAI reinforces its enforcement mechanism through the provisions of state-state dispute settlement procedures and investor-state dispute settlement procedures. The investor-state dispute settlement mechanism, together with the MAI's substantive provisions, enables foreign investors to challenge host states' regulations, legal systems and policies easily.
- In the current circumstances, developing countries should do more study on international investment instruments and thus be prepared for any future negotiation on investment rules. It would do developing countries good if they can render a negotiating text that reflects their own positions and interests at the beginning of negotiations.

Bibliography

A. A. Fatouros, Government Guarantees to Foreign Investors, Columbia University Press, 1962.

A. Böhmer, "The Struggle for a Multilateral Agreement on Investment–an Assessment of the Negotiation Process in the OECD", 41 German Yearbook of International Law (1998).

A. R. Parra, "The Principles Governing Foreign Investment, As Reflected in National Investment Codes", 7 ICSID Review—Foreign Investment Law Journal (1992), no. 2.

B. Bracewell-Milnes & J. C. L. Huiskamp, Investment Incentives: A comparative analysis of the systems in the EEC, the USA and Sweden, Kluwer, Deventer, The Netherlands, 1977.

C. Baumgartner, "The Demise of the Multilateral Agreement on Investment", Colorado Journal of International Environmental Law & Policy Yearbook (1998).

C. P. Andrews-Speed & T. W. Waelde, "Will the Energy Charter Treaty help international energy investors?", 5 Transnational Corporations, no. 3 (December 1996).

C. Raghavan, "Investment rules not dead, yet", South–North Development Monitor (SUNS) (Email edition), Issue 4156, Feb. 20, 1998.

Chen An (ed.), Arbitration of International Investment Disputes—A Research on ICSID Mechanism (Chinese edition), Fudan University Press, 2001.

Chen An, & Zeng Huaqun (ed.), International Investment Law (Chinese edition), Peking University Press, 1999.

Chen Huiping, New Trends of Multilateral Investment Framework (1999) (Chinese edition, unpublished Ph.D. Dissertation)

E. V. K. FitzGerald, R. Cubero-Brealey and A. Lehmann, "The Development Implications of the Multilateral Agreement on Investment: A Report Commissioned by the UK Department for International Development" (21 March 1998).

E. C. Nieuwenhuys & M. M. T. A. Brus (ed.), Multilateral Regulation of Investment, Kluwer Law International, 2001.

F. Engering, "The Multilateral Investment Agreement", 5 Transnational Corporations, no. 3 (December 1996).

F. Sader, Privatization and Foreign Investment in the Developing World, 1988–92, Working Papers of International Economics Department, the World Bank, October 1993.

G. Sacerdoti, "Bilateral Treaties and Multilateral Instruments on Investment Protection," Recueil Des Cours: Collected Courses of the Hague Academy of International Law (1997), Martinus Nijhhoff Publishers, 1998.

G. Schwarzenberger, "The Most-Favored-Nation Standard in British State Practice", 22 British Year Book of International Law (1945).

IPS/D. D. Sarkar, "MAI principles alive and kicking, analysts say", 4310 SUNS, Oct. 27, 1998.

IPS/J. Achieng, "Experts snub OECD's proposed investment pact", 4109 SUNS, Dec. 2, 1997.

K. J. Vandevelde, United States Investment Treaties: Policy and Practice, Kluwer Law and Taxation Publishers, Deventer, the Netherlands, 1992.

K. S. Gudgeon, "United States Bilateral Investment Treaties: Comments on the Origins, Purpose and General Treatment Standard", 4 International Tax and Business Lawyer (1986).

L. Wallach, "For the Multilateral Agreement on Investment", The NGO Pocket Trade Lawyer.

L. Wallach, "Testimony of Lori Wallach", Thursday, March 5, 1998.

M. A. Wiss, "Book Review and Note: World Investment Report 1995," 90 The American Journal of International Law (1996).

M. Daiy, "Investment Incentives and the Multilateral Agreement on Investment", 32 Journal of World Trade (1998), no. 2.

M. Khor, "NGOs in OECD countries protest MAI", 4155 SUNS, Feb. 19, 1998.

M. Sforza, "MAI Provisions and Proposals: An Analysis of the April 1998 Text", Public Citizen's Global Trade Watch, July 1998.

M. Sornarajah, "Nationalization of Foreign Investment", International Transactions, Trade and Investment, law and Finance, K. C. D. M. Wilde (ed.), The Law Book Company Limited, 1993.

M. Sornarajah, The International Law on Foreign Investment, Cambridge University, 1994.

M. Vallianatos, "Update on MAI Negotiations", Oct. 27, 1998.

OECD, "A Multilateral Agreement on Investment: Report by the MAI Negotiating Group", May 1996.

OECD, "Ministerial Statement on the Multilateral Agreement on Investment (MAI)" (28 April, 1998).

OECD, "Multilateral Agreement on Investment: Report by the Chairman of the Negotiating Group", 28 April 1998.

OECD, "Multilateral Agreement on Investment: Report by the Committee on International Investment and Multilateral Enterprises (CIME)/and the Committee on Capital Movements and Invisible Transactions (CMIT)", May 1995.

OECD, "Multilateral Agreement on Investment: Report by the MAI Negotiating Group", May 1997.

OECD, "Ministerial Statement on the Multilateral Agreement on Investment: OECD Council at Ministerial level", 26 May 1997.

OECD, "OECD Chairman's Statement under Secretary of State Stuart Eizenstat (USA) Executive Committee in Special Session", Paris, 23 October 1998.

OECD, "OECD Informal Consultations on International Investment", 3 December 1998.

OECD, "OECD Ministerial Statement on the Multilateral Agreement on Investment (MAI)".

OECD, "Opening Statement by Mr. Donald J. John, Secretary-General Consultations on the Multilateral Agreement on Investment", Paris, 20 October 1998.

OECD, "Opening To Non-members for Investment Agreement", OECD Letter, vol. 5/5, June 1996.

OECD, "Symposium on the MAI", 20 October 1997, Cairo, Egypt.

OECD, "The Original Mandate" of the MAI.

OECD, Commentary to the MAI Negotiating Text (as of 24 April 1998).

OECD, Proceedings of the Special Session on the Multilateral Agreement on Investment Held in Paris on 17 September 1997, OCDE/GD (97)187.

OECD, The MAI Negotiating Text (as of 24 April 1998).

OECD, The multilateral Agreement on Investment: State of Play as in April 1997, OCDE/GD (97)114.

OECD, The multilateral Agreement on Investment: State of Play as of February 1997, OCDE/GD (97)38.

OECD, Towards Multilateral Investment Rules, 1996.

P. Ford, "A Pact to Guide Global Investing Promised Jobs—But at What Cost?", The Christian Science Monitor International, 25 February 1998.

P. Peters, "Recent Developments in Expropriation Clauses of Asian Investment Treaties", 5 Asian Yearbook of International Law (1997).

R. Geiger, "Towards a Multilateral Agreement on Investment", 31 Cornell International Law Journal (1998), no. 3.

R. H. Thomas, "The Need for a Southern African Development Community Response to Proposals for a Multilateral Agreement on Investment," 21 World Competition (1998), no. 4.

S. Mo, "Some Aspects of the Australia-China Investment Protection Treaty", 1 Journal of World Trade (1991).

S. Muhammad, The Legal Framework of World Trade, London, Stevens and Sons Ltd., 1958.

S. Picciotto, "Linkages in International Investment Regulation: the Antinomies of the Draft Multilateral Agreement on Investment", 19 University of Pennsylvania Journal of international Economic Law (1998), no. 3.

T. H. Moran, "The impact of TRIMs on trade and development," 1 Transnational Corporations, no. 1 (February 1992).

T. Levy, "NAFTA's Provision for Compensation in the Event of Expropriation: A Reassessment of the "Prompt, Adequate and Effective" Standard", 31 Stanford Journal of International Law, no. 2.

T. W. Waelde & K. M. Christie (ed.), Energy Charter Treaty: Selected Topics, 1995.

T. W. Waelde, "International Investment under the 1994 Energy Charter Treaty: Legal, Negotiating and Policy Implications for international Investors within Western and Commonwealth of Independent States/Eastern European Countries", 29 Journal of World Trade (1995), no. 5.

TWN, "NGOs criticize MAI-type investment approach at UNCTAD", 4230 SUNS, Jun. 12, 1998.

TWN/R. Bissio, "NGOs gear up to start anti-MAI campaign", 4091 SUNS, Nov. 6, 1997.

UNCTAD, Admission and Establishment, New York and Geneva, 1999.

UNCTAD, Bilateral Investment Treaties in the Mid-1990s, United Nations, New York and Geneva, 1998.

UNCTAD, Comparative Experiences with Privatization: Policy Insights and Lessons Learned, United Nations, 1995.

UNCTAD, Existing Regional And Multilateral Investment Agreements And Their Relevance to A Possible Multilateral Framework on Investment: Issues and Questions, 21 January 1998, TD/B/COM.2/EM.3/2.

UNCTAD, Incentives and Foreign Direct Investment, United Nations, 1996.

UNCTAD, International Investment Instruments: A Compendium, 1996–2002.

UNCTAD, Most-Favored-Nation Treatment, New York and Geneva, 1999.

UNCTAD, National Treatment, New York and Geneva, 1999.

UNCTAD, Report of the Expert Meeting on Existing Regional and Multilateral Investment Agreements and Their Development Dimensions, 22 April 1998, TD/B/COM.2/EM.3/3.

UNCTAD, Scope and Definition, United Nations, New York and Geneva, 1999.

UNCTAD, Trends in International Investment Agreements: An Overview, New York and Geneva, 1999.

UNCTAD, World Investment Report 1995.

UNCTAD, World Investment Report 1996.

UNCTAD, World Investment Report 1998.

UNCTC, Bilateral Investment Treaties, United Nations, New York, 1988.

W. Greider, "The Right and US Trade law: Invalidating the 20th century", Oct. 15, 2001.

W. H. Witherell, "The OECD Multilateral Agreement on Investment", 4 Transnational Corporations, no. 2 (August 1995).

World Bank, Legal Framework for the Treatment of Foreign Investment, Volume I: Survey of Existing Instruments, 1992.

WTO, Report of the Working Group on the Relationship between Trade and Investment to the General Council (1998).

Xu Chongli, "Controversial Issues in International Investment Law and China's Countermeasures" (Chinese edition), 1 Chinese Social Science (1994).

Xu Chongli, A Study on Bilateral Investment Treaties (1996) (Chinese edition, unpublished Ph.D. Dissertation).

Y. Mitrofanskaya, "Privatization as an International Phenomenon: Kazakhstan", 14 American University International Law Review (1999).

Yu Jingshong, "Basis of the Compensation of Nationalizaion in International Investment Law" (Chinese edition), 2 Chinese Social Science (1986).